THE CURIOUS
BARTENDER
AN ODYSSEY OF
MALT, BOURBON & RYE
WHISKIES

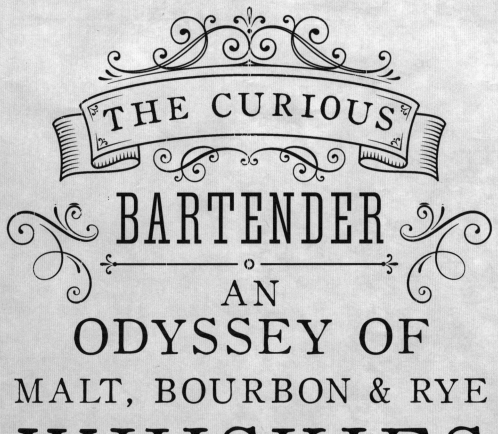

THE CURIOUS

BARTENDER

AN ODYSSEY OF MALT, BOURBON & RYE WHISKIES

TRISTAN STEPHENSON

WITH PHOTOGRAPHY BY ADDIE CHINN

Designer Geoff Borin
Commissioning Editor Nathan Joyce
Head of Production Patricia Harrington
Art Director Leslie Harrington
Editorial Director Julia Charles
Publisher Cindy Richards

Prop Stylist Sarianne Plaisant
Indexer Diana Le Core

First published in 2014 by
Ryland Peters & Small
20–21 Jockey's Fields
London WC1R 4BW
and
341 E 116th St
New York, NY 10029

www.rylandpeters.com

10 9 8 7

ISBN: 978-1-84975-562-7

A CIP record for this book is available from the
British Library.

US Library of Congress CIP data has been applied for.

Printed in China

CONTENTS

FOREWORD

'I'm writing a whisky book'

I said cheerfully to the distiller standing in front of me.

'Ah, another one'

He replied with a frown,

'Why d'ya want to do that? There's plenty enough already and they're all just lists of lists!'

Good point, I thought. I was at the Kilchoman Distillery on the island of Islay, just off the west coast of Scotland. My companions and I were in the middle of a four-day tour that covered around 20 of the 100-or-so malt whisky distilleries currently operational in Scotland today. It was blowing a gale and lashing down with rain outside on a morning in December, and we were warming ourselves by the glow of the two small copper pot stills.

I didn't really know how to reply to the man's question. He was probably twice my age and possessed limitless experience and knowledge of the whisky industry. And he was right; the subject of whisky is an impressively well-documented one. More books have already been dedicated to this category of spirits than any other I know of, and on the face of it, there is little need for another one.

But the same could have been said about Kilchoman Distillery, the very place I was standing when the question was posed to me. Here was a whisky distillery on the tip of everyone's tongue, attracting visitors from far and wide, yet Kilchoman only began making whisky in 2007. You could have argued that Islay didn't need another distillery; the seven other operational distilleries on the island

had got along quite happily for over 100 years (some of them much longer). Why start a new distillery there now? Whatever the reason it was an astute move. Folk are buying up Kilchoman as fast as they can make it, which is even more surprising given the £50 ($85) price tag for what is, by anyone's standards, a very young Scotch whisky.

So perhaps a new slant on an old favourite can be an agreeable thing? That's my hope anyway – that the same thing gravitating us towards the fresh approach that Kilchoman offers also inspires you to pick up this book and discover (or rediscover) the whisky category at a time when it is rediscovering itself.

Whether you are curious about how a young whisky from Islay might taste, or interested in how history shaped whisky in to the world's largest premium drinks category, puzzled about how a barrel turns a fiery white spirit into a mellow yet complex expression of time, or searching for better ways to enjoy drinking whisky, it's all in here, because I was curious about these things and the odyssey that I embarked upon helped me answer these questions and many more besides.

This journey has taken me to some of the absolute extremities of the United Kingdom, through the 'bible-belt' states of Tennessee and Kentucky, on to the whisky bars of Taiwan and the bullet train rides along the length of Japan. I've rooted through the history books and into the origins of human civilization, and visited state-of-the-art laboratories equipped with flavour-detecting-and-creating technology concerned with whisky making. I have consumed whisky on remote wind-torn beaches as the sun rises, and in the world's tallest buildings as the sun sets. I've tasted £10,000 ($17,000) bottles and £10 ($17) bottles and found value in both of them. I've also made lifelong friends on this journey and spent a lot of time simply sitting, sipping and thinking about whisky all by myself.

How To Use This Book

This book can be broadly separated into four different sections, each of them a useful referencing source in their own right, but when put together they form a sweeping campaign of whisky propaganda, general musings, original photography and scientific know-how.

In the first section of this book, I have endeavoured to thoroughly explore the history of whisky, from the origins of alcoholic beverages and distillation and their seemingly inseparable connections to religion, philosophy and spirituality, through to the emergence of medicinal *aqua vitae*, *uisgebaugh* and 'whisky' itself. In more recent history, I explore some of the cultures, people and politics that have moulded whisky into the global product that we know today.

Then we take an in-depth look into whisky production, from a simple barley grain through to an amber liquid with unparalleled levels of complexity and intricacy. We also look at how some of the most traditional techniques, that still remain in practice today, are now balanced with state-of-the-art renewable energy standards and precise manipulation methods that craft distinct products over a period of years and decades.

In the third section I explore over 55 of the world's most incredible distilleries, across nine countries and 19 distinct whisky-producing regions. Here we discover what makes these producers create the spirit that they do and how seemingly tiny deviations can dramatically affect the final outcome. I've aimed to shed new light on some of the oldest distilleries in the world, and championed some of the newest, too. Attention has been devoted equally to both small and large operations, and up-to-date tasting notes are included for some of my favourite expressions.

The final section includes some information on how best to drink whisky, including some original cocktail recipes, innovative whisky serves, and a couple of drinks that history has chosen to misplace. Finally, the book ends on five unique whisky blend recipes, which can be constructed by anyone, and are made from whiskies that are readily available to everyone.

Also included in the back of the book is a glossary of terms that will no doubt become a useful referencing point, and a glossary of distilleries, encompassing over 220 active whisky distilleries from around the world.

PART ONE
THE HISTORY OF WHISKY

The Origins of Distillation

Distillation is an art based around scientific principles. Its history is a story of scientific technology and the cultural background of the various people who have attempted to master it. In the broadest sense it is a way of separating components of a liquid using heat, be it to purify or 'split' a liquid, or to extract the essence of a flower, leaf, fruit or plant in its potent vapours. It is this broad scope of distilling applications that has piqued mankind's curiosity for the past 5,000 years or so – whether it was a Chinese herbalist concentrating aromatic herbs into boozy steam, a Mesopotamian physician compounding roots and barks into a medicinal tincture, or a Greek philosopher defining the elements upon which the world is founded. The ins and outs of all of these antics will continue to be debated for the next 5,000 years no doubt, but the state of distillation today stands as a legacy to those crackpot experimenters who paved the way.

Ancient Distilling

It seems that most things of any great significance can be traced back to ancient Chinese civilization, and certainly the Chinese have a long history with alcohol. One excavation of a Neolithic settlement in China found a 9,000-year-old clay pot containing fermented rice remnants – presumably they didn't clean their pots very well, or perhaps the entire village dropped dead before anyone had a chance. Strange, though, that the first two literary references of Chinese distillation come from as late as the 12th century AD. It is possible that they were just late developers on this occasion, but both of the aforementioned references provide great detail of the ingredients, methods and various types of distillation, giving this reader the impression that by the 12th century these were very well-established practices indeed. Traditional Chinese literature is thin on the ground when it comes to technology and science in general – the penning of classical literature has always been held in much higher regard in China – and adds further

weight to the argument that they were more than familiar with alchemical arts at this time.

Some scholars believe that the Chinese knowledge of distillation was shared with Persian, Babylonian, Arabian and Egyptian merchants through their contact along the ancient silk-trading routes that trickled into the Middle East. These 3,200-km/2,000-mile trails were first carved out around the 10th century BC, but it took a good 700 years to really get established. Gold, jade, silk and spices were all up for grabs, but it was as a hub of cultural networking that the silk route really came into its own. It was, in effect, the information superhighway of its time.

Whether the Chinese got the know-how from the Indo-Iranian people, or the other way around, the secret knowledge of ardent waters and botanical vapours was beginning to condense down into the classical civilizations. And the pre-eminent philosophers, alchemists and botanists of these civilizations took great interest in it.

The Greek philosopher Aristotle was certainly aware of distillation in one shape or another. One section of his *Meteorologica* (circa 340 BC) concerns experiments that he undertook to distil liquids, discovering that 'wine and all fluids that evaporate and condense into a liquid state become water.'

In 28 BC a practising magus (magician) known as Anaxilaus of Thessaly was expelled from Rome for performing his magical arts, which included setting fire to

Aristotle

what appeared to be water. The secrets of the trick were later translated into Greek and published around 200 AD by Hippolytus, presbyter of Rome. It turned out Anaxilaus had used distilled wine. Around the same time the Roman philosopher known as 'Pliny the Elder' (with a name like that he was surely endowed with a substantial beard) experimented with hanging fleeces above cauldrons of bubbling resin, and using the expansive surface area of the wool to catch the vapour and condense it into turpentine.

The world's first (self-proclaimed) alchemist, Zosimos of Panopolis, was also thought to be something of a wizard. He provided one of the first definitions of alchemy as the study of 'the composition of waters, movement, growth, embodying and disembodying, drawing the spirits from bodies and bonding the spirits within bodies.' It was Zosimos' belief that distillation in some way liberated the essence of a body or object that has led to our definition of alcoholic beverages as

The Great Library of Alexandria

'spirits' today.

The scrolls and ledgers that documented all these works were largely preserved in the great libraries of the time. There is no better example of this than the ancient and epic Great Library of Alexandria, which was thought to have contained over 500,000 scrolls. That was until successive religious and political power struggles during the first half of the first millennium AD caused them to be either sold, stolen or, as was the case with Cleopatra and Julius Caesar, simply given away only to be burned. In the year 642 AD, Alexandria was captured by a Muslim army and the last remaining remnants of the library were destroyed, and along with it the collective knowledge of much of the ancient world. Or so we thought... It would seem that some scraps of information and hastily copied texts still remained, written in ancient languages by long-dead men. The secrets to the mysteries of ardent waters and humid vapours did still exist, secreted away in monasteries and temples of learning dotted around Europe and the Middle East.

ISLAM

It was from these copied documents, amid the rise of the Islamic renaissance, that one fellow, Abu Musa Jabir ibn Hayyan (who in time became known simply as Geber), emerged in what stands as modern-day Iraq as the undisputed father of distillation. It is ironic that we have Islam, a religion that prohibits the drinking of alcohol, to thank for one of alcohol's most important breakthroughs. Some time around the end of the eighth century AD, Geber invented the first alembic still, which remains the basic form for all pot stills today. The major breakthrough in his still was that rather than using bits of sheep hair or an old rag to collect the spirit vapours, Geber's *al-ambiq* incorporated a condensing retort connected by a pipe. With the alembic still, Geber came tantalizingly close to understanding the full potential of distillation in what has to be one of the greatest understatements of all time: 'And fire which burns on the mouths of bottles due to boiled wine and salt, and similar things with nice characteristics which are thought to be of little use, but are of great significance in these sciences.'

It is thought that Geber's discoveries were influenced by the works of Zosimos of Panopolis, and that it was not spirits he sought, but the philosopher's stone and the secret of turning base metals into gold. Geber was misguided in this particular instance, but his work on distillation inspired other Arab thinkers and tinkerers of the time to experiment with the art.

Possibly the earliest example we have of distilled spirits being consumed for enjoyment, rather than medicinally, comes from a poem written in Arabic by Abū Nuwās, who died in 814. In one poem he describes ordering three types of wine, each of which becomes stronger as the poem continues. For the final drink he asks for a wine that 'has the colour of rainwater but is as hot inside the ribs as a burning firebrand'.

But for the most part, through the ninth and 10th centuries, distilled spirit was used for medicinal purposes only. This was a time of great unsettlement in the world, however. Vikings raided and Crusades gathered momentum, and as armies clashed and merchants traded, the seeds of understanding began to filter even into Dark Age Europe, where Latin-speaking scholarly monks had been waiting with eager patience for this wisdom of the ancients.

The knowledge remained exclusive to only the most worthy individuals, however. The 12th century Italian chemist Michael Salernus wrote of 'liquid which will flame up when set on fire' but took measures to write his findings in code lest the information get into the wrong hands. Around 100 years later Arnaldus de Villa Nova, a professor from the University of Montpellier, successfully translated Arabic texts that revealed some secrets of distillation. He went on to write one of the first complete sets of instructions on the distillation of wine, and it is this man that we have to thank for the term *aqua vitae* (water of life), a name which stuck in the Scandinavian *akvavit*, French *eaux de vie*, and of course the Scottish *uisge beatha*, which was later corrupted to whisky. Around 1300 AD he wrote: 'we call it *aqua vitae*, and this name is remarkably suitable, since it really is the water of immortality. It prolongs life, clears away ill humours, strengthens the heart, and maintains youth.'

Above A 17th century copper engraving of Arabian pioneer Abu Musa Jabir ibn Hayyan (Geber).

Right The title page from German physician Hieronymus Brunschwig's famous book of 1500 entitled *Liber de arte distillandi simplicia et composita*, also known as the Little Book of Distillation. It was one of the first books about chemistry and included instructions on how to distil *aqua vitae*.

EARLY GAELIC SPIRITS

FROM AQUA VITAE TO WHISKY

The big question that we need ask ourselves, though, is what were they doing with *aqua vitae*? The 14th and 15th centuries seem to be a transitional time for *aqua vitae* from its traditional use as a medical drug to it becoming a rather addictive social drug. Let us now focus on the British Isles, and chart the evolution of *aqua vitae* into the beverage known by the gaelic name *uisge beatha* and its coming of age, as the world is introduced to whisky.

Irish legend cites that Saint Patrick brought distilling to Ireland in the fifth century. This seems like a bit of a stretch to me and a likely case of crediting the man simply because he is a prominent historical figure and, in fairness, a useful bloke to have around (especially where snakes were concerned). I have seen reference made to bronze distilling artefacts found around the ecclesiastical province of Cashel in Tipperary, but hard evidence of this is thin on the ground. What is a likely fact, however, is that Henry II discovered grain-distilling practices when he took the liberty of invading Ireland in 1172. If Henry got it right, it would indeed be one of the earliest examples of distilling in the British Isles that we know of.

There is some evidence to suggest that *aqua vitae* was being distilled in Ireland for non-medicinal use as far back as the 14th century. *The Red Book of Ossoly* (1317–1360), was a record of the diocese written by Richard Ledred, who was the bishop, and it includes a treatise on *aqua vitae* made from wine, but makes no mention of grain-based spirits. In Edmund Campion's *History of Ireland*, which was published in 1571, he remarks that during the 1316 Irish Famine that was caused by a war with Scots soldiers, the miserable Irish comforted themselves 'with aqua vitae Lent long'. He also goes on to mention a knight from shortly after the same time, who would serve to his soldiers 'a mighty draught of aqua vitae, wine, or old ale.'

This, of course, is not proof by itself of the consumption of *aqua vitae*, since Campion wrote the book a clear 200 years after the event. Neither is the following eulogy, which is taken from a 1627 translation of *The Annals of Clonmacnoise*, originally published in 1408: 'Richard Magranell, Chieftain of Moyntyreolas, died at Christmas by taking a surfeit of aqua vitae, to him aqua mortis.'

Since the original 15th-century manuscript is lost, we can only guess at the accuracy of the translation and the poetic licence taken. The author's sense of humour in the pun '*aqua mortis*' (water of death) has not faded over the years, however, and surely there can be no greater testimony to the recreational enjoyment of *aqua vitae* at the start of the 15th century than the evidence of death through overindulgence during the festive period. Sadly, some things never change.

Raphael Holinshed describes the *aqua vitae* he finds in Ireland as a veritable cure-all for the 16th-century man, in his *Chronicles of England, Scotland and Ireland* (1577):

'Being moderatlie taken it sloweth age, it strengthneth youth, it helpeth digestion, it cureth flegme, it abandoneth melancholic, it relisheth the heart, it lighteneth the mind, it quickeneth the spirits, it cureth the hydropsie, it keepeth and preserveth the head from whirling, the eyes from dazeling, the tongue from lisping, the teeth from chattering, and the throte from ratling: the stomach from womblying, and the heart from swelling, the belly from retching, the guts from rumbling, the hands from shivering, & the sinews from shrinking, the veins from crumpling, the bones from aching, & the marrow from soaking.'

Taking the early Irish references at face value, it would seem that Scotland was a little slower on the uptake. The first reference to *aqua vitae* in Scotland comes from the Royal Exchequer Rolls of 1494 – which lists the sale of 500kg (1,120 lbs.) of malt to one Friar John Corr 'wherewith to make aqua vitae'. This order of *aqua vitae* was to be delivered to King James IV of Scotland no less. The story goes that King James had been campaigning on the island of Islay in the previous year and at some time or other got a taste for the spirit made there. A taste for it indeed, since the order placed in 1494 would be enough to manufacture over 1,200 bottles of whisky by today's standards!

Despite its apparent popularity with the royal household, it still took a while for *aqua vitae* to leave a mark on Scottish drinking habits. Most of the references to Scottish alcohol consumption during the following 50 years still refer to beer as the reliable beverage of the masses. *Aqua vitae* did, however, continue to exist for medical purposes. In 1505 a seal was granted by James IV of Scotland, which gave the Guild of Surgeon Barbers of Edinburgh (barbers were held in high regard back then) a monopoly over the manufacture of aqua vitae, stating that 'na [other] persons man nor woman within this Burgh make nor sell any aqua vitae within the samen'. And the Scots continued to find other uses for the stuff besides drinking it.

In 1540 the treasurer's accounts contain an entry relating to the supply of *aqua vitae* for the manufacture of gunpowder.

Around the same time we saw Henry VIII, King of England, begin his long succession of failed relationships. When the Pope denied Henry a divorce from his first wife, Catherine of Aragon, Henry took matters into his own hands, and in 1534, made the unprecedented step of separating the Church of England from the Roman Catholic Church. Just to make sure the point was clear, he disbanded monasteries, priories, convents and friaries, leaving a lot of learned monks out in the cold on their own. Some of these learned men

Below Henry VIII's dissolution of the monasteries drastically altered the landscape of England; one of its by-products was the dissemination of distillation knowledge among common folk, rather than just among monks.

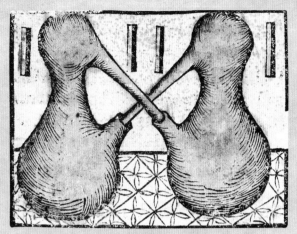

Early stills
Distillation techniques using 'double pelicans' (above) and the '*Rosenhut*' (right), from Brunschwig's pioneering book.

integrated into the local communities and the knowledge that had previously been the preserve only of these religious institutes began to filter through the land and into the farms and workshops of the very grateful common folk. Distilling gradually became a common farmyard practice, alongside brewing beer, churning butter and baking bread.

During the same period it is likely that there were some significant advances in the equipment used to make drinkable spirits. Alcohol for medicinal purposes required very little in the way of still management, but if people were expected to drink and enjoy this peculiar tonic, the equipment would need to be slightly more tailored to the needs of safety and taste. Alembic stills became bigger, due to demand, which in turn improved the quality of the distillate through longer still necks. Conical-shaped stills, ranging up to some 44 gallons/53 US gallons in capacity became the industry – I use the term loosely – standard. 'Worm'-style condensers (see page 75) were also probably introduced, since they were known to be in use in France and Italy.

Fynes Moryson's *Itinerary of Ireland* (1603) gives us an early taste of the production method of 'good' Irish *aqua vitae* at this time, and provides us with one of the earliest examples of the corruption of the gaelic name for 'water of life', *uisge beatha* (pronounced *ooshky-bay*):

'The Irish aqua vita, vulgarly called Usquebagh, is held in the best in the world of that kind, which is made also in England, but nothing so good as that which is brought out of Ireland. Usquebagh is preferred before our aqua vitas because the mingling of Raysons, Fennell seed and other things, mitigating the heat and making the taste pleasant, makes it lesse inflame and yet refresh the weake stomache with moderate heat and good relish.'

If you are thinking that this flavoured spirit sounds nothing at all like the whisky you enjoy today, you're not alone. It would seem that not everyone got the memo about whisky being made from only barley. In 1772 when Thomas Pennant visited the island of Islay he recorded that 'in old times the distillation was from thyme, mint, anise, and other fragrant herbs'. George Smith's *Compleat Body of Distilling* (1766) has a recipe and cost breakdown for 'Fine Usquebaugh' that has among its ingredients malt spirits, molasses spirits, mace, cloves, nuts, cinnamon, coriander, cubeb, raisins, dates, liquorice/licorice, saffron and sugar. This, to me, sounds remarkably like a (bad) gin, which is not at all surprising given the goings on of the gin craze that had been overwhelming London for the past half-century. Flavouring spirits was not only frequent during this time, but downright essential if one was inclined to make the concoction drinkable.

So there was no clear identity for *uisge beatha* during the 1600s, but that didn't hamper its steady integration into the fabric of society. More and more farms turned more of their attention to the profitable liquor and it developed into an important economic commodity, even being used as part of a rental payment for properties in Scotland and trading with Irish merchants – despite the apparent enthusiasm that the Irish held for making their own. And with the recognition of a growing industry, so too came the inevitable: taxes.

TAXES AND SMUGGLING

The first tax on spirits in Scotland was set in 1644 at a rate of 2 shillings and 8 pence for 'everie pynt of aquavytie or strong watteries sold within the countrey', with further increases half-a-dozen times over the following 60 years. After the Act of Union in 1707, the parliaments of England and Scotland were brought together as one, and the same taxes on distillation applied to both. In 1715, the English Malt Tax was put into effect in Scotland, too, and then increased in 1725, making it one of the major contributing factors to the Jacobite uprising and riots that were frequent at the time. But even with heavier taxes, the distilling industry continued to prosper, since *uisgebah* could also be made from other cereals. This fact also encouraged many of the brewers to turn to distilling.

Let's get one thing straight, though. For most of the 18th century, this still wasn't whisky as you know it. It was crudely distilled from a mixture of cereals in a rigged together tin can. The spirit wouldn't have been cut correctly, at best making it foul and at worst lethal; it was most likely flavoured, and certainly wouldn't have been intentionally rested in oak barrels. Besides, nearly all of the whisky produced during this time would have been for Scottish or Irish consumption, with London certainly needing no further encouragement to drink as its inhabitants wallowed in the midst of a gin craze.

There were exceptions to the backyard rule, of course. One of history's most prominent malt distilleries from the same period, and the first large distillery to flourish in Scotland, was Ferintosh. The distillery at Ferintosh became an incredibly lucrative operation after its owner was granted a tax break for support of the new Dutch king, William of Orange, who acceded to the British throne in 1689. No taxes meant the product could be sold cheaply, meaning the other tax-paying distilleries could not compete with Ferintosh.

Growth for Scottish distillers continued up until 1752, with the annual output almost doubling in the space of 10 years. The future looked good until disaster struck in 1757, marked by a massive crop failure that forced the British government to prohibit the sale of distilled spirits for three years. The use of a private still was not prohibited, however, and so long as its wares were used only for household consumption, no law was broken. No enterprising Scotsman in his right mind would lie down just like that and so illicit distilling and smuggling began on a massive scale.

By the time the ban was lifted it was already too late – duty-free whisky had a good taste to it and men had little inclination towards paying taxes. And it was the game of taxation that seemed to govern the prevalence of illicit operations for the next 50 years, increasing dramatically when the risk of being caught was outweighed by the significant rewards. A sudden increase in duty meant the sprouting up of new illicit distilleries by the thousand.

It seems the government was too slow to recognize that things were getting out of hand and excise officers were simply too lenient on those caught in the act of illicit distilling, with early records of some individuals being caught three or four times in a short period. When the authorities did get a handle on the sheer scale of the problem, it was already endemic and far too big to police or manage, regardless of the severity of the punishment.

Above Seventeenth and 18th-century buildings, thought to be part of the old Ferintosh distillery in the Scottish Highlands.

The risk to the clandestine operatives, of course, was not a particularly great one. The various inaccessible islands, glens and crags of the Highlands (many of which have given their names to present-day legitimate distilleries) provided ample seclusion from the prying eyes of the excise officers, who were also known as gaugers – named for their 'gauging' of the malt to assess its duty. The Glendronach Distillery in Speyside is one such operation that picked its location very carefully. Situated adjacent to natural springs, it meant that there was an abundance of clean water, but even better than that was the colony of rooks which nested nearby and were prone to screaming whenever anyone approached at night – as good a security alarm as anyone could wish for.

The 'legal' distilleries now had to compete on price with both the duty-free Ferintosh distillery, as well as illicit operations. Many of them reacted the only way that they could, and took measures to fake their customs and excise production declarations in an attempt to reduce their tax bill. The government got wise to this pretty quickly, though, and enforced a series of strict and oppressive measures that aimed to control the few remaining legitimate operations. In 1774 William Pitt's Wash Act was passed, which required Lowland stills to be a minimum of 400 litres/106 US gallons in capacity and taxed on their size, not their output. Highland distillers were granted more lenient taxes, based on the volume produced, and were permitted to use smaller stills of a minimum 91 litres/24 US gallons. The only problem was that they weren't allowed to sell it outside of the Highlands. The Wash Act drew a deep line in the sand between how Lowland and Highland distilleries operated, encouraging the distillers in the south to build stills that could distil very quickly, albeit with a significant drop in quality. In the Highlands there was less rush, and the spirit was said to be of a much greater standard than the Lowland swill... but available only in the Highlands.

Distilling for personal consumption was outlawed in 1781. If the illegitimate distillers had ever thought about going back to the straight and narrow, those thoughts had completely gone out of the window by this point. As the 18th century drew to a close, the ongoing Highland Clearances, also known as the 'expulsion of the Gael', only served to fuel the fire of resentment that burned for the British government. Any perception in the Highlands that smugglers were wrongdoers or law breakers had been replaced by an acceptance of it as a profession and even as a god-given Gaelic right. Both the duty and the punishment for non-compliance were further increased, and Scots rebelled, resulting in what nearly amounted to all-out warfare.

The rate of taxation on whisky fluctuated greatly over the years, as much as tripling in war time when the British government needed the cash, and settling down again during times of peace.

Whisky would be distributed among towns and villages by 'bladdermen', so-called because concealed beneath their britches would be a bladder full of *uisge beatha*. Highland Park Distillery on the Orkney Islands (see page 160) was known to conceal casks of whisky in the hollow pillars of nearby St. Magnus Cathedral, despite the attending reverend reaffirming 'thou shalt not make whisky' in his Sunday service. During the same period it has been estimated that Edinburgh had around 400 distilleries; 11 of which were licensed.

The 1823 Excise Act changed everything, however. Duty on Scottish whisky was cut by more than 50%, down to the manageable rate of 2 shillings and 5 pence per gallon. For many business-minded distillers this was an opportunity to legitimize their operations and increase their business. The Glenlivet, Fettercairn, Cardhu, Balmenach and Ben Nevis are just some of the distilleries that are still operational today which saw their chance and licensed their operations during this time. By 1825 there were 263 licensed distilleries in Scotland, all of them free to produce whatever volume of spirit they wished. Quality naturally improved – since it is so much easier to make good whisky when you don't have to hide it from anyone – as did quantity, and the operations that chose to avoid the duty were soon forced out of the marketplace, with records of seizure in Scotland dropping from a post-Excise Act high of 764 in 1835 to only two in 1875.

However, the less documented illicit activity in Ireland was either on a considerably larger scale, or policed more vigorously (or both). In 1833 there were 8,233 reported cases of seizure of illicit distilling equipment and the numbers remained in the thousands even up until the 1870s.

The smuggling in Scotland didn't stop there, mind you, as tax on spirits was much higher in England than Scotland during the 19th century, by over 8 shillings a gallon. Licensed Scotch distillers, many of whom had plenty of experience of the smuggling lifestyle, developed ever more ingenious methods to smuggle their 'mountain dew' over the border, even going as far as to train dogs to swim across rivers with pig bladders full of whisky in tow. Practices like that were small time, however. There were bigger operations taking place as some estimates place the volume of Scottish duty-paid whisky crossing the border in the 1820s as upwards of 50,000 litres/10,000 US gallons every week (that's a lot of dogs). Many of the distillers would travel in armed groups, each carrying 30 litres/8 US gallons of spirit tied to themselves in metal canisters. Most of the time, excise officers were simply too scared to approach them – and who can blame them?

Even up until the 1980s it was normal for excise officers to live 'on site' at the distillery. One distillery manager once candidly told me that 'To be a distillery worker you have to have a real genuine love for drinking whisky, but to be an excise officer you have to have an even bigger love.'

Back in the 1970s at The Bowmore Distillery on Islay, twin brothers John and Roger McDougall were the acting customs excise officers – just to make things even more confusing. The brothers apparently had a passion for making their own spirits, Alastair McDonald from Auchentoshan tells me. While working at The Bowmore at the tender age of 17, he was cornered by the two big officers and asked: 'What do you drink, McDonald?' Alastair assumed that something had gone missing in the

Above The pillars of St. Magnus Cathedral on the Orkney Islands, some of which would have been secretly filled with casks of Highland Park whisky in the early years of the 19th century, unbeknownst to the vicar!

distillery and quickly replied, 'Nothing.' The brothers produced a bottle of something dark and held it under his nose, apparently looking for a response. When none was given they told young Alastair to drink the liquid, which tasted like coffee. Alastair gave the pair a pleading look, and they responded by telling him 'It's our homemade Tia Maria – d'ya like it?'

The story of distillation in North America starts with rum. The early colonists didn't trust water, so turned to hard cider and beer as their staple beverages. However, something stronger was needed for the cold winter nights, and rum was the answer. Rum flooded into North America from the Caribbean during the 1600s, as well as sugar and molasses – the building blocks required to make one's own rum. Many households owned rickety alembic stills that could be used to distil mead, pear cider and hard cider into spirit – a job invariably conducted by the woman of the house – but the cheap and ready supply of molasses made rum the most economic choice for those seeking intoxication. In 1750 Peter Kalm, a Swedish-Finnish traveller, noted in his *Travels into North America* that colonists believed rum to be a healthier choice over imported spirits made from grain, even going as far as to point out that fresh meat stored in rum will 'keep as it was' while in other spirits it would be 'eaten full of holes.'

Nevertheless, there are records of corn and rye beers being made in Connecticut from the middle of the 17th century. In fact, the earliest known record of any kind of distillation in North America is of the Dutch on Staten Island (which was a Dutch Colony at the time) in 1640. The distiller was William Kieft, and he also owned a tavern, which was the only place you could buy his creations. Bottled products included brandy and some kind of crude whiskey made from the leftover dregs of beer. This was a relatively common practice in the years to come, since grain was much more expensive than molasses.

Jump forward 100 years, and not much on the back bar has changed, but rye and corn-based spirits were beginning to gain popularity. George Washington, a man who clearly liked a drink, operated one of the largest distilleries in North America out of his Mount Vernon Estate in Virginia; it was making rye whiskey. During the American War of Independence he was known to remark that 'The benefits arising from the moderate use of strong liquor have been experienced in all armies and are not to be disputed.' The same man had a barrel of Barbados rum delivered to celebrate his inauguration as the first President of the United States in 1789.

Corn whiskey probably lagged behind rye a bit. Maize was still an exotic, New World commodity, whilst the rye that had been brought over by German settlers originally was a familiar Old World product that was easy to cultivate and familiar to brewers and distillers.

As settlers expanded the frontiers, moving southwards into modern-day Kentucky and Tennessee, the soil and climate changed. Where rye flourished in the colder north, colonists soon learned from native Americans that 'Indian Corn' crops grew better in the humid heat. Not only that, but corn could even be planted in-between other crops and even trees without the need for levelling off the land beforehand. Just like the gold rush of the mid-1800s, the difference being that this gold was edible, New-Worlders flocked to the area to stake their claim on land and to grow this energy-packed, new fangled food source. Some of these early settlers had familiar names like Beam and

Above George Washington's Mount Vernon mansion in Virginia in the late 18th century. In 1797, he hired a Scottish plantation manager, who encouraged him to build a whiskey distillery. By 1799, the distillery they had created was the largest in the United States.

Weller. They, along with many others, were the forefathers of the great whiskey tycoons of the 19th century.

Corn was exported by the boat- and barrel-load. The two major trading routes from the western frontier went either to the Eastern seaboard, or down-river to New Orleans. Without railroads or motor vehicles, both were long, arduous journeys that required a significant animal and human workforce to cart the barrels of milled corn. It made far more sense to convert the corn into liquor and pop that in the barrel instead. With the weight reduced by 80%, but the value remaining the same, a horse could effectively carry five times the load. Distillation operations popped up like worms out of the ground: basic as can be and dangerous to boot. These were not artisans crafting fine-quality liquor; they were always ancillary to farm operations, made by business-minded farmers, reducing costs and maximizing profit.

The production network was established. What was needed next was a market for the product. Politics was the answer – America gained its independence in 1789. The 'Demon Rum' that had built the colonies was a British invention and a recent memory of colonial rule that had birthed the slogan 'No taxation without representation'. President John Adams himself admitted that 'Molasses was an essential ingredient in American Independence.' Rum was most definitely out of favour. The United States looked inwards for a new spirit of America. The answer was whiskey.

Above A tax collector is tarred and feathered in Pennsylvania in 1794 during the Whiskey Rebellion.

It is a historical fact that when there is big demand for a product, as there was with whiskey during this time, there will always be a taxman ready to take his cut. Continuing to mirror the goings on in Scotland 150 years previously, in 1791, only two years after independence, an excise duty on spirits was passed that required cash payment to the government based on the production of spirits. The aim was to make up the huge deficit that the war had cost the nation, but farmer-distillers felt cheated – the independence that many of them had fought for during the war was being pulled out from underneath them. It sparked rebellion, which was particularly prevalent on the southwestern frontier and across the Appalachian region that stretched all the way from New York down to South Carolina. The new government demonstrated for the first time that it was willing to use violence to suppress the uprising, but collection of taxes was minimal and the tax was repealed in 1802. Sixty years later it was reinstated, but it was much less of a problem at that time, since the government was buying huge stocks of whiskey to fire up its Civil War troops.

BOURBON

It's fairly easy to work out where rye, corn, Canadian *et al.* got their names, but to Brits, bourbon is a type of chocolate biscuit/cookie, right? To tell that tale we must first look to France. Louis XVI was King of France from 1774 to 1792, and a strong ally of George Washington during the War of Independence. As a sign of America's gratitude to Louis – mostly for supplying weapons – after the war, a huge swathe of land that included 34 modern-day Kentucky counties was named after Louis' house name, Bourbon. Some say that it was actually the French general and war hero Lafayette, also descended from the French royal house, who the county was named after. Either way, the Americans liked the French during this period – Bourbon County was an obvious reflection of that.

As time went on, the French connection was forgotten and Bourbon County got smaller. The state of Kentucky was formed, but 'Old Bourbon County' whiskey continued to be traded in New Orleans. As the barrels of liquor bobbed up and down the Mississippi River (not literally – they would of course have been on a boat) towards the port, they had lots of time to mellow and integrate with the wood in the southern sun. The whiskey became famous for its quality and the name of bourbon became synonymous with it.

The title of being the first producer of bourbon is a hotly contested one. Many attribute it to Evan Williams in 1783, though solid evidence to back it up is scarce. Others pick out the preacher, Elijah Craig, claiming that he was the first to age whiskey in barrels. Allegedly, Craig used barrels that previously held pickled fish (for reasons of

economics, not flavour); so as to remove the smell, he would char the inside. The simple act of charring a barrel opened up a whole new world of whiskey complexity to his liquid. Other historians believe that the char was a sterilizing measure, put in place during a time when casks were used for fermentation of the wash. Then there are Oscar Pepper and James Crow, distillers through the 1830s and 1840s who perfected many of the methods that are essential to good bourbon production today. Bourbon whiskey is not a product of any single man's endeavours, but a concerted effort by many men, across multiple generations, compelled and coerced for reasons of economics, geography and the pursuit of a better product and a stronger brand. And what we do know is that the first known advertisement for bourbon whiskey was published in the *Western Citizen* newspaper, in Paris, Kentucky in 1821.

The mid-1800s saw the introduction of the column still, which now features in many modern-day bourbon whiskey distilleries. This meant an increase in production, due to the continuous nature of the apparatus. It also meant greater consistency – another strong selling point to the thirsty public. As frontiers stretched out to the Old West, it was bourbon whiskey that cowboys called for in saloons.

In 1850, the Louisville & Nashville Railroad was chartered and began connecting Louisville to markets not serviced by the traditional steamboat trade. The growing railway system caused a significant change in the bourbon industry. Distilleries no longer had to be located near gristmills or flowing streams or rivers. The railroad could bring large quantities of grain to nearly any location in the state and could transport full barrels of whiskey to market. This allowed bourbon distilleries to locate in Louisville and offer a better service to the whiskey merchants on 'Whiskey Row'. For example, the Old Kentucky Distillery was established in 1855 along a railway on the outskirts of Louisville. And in 1860, the Early Times Distillery was built at the Early Times Rail Station in nearby Nelson County – it is still there today.

When the Civil War broke out in 1861, Kentucky, a border state, found itself trapped between both sides of the conflict. The fact that

Above Bourbon County in Kentucky is named in honour of Louis XVI's family name, in thanks for supplying weapons to George Washington during the War of Independence.

Kentucky remained part of the Union, but still permitted the ownership of slaves, made it about as neutral as was possible. Some stories from that time suggest that when Union soldiers were in town it would be the American flag that was flown, and when Confederates came by it would be the Confederate flag. Both armies drank bourbon recreationally, as well as using it for cleaning wounds and no doubt raising spirits.

The end of the Civil War also saw the introduction of a government-controlled distillery licensing system. This system made small-scale distilling a legally cumbersome and expensive activity. The days of small-batch production and the farmer-distiller tradition were numbered.

In Louisville, the bourbon business saw the development of new trading houses, including J. T. S. Brown (later Brown-Forman). These companies resumed the practice of buying whiskey in bulk from rural and city-based distillers and vatting them together to create proprietary flavour profiles. The vatted whiskies were then rebarreled for sale in bulk lots to wholesalers, retailers, doctors and pharmacists.

As a new century closed in, everything was looking good for American whiskey. In fact, it would have been perfect were it not for the murmurs of temperance coming from the sidelines. Those murmurs were gradually turning into shouts, and it slowly became clear that Prohibition wasn't far away. And with it would come the near-complete collapse of the entire whiskey industry. Things would never be the same again.

CANADA

In Canada, the earliest known occurrence of distilling goes back to James Grant's rum distillery in Quebec City, around 1767. As is usual, it is the cheapest ingredient that gets distilled first, and during that period it was molasses. But one thing

Above Gold prospectors in Canada in 1900, following in the footsteps of George Carmack, who struck it rich on a stream in the Yukon four years' earlier. Many prospectors struggled to get by, and often spent the little they had on whisky.

Canada was not short of was land, and the colonists soon got to work planting all manner of crops.

In terms of brewing and distilling, it was probably Scottish immigrants who kicked things off, which might be why Canadians, like the Scots, drop the 'e' from their spelling of whisky. Either way, Canada was a melting pot of experienced booze producers from France, Scotland, Ireland and England. Each European nation had brought its own cereal offering to the table, too. The Dutch and Germans came with rye; the English brought barley and wheat. Indigenous corn flourished in the south and rye did just as well in the cooler northern areas.

But the most popular cereal for distilling in the early 1800s was wheat. Wheat was milled down for bread-making and the glamorous-sounding but apparently not particularly useful 'wheat middlings' were sent to be mashed and distilled. Barley was malted and used for its enzymatic benefits, and eventually rye became a seasoning of pepper over the top of the 'mash bill': the different grains used for mashing.

One of the first whisky distilleries, and certainly the most successful of its era, was that of the Molson family of Montreal. Molson is the second-oldest company in all of Canada and better known for its brewing empire. But before beer became their bread and butter, Thomas, the son of founder John Molson, took a trip to Scotland in 1816 and embarked on a tour around a bunch of distilleries. He recorded what he saw, and, convinced that whisky was the next big thing in Canada, built his own distillery a few years later. Other whisky distilleries materialized, keen to get a piece of the pie, and in 1827, only six years after Molson had sold his first bottle, there were 31 known distilleries in lower Canada. Another six years later and that number is believed to have tripled in size.

Reports from this time indicate that this 'whisky' may have only been distilled once, meaning that it was likely no more than 20% ABV and more than a little 'ragged' around the edges. Exported stuff, by Molson at least, was apparently distilled twice in order to ensure its survival on the long voyage over to the United Kingdom or across the United States.

In 1840, distilling licences were up for grabs and reports from the time show that there were over 200 distilleries across Canada; today there are fewer than a dozen. The demand for Canadian 'rye' whisky (see page 204) was high as well. In 1861, America was thrown into Civil War, where whiskey distilling was outlawed in the South (stills were used to make cannons) and heavily taxed in the North. Canadian whisky happily picked up the slack and the void was filled. In 1887 Canada was the first nation to put a minimum ageing requirement on whisky. The minimum age was one year, which was increased to two years in 1890.

Canada played an important role during Prohibition in the USA, providing a steady flow of liquor, namely Canadian Club – which has had a strong following ever since, to thirsty American people. At the height of Prohibition there were thought to be over 1,000 bottles of Canadian Club crossing the US border every day.

These days, Canadian whiskies share similar mash bills to that of bourbon – corn-dominated, but with some rye or wheat overtones. There are some 100% rye whiskies, too, most notably those produced by Alberta Distillers Ltd.

What is Whisky?

Up until this stage in our story, whisky made in Scotland was sold and produced only as a single product from a single distillery. The Excise Act of 1823 encouraged illicit distillers to hit the straight and narrow, and many did, but even after that you would have been hard-pushed to find a bottle of Scotch whisky outside of Scotland, and over 90% of the malt whisky made in Scotland never crossed the border. Winston Churchill once attested to this: 'My father would never have drunk whisky, except when shooting on a moor or in some very dull, chilly place. He lived in an age of brandy and soda.' The truth is that the whisky of the early 19th century could not compete with the finesse of French brandies. The changeover kicked off in 1830, but it would take another 60 years for all of the cogs to align correctly and Scotch to make its true impact on the world.

The Development of the Continuous Still

It started with new advances in distillation. Whisky had always been made the same way, fermented from malted barley and distilled in a big onion-shaped kettle. It was a time-consuming 'batch' process that produced only a little liquor for a lot of effort, and required the cleaning and resetting of all the equipment before it could be repeated. At the time it was also highly inconsistent, almost all of the 330 or so distilleries had previously run as illicit smuggling operations, and despite their now legitimate operations, many of their practices remained crude, inconsistent and 'boutique', to put it nicely. But this was the early 1800s and with the industrial revolution grinding into motion, an alternative was needed to the primitive ways of old: a device that could continuously distil alcohol.

Irishman Aeneas Coffey is usually credited with inventing the first continuous still in 1830. However, those of us in the know are aware that the true inventor was actually Robert Stein, in 1827. But what most people don't know is that

Stein relied on earlier designs to make his still, too. To discover more about that we must travel to 19th-century France.

Despite being illiterate, French-born Édouard Adam attended chemistry lectures under Professor Laurent Solimani at the University of Montpellier. Adam developed and patented the first type of column still in 1804, except the column was horizontal rather than vertical and based on laboratory Woulfe bottles (sequential bottles linked by pipes). It worked by linking together a series of what Adam called 'large eggs', with pipes that would transfer alcohol vapour from one to the next. The concentration of alcohol increased in each subsequent egg, while the leftover stuff was recycled back at the start. It wasn't truly continuous in its design, but it certainly paved the way for stuff that came later down the line.

Adam died in 1807, but his rivals continued to improve the design, with such inventions as the Pistorius still, patented in 1817, which was the first still to be in a column shape. Steam was pumped up from the bottom and beer from the top and distillation took place on a series of plates. The feints were recycled and fed in again at the top.

Subsequent iterations were developed by the French engineer Jean-Baptiste Cellier Blumenthal

Below Frenchman Éduoard Adam built upon the principle of the Woulfe bottle and in 1801 patented the first still to produce alcohol in one operation.

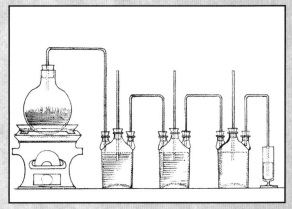

and a mysterious Englishman known only as Mr Dihi. It tended to be the case that these stills incorporated one or two elements of the continuous still as we now know it, but never all of them working in unison. It wasn't until Robert Stein came along that it eventually happened.

Robert Stein came from strong distilling stock. His father, James Stein, established the Kilbagie Distillery in Fife in 1777, one of the largest distilleries of its era. Robert went on to run it, and with the new Excise Act in place, he set about expanding his legal operation. Stein patented a new type of still, shaped like a column and split into a series of small chambers. The wash was pre-heated, then pumped into the chambers where it came into contact with steam. As the vapour rose, the steam stripped the spirit away, and anything that wasn't alcohol condensed on one of the fine hair meshes that were dotted around inside the contraption. Spirit and waste were collected separately and the process continued.

The patent still was a licence to print alcohol, but on the negative side, the purchase of a patent still was a huge investment, costing many times more than a simple pot still. But this type of distillation produced a much lighter, cleaner and more delicate spirit that was cheaper to produce and up to 94% ABV. (For a more detailed look at the continuous still, see page 78)

Just as the first orders of Stein's still were being delivered, another still was invented. An Irishman named Aeneas Coffey, who had formerly been the Inspector General of Excise in Dublin (and had no doubt seen a few stills in his time), patented his still in 1830. It had a few marked improvements over Stein's: larger processing power (3,000 gallons/3,600 US gallons of wash in an hour), greater purity of distillate (up to 96% ABV) and a much cleaner design. One of the best parts of the new 'patent still' was that pipes containing the cool wash entering the system doubled up as condensing coils for the hot alcohol vapours exiting it – like a dog eating its own tail. It was a work of genius for its time, reflected in the fact that it is still the same basic design that is used all over the world today.

The first continuous stills were made from iron, and the results were apparently disgusting – so bad, in fact, that the spirit was passed on to gin distillers to be re-distilled and flavoured. Experiments then took place with copper and wooden continuous stills, and the favourite today is, of course, steel.

Stein's design quickly lost favour, the last one being installed at Glenochil in 1846. Coffey's went on to dominate and became a favourite of the Lowland distillers, marking a clear divergence of Lowland distillers from the Highland style, which still remains in place today. This divergence from one another would later become a huge matter of dispute between the traditional malt distillers of the North, and the industrial grain distillers of the South. They were producing two entirely different products – the powerfully flavoured malt whisky was in shorter supply, inconsistent and costly, while there was an abundance of the bland grain whisky, so much so, that the distillers were finding it hard to shift it all. The solution was blending.

BLENDS

Blends, both then and now, comprised a mixture of malt and grain whiskies. The malts were mixed together to give a uniform and balanced flavour, while the grain acted as the lighter backdrop. The invention of blending was of mutual benefit to both parties, as it combined the gentle characteristics of the grain with the powerful flavours of the malt in a uniform and pliable mixture.

There is some evidence to suggest that blending was going on right at the start of the 1800s. During that time many of the most famous names in blended whisky were working in grocers' stores or as tea blenders or wine merchants. Blending back then would have been conducted on a very personal level, however, with 'A bit of this and a bit of that for you, Mr. Douglas', etc. And it wasn't until much later, in 1860, that this changed.

The Spirits Act of 1860 allowed whisky to be blended under bond, before the duty had been paid on it, meaning that blending could be done on a much larger scale. This was one of the main catalysts for the rise of the blends. The promise of blended whisky provided new avenues of trade, with larger mass appeal, larger production potential and lower costs. Also, because blends

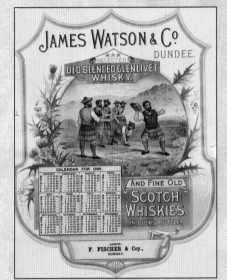

Above A selection of advertisements for well-known whisky blenders of the 19th and 20th centuries.

were more consistent, consumers could pick a favourite and know that it could be relied upon, meaning that a greater emphasis could be placed on the brand and marketing of the product.

The legislation coincided very well with the construction of Scotland's rail network and its connection with northern English cities. Rail networks were also established between Edinburgh and Glasgow, but also rail lines connecting Inverness, Aberdeen and Keith (right in the heart of Speyside) were launched in the 1850s. Suddenly it had become a lot easier to move whisky around the place.

The final piece of good fortune that set Scotch on its way was the decimation of the French wine and brandy industry by the phylloxera vine louse, an event that all but killed off brandy and set the industry back 20 years. With highly limited stocks of brandy, people turned to the next brown spirit on the list: whisky.

In my opinion it is the combination of the two factors, brandy's collapse and what was effectively

the invention of blending, that had the greatest hand in putting whisky where it is today.

Blending was also the driving force behind improving the image of Scotch whisky at a time where marketing was just as important as product quality. This drove demand for grain whisky as well as for malt, as both were needed to make blends, and in the latter part of the 19th century the whisky industry in Scotland had a clear split. For every litre/quart of pot-still malt whisky that was made, two litres/quarts of patent-still grain whisky were produced. In 1877 the six major producers of grain whisky amalgamated their operations under the title of Distillers Company Limited (DCL). They effectively became self-regulating, manufacturing all of the grain whisky for the blends.

The gold rush had begun and dozens of malt distilleries opened in Scotland during the 1890s, keen to meet the blenders' needs. Roughly one-fifth of the malt distilleries that are operational in Scotland today were opened between 1893 and 1899.

Many were doomed to fail, though, as in the following years the market became saturated with malt whisky stocks eager to find their way into the blender's bottle. Despite seemingly good prospects, the bandwagon was well and truly loaded, everyone had overestimated the demand for whisky, and well-established firms like Edinburgh-based blender, J & G Stewart, went into liquidation in 1898, taking down dozens of others with it through the network of credit. The entire industry was threatened with collapse as a result, and vast stocks of whisky remained stationary in warehouses. This event and others around it marked the beginning of 50 years of zero growth for whisky in Scotland.

The Barons of Blending

In the space of 20 years, a select group of Scots, later known as the 'whisky barons', built an unprecedented global market off of the growing popularity for blended whisky. Their good timing, coupled with a shrewd sense of self-marketing, afforded them not just worldwide domination of the drinks market, but lofty positions within high society and the eyes and ears of politicians and royalty alike. The names Buchanan, Mackie, Usher, Walker and Dewar can be seen behind the counter of off-licence and liquor stores around the world today, but only because the men behind them forged an industry for blended whisky when the world needed it most.

In 1885, Tommy Dewar, the fifth son of John Dewar of Perth, arrived in London at the tender age of 21. His mission was to make the Dewar's brand of whisky that his father had established in 1846 a household name. Allegedly Tommy had only two business contacts in London when he arrived – one of whom turned out to be bankrupt, and the other dead. Unfazed, Tommy set about

establishing himself as the premier Scotsman in London. It seems to me that Tommy's subsequent success was based upon a solid foundation of charm, wit and intelligence. It worked, though – between 1894 and 1897 Dewar's quadrupled its capital. Tommy himself was made Sheriff of London in 1896, the same year that Dewar's began building the Aberfeldy malt distillery in his home town. During that same period Tommy can also lay claim to owning the third motor vehicle ever sold in England – if such a thing as celebrities existed at the time, 'Whisky Tom' was certainly one of them. Dewar's was also the first whisky brand to use paper labels, back in 1863.

Then there was James Buchanan, another formidable character from the age of blending – with a streak of red hair, tall and wiry, and famous for his mantra 'A man must make his opportunity, as oft as find it'. If Tom Dewar was the larger-than-life Scotsman about town, Buchanan was the lean, graceful figure, demanding the attention of everyone present while he quietly smouldered in the corner of the room. After moving to London in 1879, his famous Black & White blend, originally known as 'Buchanan's Blend' but affectionately re-dubbed due to its white label on a black bottle packaging, became the official whisky of the House of Commons only a year after JB established his business in London. In 1903, Buchanan & Co went public, but all £850,000 worth of shares were purchased by the man himself – he was truly a one-man mega- corporation. A few years later, Buchanan was knighted for his services to the country and then, in 1922, awarded a peerage and the title of Lord Woolavington, a name that he apparently made up when once signing a cheque to a politician in whom he placed little trust.

Above The Scottish whisky distiller Tommy Dewar, who along with his brother John, built their family label, Dewar's, into a successful international brand.

From the town of Kilmarnock in East Ayrshire hailed the Walker family. Kilmarnock was an up-and-coming place in the early 19th century, famous in particular for its threaded rugs and carpets. The first Scottish railway was laid in the town in 1812 and it was on Kilmarnock's King Street that John Walker opened his grocer's store in 1820 at the tender age of 15. One of the services Walker was famed for was his tea blending – he later applied the same methods to blending whisky. John's son, Alexander, joined the business around the same time that the blending laws were slackened. Alexander was every bit the visionary as Dewar and Buchanan, even in the early days of the humble Kilmarnock grocers. Alexander looked outwards and to the potential of Walker's Kilmarnock Whisky in the American and global markets. Alexander Walker was the true driving force behind his father's brand and the inspiration for his son, Alexander II, who took the reins when Alexander died in 1889. By that point the Walker brand was unstoppable. In 1893 the company bought out the entire Cardhu Distillery in Speyside, a whisky that became a key piece to its Old Highland Blend, which later became known simply as Black Label. Over the 25 years that followed, Johnnie Walker became the biggest blended whisky in the world, and a globally recognized brand name before Coca-Cola had even left Atlanta. In 1908, over a lunchtime meeting, the pre-eminent black-and-white artist of the day, Tom Brown, sketched the image of the 'striding man' on a napkin – it remains one of the most internationally recognized logos in the world today.

Dewar, Buchanan and Walker were not the only hard-working men who possessed the vision and determination to see their businesses prosper. Others equally worthy of a mention are the Haigs, Mackies and Berry Brothers. In 1824, the Haigs were also the founders of the Cameronbridge Distillery in Fife, which is today responsible for making a large proportion of Diageo's entire grain whisky, vodka and gin portfolio. Its Gold Label and Dimple brands became popular products, and in 1906 it was appointed the official purveyor of whisky to the House of Lords.

Above Buchanan's Black & White whisky achieved notoriety in literature, as it was ordered both by James Bond in *Moonraker* and Dick Driver in F. Scott Fitzgerald's *Tender is the Night*.

Glasgow-based James Mackie created his White Horse brand, unique in its use of Lagavulin in the blend. He was also at the centre of the debate around 'What is whisky?' that kicked off in 1905. At the time, Highland distillers were up in arms over the 'lesser' grain spirit that was beginning to dominate the category and a big legal battle ensued, ultimately finding that, despite being different, the patent-still spirits had every right to be classed as Scotch. Mackie, who had interests in both sides of the debate, involved himself heavily in the argument but took a neutral standpoint, arguing that, regardless of the name, Scotch whisky should always be well aged and of good quality. It was Mackie's input that ultimately led to the

"IT TAKES ME A LONG TIME TO GET ROUND"
said Johnnie Walker

"The road to Kilmarnock," said Johnnie Walker, "is a long one; in fact it takes me years to get there. For the separate whiskies, which are blended at Kilmarnock into Johnnie Walker, have first of all to mature for years in the wood. Only by ageing naturally in oak casks can these fine whiskies develop the qualities which enable them to be blended into a harmonious, 'round' whisky—so that's why it takes me so long to get 'round.'

"You will understand now why maturing and blending play such an important part in the special enjoyment you get from Johnnie Walker—and, understanding, *ask for Johnnie Walker by name.*"

JOHNNIE WALKER

Born 1820—still going strong

regulations requiring Scotch whisky to be aged for a minimum of three years.

London-based wine merchant Berry Brothers & Rudd knew a good opportunity when it saw it. The Volstead Act had taken effect in America, meaning the production, sale, import and export of alcohol over 0.5% ABV was illegal. That of course didn't stop some people, and the demand for spirits was high. In 1921, Francis Berry was introduced to one Captain William McCoy in a hotel bar in Nassau, Bahamas. The Bahamas acted as the go-between for new bootleg spirits being shipped over to American soil – a kind of middleman to ease the conscience of the importer. McCoy was the courier, one of the best there was, granting his quality products the catchphrase 'the real McCoy'. Cutty Sark became a sign of good-quality whisky on the East Coast of the US during a time where moonshiners and backroom distillers were bottling up chemical cocktails and flogging them as potable spirits.

DEFINING WHISKY

The events taking place at the time perpetuated the feeling of unease among the malt distillers, as their numerous but comparatively small operations were already at the beck and call of the huge Distillers Company and multinational blending houses. All but a few malt producers were completely reliant on selling all of their products to blenders for bottling, marketing and selling. The blenders held so much power, in fact, that they could drive down prices of malt whisky through fear that the distillery owner would no longer be able to shift his wares. But if the blending houses failed, so did the malt distilleries.

Malt whisky producers began petitioning for a firm legal definition of what whisky actually is, while grain whisky distillers advertised with slogans like 'not a headache in a gallon' as a means of baiting their pot-still cousins. What followed later became known as the 'What is whisky?' debate, led by the appointment of a royal commission on 'whisky and other potable spirits'. The malt

Left A magazine advert for Johnnie Walker from 1937.

distillers of the Highlands argued that only 100% malt whisky made in the traditional manner (pot still) should be classified as the true whisky of Scotland. Grain-whisky makers, along with blenders – who, through their prolific use of grain whisky in their blends, also had a lot at stake – argued that their product was of equal, if not greater worth, and had every right to be listed as Scotch whisky. The malt whisky producers relented slightly and admitted that any blend containing at least 50% malt whisky was alright with them, but even then they were outnumbered and outgunned. For starters, many of the Highland malt whisky distilleries had already been bought out by DCL, meaning that their forces were not at all united. Then there was the fact that their product was generally viewed as being a little rough around the edges when consumed by itself. Couple that with the fact that blended whisky accounted for almost all of the bottle sales of whisky made in Scotland and it doesn't take a genius to work out where the chips would fall.

The 1909 report effectively lumped malt, grain and blended 'whiskey' into the same category, with no minimum requirements for blending and not even a minimum age statement at this stage. It was a huge win for the grain whisky makers.

At the turn of the 20th century, the biggest whisky blenders in Scotland were Walker's, Dewar's and Buchanan's. By 1909, whisky was the most widely consumed spirit in Britain and the biggest export markets were Australia, Canada, South Africa and the United States. But despite all that, the industry had still been over-optimistic about growth and no one was running at their full production potential. Things were about to get even worse, though...

Before we go into that, here are a couple of important points on etymology. For the first time in 1715 we finally see our favourite drink referred to in a manner that seems more familiar. Below is a snippet of a verse from a military poem, which is entitled 'A Dialogue between his Grace the Duke of Argyle, and the Earl of Mar':

Perhaps we may Recruit again,
And that we'll let you ken, Sir;

If that once more we shall engage,
We shall know how it goes, Sir,
Whiskie shall put our brains in rage,
And snuff shall prime our nose, Sir,
With swords and guns into our hands
We'll stoutly venture on, Sir

The earliest reference to the word 'whisky' (with a 'y') that I could find pre-dates any that I have before seen in print or on the Internet. It comes from the letter book of Bailie John Steuart. On 13th September 1735 he writes concerning a consignment of herring designated for Loch Broom. Also on the shipment are:

... 21 pounds candles, a half stone butter, four pecks peese, thirty six pound Roll Tobacco, and five Gallon whisky;

And since we started in Ireland, we had better end there, too. By far my favourite early use of 'whisky', and yet another that I have not before seen in print, comes from a poem entitled 'The Honest Irishman's Wish', first printed in *The London Magazine and Monthly Chronologer* in 1738:

The folly of pride; for we're always allow'd
To be, first proud of nothing; then, proud of being proud.
Of Brandy, or wine, I could wish to have none,
Whether genuine or brew'd, from the Loyre (Loire) or Garrone.
Were we but as wise as we're poor,
I should think
Good beer, ale, and whisky, might serve us for drink.

The Naming of Whisky

As we already know, 'whiskey' with an 'e' is the current spelling used for Irish and American spirits and without the 'e' for Scottish, Canadian and Japanese 'whisky'. It hasn't always been this way, however, and it would seem that our forefathers were a lot less pedantic about keeping the origins segregated in the past. There are plenty of examples in the early 20th century of Irish whiskey being spelled with no 'e', and the Royal Commission of 1908 that offered the first legal definition of Scotch spelled it with an 'e'. Indeed, American whiskey, although usually spelled with an 'e' (there are a few brands such as Maker's Mark, George Dickel and Early Times that spell their product 'whisky') is by legal definition, even today, spelled with no 'e'.

So what's this all about? Well, the story goes that many Irish and American producers (particularly those of Irish descent) dropped the 'e' from their whisky in the 1870s as a means of disassociating themselves with the inferior Scottish product. Whether this is true or not, it would appear that it has stuck now, the irony being that many people consider Scotch whisky to be the prized jewel among whiskies today.

The Dark Ages

The following 20 years were a nightmare for the industry as World War I set in, and taxes were increased by the Liberal Chancellor Lloyd George in what he called the 'People's Budget' – which introduced pensions, national insurance and unemployment benefit. Lloyd George was a family man and a teetotaller, and perhaps whisky's greatest adversary at the time. During World War I, he commented that 'Drink is doing more

Below A Liberal Party campaign card for the 1909 UK General Election showing the party's vision of sunlit fields of waving corn. The slogan at the bottom reads: Vote for the People's Budget.

damage than all the German submarines put together' and proposed that the taxes on spirits (not wine and beer) be doubled.

Many malt distilleries cut their losses and merged to protect their interests. Blenders did, too, most notably Buchanan's and Dewar's, which were later joined by Walker's and DCL.

Across the pond things were even worse. Many bourbon distilleries were forced to manufacture gunpowder in place of whiskey. What came next, though, all but killed the entire industry.

Prohibition came into effect on 17th January 1920 and lasted a full 13 years. The sale, consumption, importation and manufacture of alcohol in the USA became illegal and almost all of the American whiskey distilleries were forced to close, never to re-open. There were a few exceptions, however, and some distilleries were kept afloat by applying for a medical licence, since even then, whiskey was considered to be of use to the medical industry. Brown-Forman was among them, but it bought the Early Time distillery to help bolster its stocks.

Scotch whisky had only achieved limited success up until that point anyway, while bourbon remained the American staple. The same rules that applied to bourbon applied to Scotch, however, so blenders clambered to make their product available medicinally and used phrases like 'first-class digestive' and 'a good heart tonic' in their advertising campaigns. Those slogans herald from advertisements for 'White Horse', which also around this time became the first brand to use a screw-cap in place of a cork – sales doubled in a year following this innovation.

Prohibition, at the time, seemed like yet another disaster for the Scotch whisky industry, but of course it, unlike the vast majority of the bourbon distilleries, were able to continue producing stock. When Prohibition ended, the Scotch whisky industry was ready. The determination of the blenders to fulfil their customers' needs during that dark time was an effort that would one day be richly rewarded by the American people.

In Scotland, DCL made various other purchases throughout the 1920s, and despite sitting in a position of great power, it would appear that

Above A US magazine advert of 1919 encouraging customers to buy what they can before Prohibition.

under the watchful eyes of William Ross (the hero to Lloyd George's villain), took charge of the ongoing crisis with the greater good of the industry in mind by doing the only thing that it knew how – purchasing smaller operations when they were doomed to fail. It is thought by many that the careful steering conducted by DCL during this period contributed greatly towards the shape of the industry today.

The end of Prohibition and a drop in taxes gave new hope to the Scottish distilleries that had just about managed to weather the storm. But the wreckage from the previous 30 years was substantial. Only two of Campbeltown's 30+ distilleries remained in business. In addition to that, many of the Highland and Island distilleries had been hit hard, too, in favour of the delicate Speyside malts, again establishing the playing field for the present day.

The early 19th century saw the first mutterings of temperance in the United States. At first the movements, based out of Connecticut, Virginia and New York, advocated the restraint of alcohol consumption, but soon it turned into all-out abstinence. All alcoholic beverages were drawn into this, but spirits, and especially whiskey, were the primary target. The reasons that many people argued in favour of teetotalism were numerous. Much of the energy came from religious leaders, teachers, women's rights activists and women themselves, many of whom experienced the negative effects that alcohol had on their partners on a daily basis. This was reflected in largely women-based organisations, such as the Anti-Saloon League, who devised accompanying placards touting such phrases as:

'Lips that touch liquor shall not touch ours!'

For male and female members of the working class, alcohol had become a major part of everyday life and abstinence was a means of proving themselves worthy of the vote, a privilege that they were denied at the time. Temperance, it seemed, could solve these problems and much more.

Most of us consider 1919 as the beginning of Prohibition in America. It was in this year on January 16th that Nebraska became the 36th state to ratify the 18th amendment, and a year and a day later, the Volstead Act was put into effect. But in truth, it was not the sudden and shocking event that many would have you believe. Numerous states experimented with prohibition and prohibitive measures throughout the 1800s and, by 1913, nine states were already committed to the prohibition of alcohol. Nationwide prohibition was a dead certainty by this point – it just took a few more years for Congress to approve the submittal of an amendment to the constitution of the United

States. It was the 18th amendment, which prohibited 'the manufacture, sale, or transportation of intoxicating liquors within, the importation thereof into, or the exportation thereof from the United States and all territory subject to the jurisdiction thereof for beverage purposes.' Everyone assumed Prohibition would be short-lived and many people simply laughed it off to begin with. Nobody expected it to go on for 13 years.

The effect on Kentucky was, needless to say, cataclysmic. Prohibition didn't just alter the lives of distillers and brewers, but also farmers, truck drivers, shipping companies, saloon keepers, and restaurateurs, as tax revenues dropped and the cost of policing increased.

Prohibition was designed to cure the ills of society by ridding it of the temptation associated with the evils of alcohol. Instead, it had the

Right A 19th century temperance pledge certificate, promising abstinence from alcohol consumption.

opposite effect. Crime soared and criminals built empires through the illegitimate importation and production of alcohol, along with other profitable criminal activities.

All except a handful of distilleries were forced to close their doors and in Kentucky alone, 59 whiskey distilleries were shut down between 1918 and 1919, including H. Sutherland in Bardstown, a distillery that had been in business since before America even gained its independence. The Buffalo Trace Distillery, which at the time was called 'Stagg', was one of a handful of exceptions and remained semi-operational during the 13-year period, firing up its stills on at least four occasions. The government seized control of 'concentration warehouses' that contained whiskey stocks and allowed the spirit to be bottled for medical purposes only. Some of the familiar brand names, like 'Old Grandad', appeared on pharmacists' shelves, albeit with dumbed-down branding and more of a 'drugstore' look about them. Doctors could prescribe whiskey to patients for a variety of illnesses and ailments. Some were no doubt keener than others, and I suspect that certain doctors were offered both the carrot and the stick in return for cooperation.

Despite distilleries like Stagg topping up stocks for the medical industry, the level of whiskey in warehouses dropped steadily over the years and the average age of the product

Top left Federal agents pour illegal liquor into a sewer during the Prohibition.

Top right Bystanders attempt to catch in cups moonshine being poured out of a window by federal agents during a raid on an illegal still in 1925.

Above After a raid on a private home that served as a distribution warehouse for illegal liquor, a federal agent carries boxes of whiskey to load into his car before disposing of them.

For a Cold

OLD Overholt Rye and quinine is an unfailing remedy in curing colds and preventing serious developments.

Old Overholt Rye

"Same for 100 years"

proves invaluable and saves many a doctor's bill. It possesses decidedly strengthening qualities and should be in the home, at all times, for emergencies. Aged in the wood, bottled in bond.

A.Overholt & Co., Pittsburgh, Pa.

Above A magazine advert in the 1930s extolling the health benefits of Old Overholt Rye, the brand that became the 'medicinal alcohol' used by the US Navy during World War II.

increased. By the time Prohibition ended, almost all of the pre-Prohibition stocks had been exhausted. Demand during Prohibition was high of course, and today pre-Prohibition bottles of bourbon are very rare indeed. Any stocks that might have remained in unpillaged warehouses were, by 1933, very old and would have been blended with unaged or very young whiskies as producers hurried to fill the marketplace with any legal product that they could.

Smuggling whisky into the USA during the 1920s became a big business for some. Canada, where alcohol remained legal, played a particularly important role, providing a steady flow of liquor, namely Canadian Club, to thirsty American people. At the height of Prohibition there were thought to be over 1,000 bottles of Canadian Club crossing the US border every day. The popularity of Canadian, Scotch and Irish whiskies in America today can be attributed to its availability at a time when no domestic products were on the market.

The moonshiners were named after their preferred practice of night-time distilling, lit only by the light of the glowing moon. Ignoring for now the fact that the liquor was unquestionably low in quality and more than likely quite dangerous, the romance associated with moonshining is undeniable.

Ever since whiskey had been taxed, moonshining had been going on, but when Prohibition took effect, many farmers acknowledged the threat of poverty and did what they could to stay afloat. In other words, they turned anything fermentable into liquor. Moonshining went on all over America, but was endemic to states like Indiana, Virginia and Kentucky. In risking it all for distillation, these men became very resourceful at concealing their operations and making a quick getaway when the circumstances required it. Distillery set-ups were often designed to be loaded and unloaded quickly, and moonshiners used back roads and souped-up vehicles to transport their cargo from state to state. Fast and fearless drivers were prized for their abilities to outrun the cops, including Junior Johnson, who was never caught despite many years of transporting bootleg liquor at very high speed. After Prohibition ended, he transferred his formidable skills to professional motorsports driving and became a NASCAR legend.

Moonshining was dangerous in many ways, but perhaps none more so than in the act of drinking the stuff. Even unadulterated products were risky, due to the presence of methanol and higher-proof alcohols. Some moonshiners coloured their hooch with iodine and tobacco in efforts to pseudo-age the liquor. One report from New York in 1926 found that of the 576,000 gallons of moonshine seized that year, all contained traces of poisonous ingredients. In

New York alone there were up to 40 moonshine-related deaths a day during the 1920s.

The 'Noble Experiment', as Prohibition is often referred to, was ultimately a failure. Crime rates went up and criminals got rich; it ravaged the economy, created civil unrest, lowered government tax revenues and caused unemployment to skyrocket, hitting an all time high of 23.6% in 1932.

Right Izzy Einstein (left) sharing a toast with his partner, Moe Smith in a New York bar in 1935. In the 1920s, Izzy and Moe were the most effective team of Prohibition agents, using disguises to arrest bootleggers, close speakeasies and dispose of illegal liquor.

Below Unloading a consignment of newly legal whiskey after the end of the Prohibition in 1933.

THE TWENTIETH CENTURY AND BEYOND

The Great Depression of the 1930s trimmed Scotch production to an all-time low, forcing all but The Glenlivet and Glen Grant to close. The end of Prohibition signalled some changes, however, and despite rising taxes the industry grew strongly until World War II hit. Taxes increased to fund the war effort and foreign barley shortages spelled another period of decline in sales and an increase in prices. The price of a bottle in 1946 was around twice that of a pre-war bottle. Taxes increased by another 30% in 1947, but as more barley became available, production increased at a furious rate. This can be put largely down to demand for Scotch from the US, who no doubt felt it only right to reward the supply of whisky through the Prohibition years. There was an emotional connection to Scotland too, fostered by the US servicemen who passed through Scotland during World War II, no doubt sampling the spirit of the Highlands.

Japan's whisky story really got going in October 1923. Shinjiro Torii, an experienced whisky merchant and wine maker, began building the Yamazaki distillery and employed 29 year-old Masataka Taketsuru as his distillery manager. Five years previously, Taketsuru had travelled to Glasgow where he had enrolled in a chemistry course at the University. The real reason for his trip to Scotland though was a more practical kind of chemistry. This young Japanese man intended to learn the specific secrets of Scotch whisky making. By the time he left Scotland to go home in November 1920, he was likely the most accomplished distiller in Japan; not to mention husband to a Scottish wife, Rita. The experience that Taketsuru brought with him not only established the blueprint for the Yamazaki distillery, but also formed the mantra for Japanese whisky production to this day. Upon his return to Japan, Taketsuru insisted that the distillery be set up in north Japan, where the climate was most similar to Scotland. Torii, ever the pragmatist, preferred the transport links and clean waters that could be found near Osaka. Torii won the argument, for at least ten years anyway, at which time Taketsuru set his own distillery up on the Northern island of Hokkaido. These rival distilleries at Yamazaki and Yoichi formed the basis of the Japanese whisky industry and marked the origins of Suntory and Nikka.

Until the middle of the twentieth century, nearly all of the whisky in Scotland was matured in ex-Sherry casks. It had been an excellent arrangement but Sherry was becoming unfashionable with consumers in Europe, as well as in the US and Asia (whilst whisky was gaining popularity) so supplies began to dwindle. Many producers turned to bourbon barrels, but there was not a great supply of these either, since Prohibition and World War II had more or less destroyed the American spirits industry. Larger distillers, and especially grain operations, are known to have filled casks at much higher strength to compensate for the lack of wood.

Thanks to the work of Walker's, Dewar's Mackie's and Buchanan's, it was blended whisky that continued to lead the way, typically drunk with a splash of soda. This 'whisky highball' became an American staple in the 1950s. However, not to be outdone, the USSR made their mark in the international spirits world, with vodka, quietly absorbing a massive chunk of the market.

The response from Scotland was already on its way. Rather than tackle the vodka highball head on, a new plan of attack was required and, in effect, a new style of beverage was created – neat whisky. In 1963, Glenfiddich became the first distillery to market a 'straight' malt whisky. It was eight years old and packaged in the distinctive triangular bottle shape. The campaign focused on single malt as a well-kept secret of the Scots and great emphasis was placed on its history, location, ingredients and intensity of flavour. The Glenlivet (arguably the definitive single malt) followed with similar marketing campaigns for their own single malt, along with Glen Grant and Macallan. The single malt market was still tiny compared to that of blends, but a trickle-down effect was hoped for – something that would re-ignite the enthusiasm that had existed for the blends.

The American spirits industry watched the events unfolding in Scotland with great interest. The single malt posed a threat to their bourbon market, which had enjoyed steady growth since the war. A competitive edge was needed and it announced itself in the form of a single barrel. Single barrel bourbons were of course, not new; the likelihood is in fact that many of the earliest aged whiskies were not blended at all, but bottled directly from the cask. But Elmer T. Lee of the Buffalo Trace distillery (then Age International) remembered Colonel Albert Blanton, a former manager of the distillery in the 1930s (then Schenley) had, on occasion, bottled the liquid from exceptional barrels as special gifts. Lee bottled the first Blanton's Single Barrel Bourbon in 1984. With an emphasis on the single, it was closely followed by a Maker's Mark bottling and was the perfect counterattack to the growing single malt whisky that was being bottled across the pond. These products did especially well in Japan and quickly encouraged other producers to expand their range of bottlings. In turn, the small batch was born too, placing emphasis on the craft of the blender, who would use a comparatively small selection of barrels to blend a specific flavour profile that typically has an older average age and is higher in strength than standard labels. Jim Beam got in there early in the late 1980s and early 1990s, launching in quick succession Basil Hayden's, Booker's, Baker's and Knob Creek. Heaven Hill had already launched their Elijah Craig brand by 1986. Not only did these high-end products add additional strings to the bourbon bow, but they also encouraged consumers to give the producers' core expressions (Jim Beam White label, for example) a second look.

In Japan, Keizo Saji, the second son of Shinjiro Torii, became president of his father's company in 1961. Saji is the man responsible both for propelling Suntory into its current stratospheric status, and for being the original driving force behind Japanese single malt whisky. Saji launched Yamazaki 12 in 1984 and at the time it was the first mass-marketed single malt around.

Meanwhile, Scotch whisky producers trudged on blindly into the dark, over-optimistic and blissfully ignorant to the impending downturn, as more and more drinkers turned their noses up at the prospect of the old man's drink. Overproduction ensued throughout the 1970s and 1980s and something had to give. In a repeat of what had happened in the 1920s, over 20 distilleries closed down in the years between 1981 and 1996, including legendary operations like Brora, Port Ellen and Rosebank.

Whisky's ability to adapt and evolve, to duck and dive, has enabled it to weather this latest storm as a more versatile and self-aware product. Whisky today understands its market, demands mass appeal and affords its drinkers an immense range of choice through different producing countries, distilleries, production methods and people.

Ultimately it is the whisky highball that commands the lion's share of whisky sales around the world today. I have for a long time believed that the younger generation will embrace the drinks their grandparents enjoyed and eschew the favourite drinks of their parents – it's a rebellion thing. The highball of the 1950s lives on, but in various shapes and forms, each dictated by local flavours and preference, but each steered by the common theme of whisky. Hipsters have shunned the grape-based products of their parents and turned to whisky and coke (as well as gin and tonic) as their choice refreshment. In China, you'll find whisky mixed with green tea; in Japan it's often mixed with lots of cold water and increasingly served with food. In Latin America, it's mixed with coconut water and in South Africa you'll find it partnered with Appletiser. The UK consumes almost half of all the world's Jack Daniel's... with coke, of course. These kind of drinks allow the blends and bourbons to do what they do best, integrate, accentuate and stimulate, resulting in a drink that is greater than the sum of its parts.

It's good news for single malt whisky too, where developed markets continue to demand a greater range of bottlings and producers are only too happy to fulfil the request at increasingly higher prices. Single Malt has become a vessel for celebration in countries like Russia, Taiwan and Japan, the latter of which are doing a very good job of producing their own stocks of top-quality malt.

As I write, malt whisky is being made in over 25 countries around the world, including almost every country in Western Europe, Australia, New Zealand, South Africa, Pakistan, India and even Argentina. On top of that, five of the top ten fastest growing global spirits brands in 2012 were whisky products.

Part Two
How Whisky is made

INTRODUCTION

Most people will tell you that whisky is a product made from only three ingredients: cereal, water and yeast. I would argue that wood deserves a place on that list, too, since it is the influence of wood that provides the larger part of whisky's character. For some whiskies, most notably those from Scotland, there is arguably a fifth ingredient in the form of peat smoke, which can be a major flavour player in the finished product. Others may contest that the people who make whisky actually constitute an ingredient; after all it's their knowledge and experience that shape the character of the product. While I agree that people are critical to every stage of whisky production, from growing the cereals, right through to blending and bottling, I see them rather like ice in a cocktail: an integral and intrinsic part of the process, but a means to an outcome rather than a component of it.

The exciting thing about whisky making is that every stage of the process is meaningful and directly impacts the next stage. Of the four ingredients, wood is by far the most complex and unequivocally the most important. It is so familiar to us, yet somehow cryptic and arcane in its interaction with spirits. What we know for sure is that whisky gets a good proportion of its flavour and all of its colour from time spent encased in wood – without it we'd all be drinking white spirit and pulling strange faces.

Cereals are important, too, at least in the sense that they provide the energy source required to make alcohol in the first instance, and at most for the mouthfeel and lingering finish that they can contribute; the type of cereal used, be it malted barley, corn, rye, or wheat, does impart some flavour and textural nuances to the whisky. Bourbon sometimes has a sweet, popcorn-like quality, partly due to its 'mash-bill' (the proportion of different grains used during the mashing process), of which corn forms the majority. Rye produces a dry, nutty, pepper-like character, and malt whisky a fruity, breakfast-cereal tone that underpins the other goings-on. However, detecting the mash bill of a Bourbon in blind tasting is not always straightforward, since many other factors come into play. Assessing whether a 20-year-old grain whisky is made from corn or wheat is no easier. For this reason, cereal is important from a practical point of view, but still limited in its contribution to the character of the final product.

Water, while crucial for virtually every stage of the whisky-making process, is not something that we should get too excited about or romance over. Assuming that the water is of acceptable quality and free from excessive bacteria or pollution, a distillery only needs to meet a limited number of parameters for the water to do its job. Pay no heed to talk of artesian wells and 1,000-year-old springs; it has little to do with the final product.

Yeast is the hardest ingredient of the four for us to relate to, and yet one of the more influential, in my opinion. Microscopic and numerous, it's only recently that distillers have begun to accept that the type of yeast can have a lasting impact on the character of the bottle. We don't hear much about yeast in day-to-day life, however; arousing excitement over a discussion centred around yeast culture is a luxury reserved only for the geekiest of whisky geeks.

Besides the raw ingredients that provide whisky with its substance and mass, there are various tools and techniques that also shape the final outcome. Like wood, many of these practices straddle the void of mysticism that connects our world and that of the whisky gods. Many of the older whisky distilleries of the world are heavily laden with superstition and supposition; 'turn that knob first' and 'clean that vat last' are calls that can be heard not in the pursuit of correct practice, but in the adherence to *ritual*. Much has been learned through scientific pursuit, but many unexpected outcomes still leave whisky makers scratching their heads and pondering the unfathomable.

In the following chapters, we'll take an in-depth look into what whisky is made from and how it is made, covering each stage in sufficient detail to understand the state of the liquid in our glass. Here we go…

⇒⇒⇒ WATER ⇐⇐⇐

I was always led to believe that the regions of Scotland and whiskies from other parts of the world owed much of their character and style to their immediate surroundings and their water. As one of the four ingredients used to make whisky, and perhaps the one that we associate with the easiest, it's not surprising that many brands and whisky books have placed a great deal of emphasis on water-sourcing in the past; the brands, in particular, have enjoyed showering us with creative descriptions of how and where their water has been obtained – *hand-extracted from the crystal ice-clouds of Tibet's most inaccessible subterranean diamond palace*, for example (alright, I made that one up). Likewise, I have read well-respected whisky books that stress how many whiskies owe much of their character to water filtered through 'granite mountains' and 'sandstone stacks', or water sourced from 'ancient lakes'. One book even features a water heading under each distillery, complete with a life history of the water source. But around five years ago the veil of mystery that shrouded the subject of distillery water was lifted for me, when my friend Stuart Howe, one of the world's most accomplished brewers, told me that he could add and remove minerals from his water so as to emulate naturally occurring water from anywhere in the world. I was shocked and slightly concerned by his unholy claim, having been led to believe that good quality, natural water was the backbone of any great brewing or distilling operation. But the more I investigated, the more I found that many distilleries were modifying their water sources to fit their needs. And in my opinion, it makes total sense to do so.

Sure, 200 years ago, a good water source was one of the major considerations when deciding

Below The River Spey in northeastern Scotland. Good for Salmon fishing and good for whisky, it's Scotland's fastest-flowing river, and the setting for almost half of its distilleries.

upon a distillery's location, principally because water powered the wheels of the mill, which was used to grind down the cereals ready for mashing. Nowadays, the water used to make whisky is still of critical importance to the manufacturing process – it's used in every single stage of whisky production, from irrigating crops, to malting, mashing, distilling and bottling, and by my estimates it takes around 50 litres/53 quarts of 'process water' to make 1 litre/quart of whisky (and that doesn't include the water used for the various stages of cooling and cleaning that take place along the way) – but it's actually of very little consequence in terms of where it comes from. Most distilleries use tap water, while some utilize spring water.

Bourbon distillers in Kentucky have long claimed that their water, which passes through limestone, has a certain quality about it that is important to their product. Maker's Mark is one such brand that places great emphasis on the ecology of the area surrounding its water source. On the other hand, Brown-Forman, which produces Woodford Reserve, will tell you that the type of water is not an important part of its product. Harold Ferguson, the veteran distiller of Canadian Mist, once said: 'I'd choose to make whisky out of the cleanest water I could get. You can adjust everything else.'

Thankfully it's becoming rarer to hear whisky makers ramble on about their water source. I put this down to two factors, firstly because many of them simply use the tap water, and secondly because consumer understanding has improved to the point that two much more significant factors determining whisky flavour – wood and still shape – are attracting greater interest.

Using water from the tap/faucet might sound less romantic, but it makes perfect sense, because it's a very consistent supply that has already met various quality standards. Once it arrives, it is further processed to the requirements of the distillery, which means checking levels of copper and iron, stripping out chlorine and even adding minerals like zinc, calcium and magnesium that help promote enzyme activation in mashing and ensure a healthy fermentation process.

Before farming, the human race was stuck in a rut. The acts of eating and drinking were hardly ever planned more than a few days in advance and we generally munched on whatever we were capable of catching or snatching. One day, however, around 15,000 years ago, it became clear to our ancestors that something had to be done. Food seemed to be fairly essential for life and we needed more of it to avoid the repetitive nomadic stresses of migration and death by starvation (or sabre-toothed cat). So crops were purposely planted, domesticated and nurtured, the first of which were cereals, the edible seeds or grains of the grass family *Gramineae*. Barley or wheat were probably the first, sewn in the 'Fertile Crescent' of the Middle East, which later went on to become the Mesopotamian Empire. Farming, the world's second-oldest profession, had been born.

Eating cereals straight from the fields is no one's idea of a fun day out, though – they're tough, difficult to chew and digest, and almost flavourless. So history's first chefs and bartenders set about developing a menu of dishes that would both satisfy the stomach and please the palate. Water was found to be a good medium for softening the hard structure of the grain, and if heated, a kind of porridge or gruel would form. Bring some naturally occurring yeast into the fold, and you have the ingredients for two of life's most important things – bread and beer.

Evidence of cereal fermentation goes back around 8,000 years, but the earliest written record of brewing beer comes from the Sumerian Empire around 6,000 years ago. The Sumerians loved beer; it's even mentioned in their (and the world's) oldest story – *The Epic of Gilgamesh*. In the story, the bestial giant Enkidu consumed beer, shed his fur, danced and became a human. Enkidu became a metaphor for man's progress towards civilization through the merits of beer. Indeed, so precious were the building blocks of beer to prehistoric man that grain stores essentially operated like banks.

The Different Grains

Grain cereals fall into one of two categories: warm-season crops, like corn and millet, and cold-season crops, like barley, oats, rye and wheat. They are all packed with carbohydrates in the form of starch, a potent little package of energy that the plant uses to germinate and grow. It's generally accepted that the variety within the sub-family of cereal has little effect on the flavour of the final product. Indeed, by the time the grain has gone through malting, mashing, fermenting, distillation (at least twice), ageing, filtering and bottling, it would be a difficult case to argue – like insisting that the quality of the cattle feed affects the smell of the leather. Having said that, many distillers believe that the variety of the grain can be responsible for oiliness, waxy qualities and thickness on the palate.

While flavour may not be a concern, the specific cereal variety does affect the yield of alcohol, which in turn affects the amount of money that can be made from it - in this, all distillers are united. Each type of grain poses different challenges in its processing, too – see page 62 for more on this.

Barley

There are, apparently, over 300,000 varieties of barley in the world – so many that it strikes me that one person would not have long enough to count them all. Barley's excuse is that it's a type of grass, and grasses have a propensity for mutation. Barley used for malting accounts for only a small percentage of the total, but a staggering 25% of the world's total supply of barley is malted, mostly for the production of alcoholic beverages.

Barley comes in two distinct forms, 'two-row' and 'six-row', which are identifiably different because the former has two rows of seed on each spike (head), whereas the latter has six rows of seed

on each spike. Scotch distillers prefer two-row, because it's typically lower in protein and produces a higher yield of fermentable sugars. In the USA, six-row barley is preferred, since it typically contains more enzymes, which are necessary for their corn- and rye-rich mash bills (see page 52 and 62–63).

The Old English word for barley is *bære*, and one of the earliest varieties of barley grown in Scotland is an old heritage crop called bere, a six-row barley derived from the same word. Bere is thought to be the root origin of the word 'barn' and these days, it is only grown on the island of Orkney. Highland Park, one of two distilleries on Orkney (the other is Scapa) used bere up until 1929. Young upstart distillery Arran and Bruichladdich have recently launched special release bere malts. You can still buy bere bannock, a kind of flatbread made from the bere grown on Orkney. For making spirits, bere is not a sensible choice, though. Over the past 200 years new strains of barley have been cultivated that are more resilient to disease – and to the Scottish climate. What's more, they are easier to process, and produce a higher yield of alcohol per ton.

In the mid-19th century, a typical malt distillery would turn 1 bushel (8 gallons) of malted Archer or Goldthorpe barley into 2 gallons of spirit. A hundred years later, the same weight of hybrid barleys, Spratt-Archer or Plummage-Archer, would be enough to produce 3 gallons of spirit (note: these volumes are of 'potable' spirit, not pure alcohol – by today's standards, you need roughly 1kg [2.2 lbs.] of barley to make a 70cl [24 fl. oz.] bottle of whisky). These improvements in yield can also be partly attributed to better production methodology and machinery, but over the past 50 years, yield has increased by 30%, while practices have remained relatively unchanged. The introduction of the Golden Promise barley variety in 1968 marked a huge leap forward for the industry, as it matured early and thrived in the Scottish climate; 10 years later more than 90% of the malting barley used in Scotland came from Scottish-grown Golden Promise.

Golden Promise has, in turn, been surpassed; given the economic rewards involved, it's not surprising to hear that new varieties are still being developed today. Think about it: even a variety capable of producing 1% equates to tens of millions

Above Barley really is the brick that builds many of the towering whiskies that we know and love.

of pounds worth of additional spirit. At the time of writing, Optic and Decanter lead the way, but keep an eye out for next-generation varieties like Odyssey and Chronicle stealing the limelight soon.

All barley is air-dried after harvest, taking its moisture content from 20% down to 12%. Next, it is graded for size and cleaned, then cooled over a period of months from 20°C (68°F) down to 5°C (41°F). This temperature change causes the grain to start preserving itself, ready for us to trick it into thinking it's in the ground and warm, ready for germination. During its time spent in the storage facility, ventilation and condensation are closely monitored to prevent the onset of mildew.

WHEAT

Wheat is highly adaptable and numerous in its varieties, having been domesticated for at least as long as barley. It can be planted as a winter or spring crop, and as such, crops up a lot all over the world. The alcohol industry uses winter wheat almost exclusively, since it has a higher starch content and produces more alcohol per bushel. The spring wheat tends to be used for bread making, since it has the desirable higher protein content.

Most grain whiskies produced in Scotland are made from wheat (corn lost favour in the 1980s) and wheat makes up a portion of the mash bill in some American whiskies, too. Wheat was the choice grain for Canadian whiskies back in the early-1800s, but most distilleries have switched to corn now for their 'bulk alcohol' requirements.

Wheat produces a smooth distillate that adds

sweetness and a mellow characteristic that tempers the harshness that can come from corn and rye. Think about Belgian wheat beers, with their silky, delicate character, and you'll have a good idea of wheat's contribution to whisky.

Corn (Maize)

Corn, or maize, is indigenous to the warm climates of Central America, and was probably first domesticated around 2,500 BC. Native Americans relied heavily on corn, which actually featured in some of their religious practices, and were quick to convert forested areas into plantations. To this day, it makes up a huge proportion of the Mexican and Central American diet.

Native Americans first showed settlers how to cultivate corn, and today it is the most widely grown crop throughout the USA and the Americas, accounting for half of the world's production, with over one-third of that being used to make alcohol. Three of the top corn-growing states in the USA also have something else in common, in that they all begin with 'I' – Iowa, Indiana and Illinois.

The variety of corn used in the production of American whiskey is 'dent' corn, which can be easily identified by the dent in the crown of the kernel. Interestingly, corn is the one truly American ingredient used to make American whiskies. It gives a higher yield of alcohol than the other cereals mentioned here, due to its high sugar and starch content. It's also quite easy to work with, lacking some of the compounds that can cause other cereals to turn into porridge or glue. Corn makes up the majority of the mash bill in bourbon, and when doing its job properly, contributes all the sweet and buttery characteristics we expect from popcorn. If allowed to dominate, the spirit can become greasy and thin – think excessively buttered popcorn.

Corn was the primary cereal used in Scottish grain whisky until the mid-1980s, when competitively priced wheat began to take over. Until the 1980s, most of the corn was imported from the USA, but these days it is typically sourced from the warm areas of southern France.

Left Many different cereals are used to make whiskies, but it's the terroir of the of the region that dictates this more than the preference of the distiller.

Corn grows on the familiar 'cob' structure, with each cob holding up to 1,000 corn seeds, of which around 85% is starch. Corn is harvested at the end of the summer, just as the kernels are beginning to dry out. After harvesting they are dried further, down to a moisture content of approximately 14%.

Rye

Rye is the delicious cockroach of the cereal world. It's both tenacious and hardy, and more than capable of growing in snow-covered regions of Eastern Europe and in soils that no other cereal would survive in. Rye is a fully fledged winter crop, usually sewn in the autumn and harvested in the early summer. It is covered with a husk and a 'beard', and grains are arranged in an alternating pattern along the rachis (a zigzag-shaped stalk). If a wheat grain is the fat thumb of a baker, rye is the slender index finger of a *pâtissier*.

Rye is characterful and complex as an ingredient in bread, beer or whisky, but many farmers don't grow it because it's not very lucrative. Beer and spirit producers avoid it because it has a powerful flavour and it's a bit of a nightmare to brew with, as it has the absorbency of a sponge, and features particularly high levels of a starch group called beta-glucan, which means that brewing a rye-heavy wash can feel a bit like cooking a pot of bubblegum. I've heard stories of enterprising distillers using their sticky rye mash to plug holes in their stills!

In North America, where it is used to make rye whiskey and, in the past, Canadian whisky (which is sometimes referred to simply as 'rye') the crop grows in the cooler northern states like the Dakotas and Minnesota and in various parts of Canada. It makes sense, as these areas best match the cool Eastern European climates from which the grain originated.

Character is where rye comes into its own. In many bourbon mash bills, rye is used to add an element of pepperiness and dryness that balances the sweet, oily, corn. Bourbon without rye can be a bit flabby and gutless, while rye whiskey itself (which contains a minimum of 51% rye) is full of all that engine-oil heat and raw-bran nuttiness.

THE WHISKY PRODUCTION PROCESS

	MALT WHISKY	IRISH WHISKEY
Grain	Barley	
Malting	Malting	
Kiln	Unpeated or peated drying	
Milling	Ground down to grist	Milled with malted barley
Mashing	Sent to mash tun for mashing with water at 63.5°C (146.3°F)	Mashing at 55°C (131°F), rising up to 65°C (149°F) and finally 75°C (167°F)
Addition		
Fermentation	50–100 hours	60–120 hours
Distillation	1st: Copper wash still / 2nd: Copper spirits still / 3rd/additional distillation / No additional distillation	Any combination of pot and column still / 1st pot still / 2nd pot still / 3rd pot still
Filtering		
Maturation	Refill cask / Ex-bourbon cask / Finishing in wine cask or no finishing	Ex-Sherry cask
Water	Added to adjust strength	
Filtering	Chill-filtered	
Colour adjusted	Caramel (E150)	

GRAIN WHISKY		BOURBON, TENNESSEE AND RYE	
Any (typically wheat)		**Any (predominantly corn and rye)**	
Sometimes		Milled	
Cooking		Corn is cooked at a high temperature	
		No other cereals added (Bourbon and Tennessee)	Rye and/or wheat added at lower temperature
		Malted barley added	
		Sour mash/set-back added	
48 hours		Fermented without filtering for 3–5 days	
Column-still distillation		Single column distillation	
Additional column distillation	No additional columns	Thumper (only used at Early Times and Bernheim Distilleries)	Doubler
		Maple charcoal filtered (Tennessee)	
Matured in ex-bourbon casks		Cut to no more than 62.5% ABV and matured in new charred American oak casks	
Natural cask strength			
Non-chill filtered			
No caramel		None permitted	

Malting

Malting is the transformation of a grain from a lifeless seed to an energetic sack of potential. All cereals are capable of being malted, but barley is by far the best. Barley contains a higher concentration of *diastase* (a family of enzymes) that is necessary to facilitate the malting process. The aim of malting is to prepare the grain for releasing its starch, and to liberate the *diastatic* power that converts the starches into simple sugars during mashing. Once successfully malted, the barley can be mashed on its own (as when producing malt whisky), or mixed with other cereals, like corn, rye or wheat (as with bourbon, rye, Canadian whisky, and Irish whiskey), where it will provide the enzymes needed to break down the other cereals' starches, too.

All cereals have structural similarities and contain an embryo (the brains) and an endosperm (the muscle). The first stage in the growth of a barley embryo involves the embryo's hormones triggering the release of enzymes that self-destruct cell walls and proteins and ready the grain for breaking down starch stored in the endosperm into simpler sugars. If occurring naturally, this process gives the plant enough fuel to power growth until it can draw energy from the nutrients in the soil.

I once had the malting process explained to me in the context of a hazelnut chocolate bar, where the hazelnuts represented the starch. The wrapper represents the protein matrix that holds all of the cells of the plant in place. During malting, the protein is first broken down – the chocolate bar is unwrapped. Next, the individual cells are separated from one another – the chocolate bar is broken into segments. Finally, the enzymes break down the cell structure, revealing the starch – the chocolate is peeled away, leaving only the nuts.

Malting is essentially a clever growth mechanism that protects the grain's energy store until such time that it is needed. What the naive barley grain didn't plan for, though, is *us*. Through our mastery of all things botanical we have learned to trick the barley grain into believing that it's time to grow, opening the gates to its

Above Tiny rootlets emerge from a handful of 'green malt', indicating that the process is complete and the barley is now ready for drying.

Right Yours truly attempting to turn malt in the traditional manner at the Benriach distillery in Speyside. Even a couple of minutes is exhausting, which led me to the conclusion that maltmen truly are men of steel!

treasury and allowing us to raid the coffers. The secret to good malting is controlling the trickery, giving the grain all the encouragement it needs, then stopping it in its tracks before it has a chance to use its resources. What's left behind is an energy-rich package, ready for mashing and fermentation.

Most distilleries around the world buy in their malted barley from a commercial malting facility, prepared to their required grain size, nitrogen content (and indicator of starch content) and moisture levels – all important factors to determine spirit yield and, some would say, flavour. Commercially malted barley is produced on a huge scale, with state-of-the-art equipment, ensuring consistency and quality. Some Scottish distilleries, however, (six at the time of writing)

still malt a proportion of the barley they use in the traditional manner. Springbank (see page 155) is the only distillery that malts all of its own barley. Kilchoman has recently released its 100% Islay expression, where the barley is both grown and malted in its own facility. This is not without its headaches, though. Temperature control, good timing and a committed labour force are required to manage traditional floor maltings, but the romance and craft associated with the process are a big draw for many whisky drinkers.

STEEPING

The first stage of malting is the steep. Here, the dried grains are soaked in cold water for around 36–48 hours. The water is drained and refreshed a few times and oxygen is bubbled through it. These are the ideal conditions to trick the barley into germinating, as it believes that its surroundings are being subjected to natural rainfall. During this time, the grains will go from 12%–45% water content. Much is often made of the type of water used during this stage, with romantics favouring water percolating through peat bogs, but it makes no difference at all. Barley naturally filters the water, removing contaminants along the way.

GERMINATION

In traditional floor malting, the plump grains are taken from the steeps and spread across malting floors, typically 30cm/12 inches in depth. It's at this stage that a piece of genetic code within the barley whips the enzymes (diastase) into action, and biomechanical reactions begin to take place at a vigorous pace. Protein structure and cell walls are broken down, allowing access to the inner sanctum of starch, which is converted into its soluble form, dextrin, by the enzyme amylase. Moisture levels must be maintained to keep the enzymes happy, and it's common to see maltmen checking the thermometers that protrude from the barley beds (16°C [61°F] is the optimum malting temperature). They also test the sponginess (using their feet) and rake or shovel the malt (using a malt 'shiel') to prevent the clumping that occurs when rootlets emerge from the seed and grab hold of each other! This endless turning of the barley is the cause of a repetitive strain injury common to maltmen called 'monkey shoulder'; in 2005, William Grant launched an innovative blended whisky eponymous to the affliction. I'm also told that in the past, maltmen would keep one fingernail longer than the others (a bit like some Spanish guitarists), which would be used to break open the grain and check the growth.

Commercial malting takes place in either Saladin boxes or drum maltings. Both work in much the same way, with the speed of germination controlled by airflow that cools the heat produced during the process. The Saladin box is a huge circular or rectangular trough. The malting drum looks like a coffee roaster,

intermittently turning the grains and distributing the heat as the drum rotates. I was told by Ramsay Borthwick at Port Ellen Maltings that the temperature of the barley inside its drum malting once rose to 40°C (104°F) when a power cut stopped the coolers from running. The barley was half-cooked by the time the power was restored.

A good maltman can tell when the malting is complete by feeling a single grain. The plant begins to draw energy from the shoot end first, noticeably by the softening of its structure. As the germination continues, the plant softens right down to its tip, and once the whole thing can be squashed into a kind of mushy flour, it is deemed fully germinated.

Below The large steeping vessels in this room, at Port Ellen Maltings on Islay in Scotland prepare the barley for malting. Here, we see the might of industry bend a knee to the humble barley grain, all in the pursuit of liberating its valuable sugar stocks.

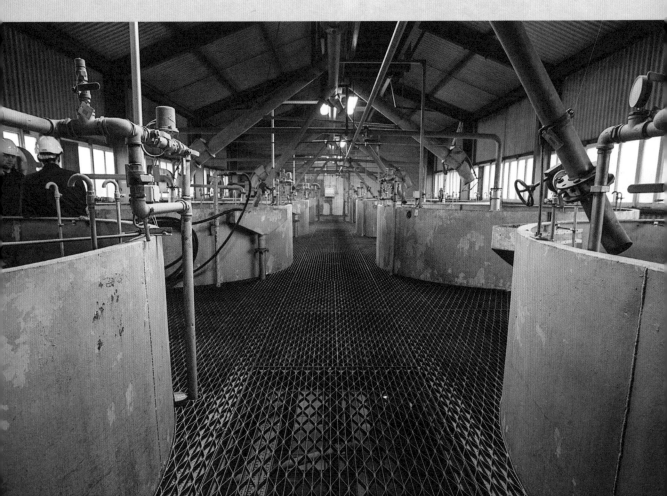

KILN DRYING

Germination can take between four and 12 days, based on humidity, temperature and airflow. By this time, the grains have sprouted tiny rootlets, which look a bit like tadpoles. Once the rootlets reach about three-quarters of the length of the grain, the 'green malt' is sent for drying. The barley has now reached the perfect balance – its structure has been sufficiently broken down, but its energy source still remains intact. The biomechanical process must now be halted and the barley's endosperm killed.

Kiln drying is a balance between airflow and temperature control. Whether conducted in a commercial maltings or at the distillery itself, kiln drying is the simple process of blowing warm air up and through the bed of green malt. Most modern kilns are fuelled by coke, rather than coal, as it is a slightly cleaner (and non-toxic) fuel that gives off only water and carbon-dioxide as by-products.

At the start of the kiln drying process, the airflow will usually be stronger and the temperature lower, which encourages moisture to migrate from the inside of the grain to the outside. Slowly the temperature is increased from 40°C (104°F) up to as high as 75°C (167°F) and the airflow reduced; the whole process takes around 36 hours in a commercial maltings. Once dried down to 4% moisture, the barley must then be

stored for a minimum of two months before being milled and mashed. The longer the better, too, as it gives the moisture content of the grain a chance to equalize, following the same principle as resting your Christmas turkey!

Many of the malt whisky distilleries of Scotland still feature one or more pagoda roofs, which pinpoint the location of the kiln room. The Dailuaine Distillery's kiln room roof was originally designed by Charles Chree Doig in 1889, emulating the tiered roof towers of eastern Asia. The premise was simple – allow good airflow up from the kiln and stop rain from getting in and wetting the barley. Nearly all the pagoda roofs in Scotland are decorative features today, since only a handful of distilleries still malt their own barley. If you do spot a pagoda chimney on top of a building, it's highly likely that the place was once used as a maltings.

Below Heavy peat 'reek' ascends up a chimney, imparting flavour into the barley above.

Left The pagoda-style chimney at Highland Park Distillery.

Below The kiln room at Highland Park: old, unchanged, and still very much in use.

PEAT

The Scots turned to peat as a fuel when it became apparent that they didn't have enough wood or coal to burn. Peat bogs are formed when plant roots, moss, heather and other vegetation decompose in an acidic environment without drainage. The vegetation eventually decomposes, because it's always wet, and over hundreds and thousands of years of crushing gravity, it forms a loose organic mass that, if dried, can be burned.

In the grand scheme of things peat is not a great fuel source. It comprises around 60% carbon, so it gives off far less heat than comparable fossil fuels – and it makes everything smell! But it's this smell that has enticed so many of us into the world of Scotch whisky. Just like barbecued food, there's something primal and fundamental about the intoxicating aroma of smoke. It feels like home.

Above Peat can be as soft as compost or hard, like clay, depending on where it came from and what depth it was dug.

CUTTING PEAT

Many years ago, I cut peat in Ireland with my father. I recall, on most occasions, being more than a little reluctant to participate in this soggy, cold and windswept practice, ironically designed to keep my grandmother's house warm. Cutting is usually done at the beginning of the summer, to give the rolls of peat time to dry out, ready for the cold winter months. There are three specialized tools that peat cutters use to lever their prize from the earth. First is a flat shovel that removes the top layer of soil; the second tool is something akin to a giant palette knife, which slices downwards and levers the slab of peat out from underneath. Finally, there's a pitchfork that's used for collecting debris.

Cutting peat by hand is a little like deconstructing a house brick-by-brick – care and attention must be taken to ensure that the next layer down is preserved so that it can be cut out in uniform pieces. I'm told that an experienced peat cutter can 'win' up to 1,200 rolls of peat on a good day. It sounds like a lot, but in the cold winter climates of Scotland and Ireland, a single household could get through 50 rolls in a single day! If you're feeling thirsty after a long day peat cutting, the traditional refreshment is a choice mixture of uncooked oats and water – delicious.

There's no question that peat cutters are tough men. My friend and whisky expert Colin Dunn was once taken on a peat-cutting expedition on Islay. He noticed that a bottle of malt whisky was loaded into the peat cutter's bag, and an hour or so into slicing away at the ground, Colin was parched and ready for a wee dram. Eventually the peat cutter stopped his work, produced the bottle, pulled the cork and proceeded to throw it over his shoulder. The man then turned to Colin and with a glint in his eye said 'Well... ye know what that means, don't ye?!'

When you bear in mind that peat was originally used to fire the stills of early malt makers in the 18th century, a considerable workforce must have been needed to cut enough peat to last the winter. I suppose it's possible that the peat smoke in these distilleries imparted a fragrant finish to the distillate, which soon became a sought-after quality. One way or another, peat was being used exclusively to dry barley by 1700. Logic tells us to expect some seriously peaty whiskies from this era, but the truth is that many of the old samples that exist are not overpoweringly peaty. The reason for this remains a mystery to whisky historians. In my view, much of it comes down to science and the

peat saturation threshold of the barley grain (see pages 60–61).

These days, most peat is often cut in a slightly less romantic fashion. Vast lengths of land are literally sawn open, the organic matter sucked out, then neatly displayed on the ground for drying. One method incorporates a modified digger shovel that acts like a giant egg slicer. Another sucks the peat out mechanically, leaving behind what looks a little like the fecal matter of several hundred elephants.

The density and composition of peat does vary based on the depth it is cut, the geology and local ecosystem of its origin. Talisker, for example, is thought to derive its slight salinity from the salty sea air and occasional spatter of seaweed that its peat is exposed to. Meanwhile, Highland Park uses only the top couple of layers of the peat bog, which feels more like soil and is rich with heather roots. Dig deeper and you'll be rewarded with a more carbonic peat that is more like coke or coal. The deeper, darker stuff, or 'black peat', contributes less phenolic flavor (see pages 60–61) than the 'brown peat' that is found closer to the surface. A combination of both types can give the necessary heat as well as the phenolic aromatics that are required to dry and flavour the barley successfully.

Top Scarred land on Orkney, where Highland Park peat cutters have taken slices of flavoursome mud from the bog on Hobbister Moor.

Above Dark smoke is preferred over paler, white smoke – a sign that the peat is impacting the maximum phenol effect onto the barley.

This page After the peat is cut by hand using specialized tools, the resulting 'sod' is left outside to dry in the open air for around two-three weeks. Following this, the peat is collected and then transported to the distillery.

PORT ELLEN
DISTILLERY
LOW ROBERTSON & CO. LTD

THE SCIENCE OF PEAT

Peat is possibly the only component of malt whisky production that is genuinely governed by terroir, but I am well aware that that statement may upset one or two people. The composition of peat smoke (aptly named 'reek') is made up various volatile compounds that give the familiar burnt mustiness of peat smoke, most notably phenols. Depending on the location and the depth of the cut, the compounds will differ. Ardmore in Speyside uses a carbon-rich peat that gives its whisky a light, 'sooty' quality that's in contrast to the more maritime and medicinal drams that you might find on Islay or the Isle of Skye.

The peatiness of a whisky is measured in phenolic parts per million (ppm). By definition this means that a whisky of 1ppm would contain one phenolic molecule for every 999,999 other molecules. The most heavily peated whisky currently available is Octomore, produced by Bruichladdich; at 169ppm it's enough to make you cough just thinking about it (see page 115).

The level of peatiness in the final product is nearly impossible to control during kilning – there are simply too many intangibles. These range from the exact moisture of the barley to the make-up of the peat itself, and how well the peat fire has been tended. A gauge can be taken by looking at the quality and density of the smoke, but that's about it. When tending a kiln you will be looking for rich, dark smoke rather than pale, white smoke, a sign that it contains plenty of phenols. Fire is not your friend as many of the more delicate aromatics can be lost if the peat gets too hot. In a good kiln, you should be able to touch the peat while it's smoking without burning your hands.

And then there's the break point, which occurs about halfway through kilning (at roughly 18 hours). This marks the stage where the barley will accept no more phenolic compounds, as a result of its ever-decreasing moisture content. Pre-break, there is plenty of moist air and the damp husk of the barley absorbs phenols like a sponge, but as the grain dries out, so to does its capacity for trapping the peat characteristics. After the break point, the air becomes drier and no amount of peat will increase the ppm any further.

Port Ellen Maltings on Islay always burn approximately 10 tons of peat for every 50 tons of barley, and the results range from as low as 30ppm right up to 80ppm. In commercial kilning, a sample of peated barley is taken after the kilning process and its ppm is measured. The batches are then blended together to create an average ppm at the desired level.

Of course, the phenolic parts in peated barley won't all make it through to the bottle. Despite being resilient little beasts, the phenols have to undergo the trials of mashing, fermentation, distillation and ageing. For example, Laphroaig peats its barley to 40ppm, its new-make spirit is 25ppm, but its finished whiskies are all below 10ppm.

It's also worth noting that the phenolic parts per million in a whisky are only a guideline to how smoky a whisky will really be when you come to taste it. Although it's possible to measure phenols accurately, the ppm does not account for other flavourful molecules that might combat the smokiness and lessen our perception of it.

Above Commercial maltings produce over 99% of the malted barley needed to make whisky.

☞ Milling and Mashing ☜

Milling

Before mashing can take place, the grains must first be milled down to size. In the case of barley, this increases surface area, but also separates the husk from the innards, allowing better conversion rates (from starch to sugar) and turning the husks into a useful filtering system that stops tiny particles draining out of the wash later down the line. Whole (split) husks are preferred as they offer a better medium for efficient percolation. For other grains like corn, wheat and rye, the milling similarly increases surface area, but also gives better access to the starch stores. Many American distilleries use a type of 'hammer' mill to powder their cereals, which pretty much does what it says on the tin and pounds the grains into a fine powder using rotating hammers – ouch! Particle size is of critical importance during mashing and fermentation, and can have a big impact on the final alcohol yield. Never underestimate the mill. Having said that, I have seen evidence to suggest that one or two grain distilleries in the UK don't actually mill at all, and instead promote longer cooking times of their wholegrains to extract the necessary starch.

In the case of malt whisky, the malt is milled down to a flaky powder called grist, and no other cereals are added. In contrast, the malted barley proportion of a typical bourbon or rye mash bill is usually about 5–15%. Irish pot still whiskey can be made up of between 40–100% malted barley, with the rest being unmalted barley.

Mashing

Mashing is a crucial stage in the pursuit of fermentable sugars before fermentation. It's where the ground-down cereals are mashed and heated with water, converting their starch into sugars, resulting in a sweet liquid called wort, which is better known as unfermented beer.

Starches are ungainly things made up of connecting chains of glucose molecules. For fermentation to work, these starches need to be broken down into more simple sugars so that the yeast can successfully 'feed' on them. During mashing, our arsenal of enzymes that were gathered during malting target starches in the mash and break them down into simple sugars.

For malt whisky, the barley is added to a mash tun mashed into hot water at 69°C (156°F), which subsequently drops to around 64°C (147°F), known as the strike point. This temperature must be maintained precisely to get the maximum levels of fermentable sugar out of the malt without damaging the enzymes. After about an hour, the wort is drained off through a mesh called a lauter screen, which filters out the husks and solids, and is then sent on to the washback for fermentation. A second and third mashing takes place to extract the maximum amount of sugar from the remaining grist. This involves increasing the mashing temperature up to 70°C (158°F) and 88°C (190°F), respectively. The final (third) mash extracts very little sugar, and is known as sparge, leaving behind the spent grist. This water is then used as part of the first water on the next mash. This is standard for most distilleries, although some get away with using only two sets of water and a 'continuous sparge', like Caol Ila; others use four sets of water, like Springbank.

For American whiskey, the non-malt cereals (corn, rye, wheat) are cooked first to gelatinize the starch, preparing them for the addition of the malt later on. Corn, in particular, has to be boiled at 100°C (212°F), which causes the starch to swell irreversibly, breaking hydrogen bonds, and causing no end of disruption to the starch matrix. Some distilleries, like Four Roses, do this in a massive pressure cooker. These beasts can heat the mash up to over 130°C (266°F), which can dramatically speed up the process. Other producers use a slightly less efficient steaming method, which is thought to be a little more gentle on the product. Rye is cooked at 78°C (172°F) and malted barley and wheat at around 65°C (149°F). The whole thing is a bit like making a casserole, where all the different ingredients must be cooked to different temperatures and times for them to be at their best. One of the main differences between mashing and fermenting American whiskey, compared to malt whisky, is the fact that the mash is not filtered in between the two stages.

Before production was scaled up, the mashmen of America used to do all their mashing and fermenting in standard wooden barrels. They would add their mash bill to a cask containing hot water and give it a good stir with a long paddle.

Above These old mills are a common site in Scottish distilleries; they were constructed so well that modern mills are a surprising rarity in this part of the world.

Left The 115-year-old mash tun at Edradour still retains its original cast-iron floor and walls, and would be difficult to replicate using modern techniques.

This page Mashing is a careful balance between the ratio of ingredients, temperature of water and milling of cereals, with the ultimate goal of converting as much starch into sugar as possible.

Yeast is a microscopic single-celled organism that exists all around us and on virtually everything we touch. It's on the pages of the book you're reading now, in the air you're breathing, and even working away inside your digestive system. You can only see yeast cells under a microscope and to give you an idea of their size, you will find approximately 100 million test cells in a single 7g/¼ oz. packet of baker's yeast that you find in a supermarket or grocery store. If you leave a covered bowl of flour and water out for a couple of days, you will see it begin to bubble and come alive. Microscopic yeast cells, descended from the air but also present on the flour itself, devour the food source, multiply in numbers, and pump out carbon dioxide and alcohol.

When yeast is added to a sugary wort (beer), three actions take place: firstly, the yeast multiplies by using the sugar to form new cell material. Secondly, the yeast 'ferments' – an anaerobic reaction involving the breakdown of glucose and its conversion to ethanol and carbon dioxide. Thirdly, the yeast respires – another aerobic reaction that happens when oxygen is available.

In the production of beer, brewers will always use their own special formula of yeast. The type of yeast used will not only affect the yield of alcohol, but it can also control the rate and intensity of fermentation, and ultimately the complex flavours that are created. Up until quite recently, distillers believed that yeast was only significantly involved with conversion rate and resilience. Yes, it must be able to convert a sugar-rich liquid containing zero alcohol up to perhaps 8% or more, and it needs to do it quickly. However, a few distilleries are starting to look a lot more closely at their yeast strain, since it's the yeast that builds the palate of flavours that the distiller has to play with. One such distillery is the London Distillery Company (see page 224), which only became licensed in 2013, but it is taking its time trialling a few different yeast strains before gambling the life of the distillery on it! The Ben Nevis Distillery in Scotland is one of the only malt producers that uses a traditional brewer's yeast rather than hard-working distillery cultures. Meanwhile, in

Above It's not always pretty (or perhaps it is), but fermentation arguably defines many of the parameters of flavour in whisky later down the line.

Wales, the Penderyn Distillery (see page 219) actually buys its beer in from the local Brains Brewery, a luxury not afforded to Scottish distilleries, which must by law mash and ferment on site. Yeast can be added to the fermenting vessel in one of two ways, either by literally tipping 20kg/44 lbs. bags of living culture in by hand, or by pumping liquid yeast in through pipes. Malt whisky requires about 20kg/44 lbs. of (dry weight) yeast per ton of barley, or roughly 5g/⅙ oz. per litre/quart of wort.

Once the yeast and wort come into contact there's a period called the 'lag', which can last between three and six hours. Here, the yeast is acclimatizing itself to its new surroundings and preparing for the challenges ahead. The next stage is the 'log', where the yeast kicks into action. Deprived

Left A yeast culture sample, jealously guarded in a locked refrigerator at Woodford Reserve Distillery in central Kentucky, USA.

fermenters and used to supply a steady feed to the continuous stills.

In bourbon and rye whiskey production, the wort is not filtered after mashing; everything gets piped through to the fermenter and the solids are only removed later, during distillation. Fermentation tends to be around 3-4 days and the beer strength slightly higher than that of malt whisky, but this is partly due to corn having a higher percentage of fermentable sugars. In North America it is sometimes necessary to stop the wash/beer from getting too hot (which would endanger the yeast cells); many American fermenters feature cold water pipes to help to control this.

Generally, the time it takes to convert the sugar will depend on the temperature of the fermentation. The optimum temperature for any distillery depends on the specific strain of yeast, the sugar content of the wort and the desired outcome in terms of flavour – but typically you're talking about a starting temperature of around 20°C (68°F) and an end temperature just above 30°C (86°F). In Scotland, there's usually little in the way of temperature control, other than lowering or increasing the starting temperature to counteract the seasons. This, in my opinion, is the first major turning point in the production process that can differentiate one distillery's character from another.

Even in longer fermentations, most of the alcohol is created in the first two days, but bacterial effects, which go on at the latter parts of the fermentation process, can help to develop wild, fruity and floral flavours that will carry through to the distillation stages. Fermentation produces many other things besides ethanol, including various other alcohols, aldehydes, acids and ketones. These are the building blocks of the final liquid's flavour profile and many of these also develop (in addition to the bacteria) in the later stages. The downside of dragging it out too long, though, is that some of the shiny new alcohol that has been created in the wash is wasted through oxidization – in other words, long fermentations make interesting flavour, but ultimately lose the distillery money.

of the oxygen it needs to sustain itself, it begins to ferment the wort, producing ethanol, carbon dioxide and heat, at a serious pace, and multiplies in number rapidly. Most washbacks are equipped with 'switchers', metal paddles that rotate around and suppress the foam that is generated. The fermentation of malt whisky usually begins to slow after 36 hours and most distilleries stop altogether at around 48–60 hours.

For malt whisky and North American whisky production the fermentation vessels are traditionally constructed of wood, but these days it's becoming more common to see steel ones, too. Glenrothes Distillery has 10 Oregon pine washbacks and eight steel. I have not personally tasted the beer produced from each side-by-side, but John MacLellan, distillery manager of Kilchoman on Islay, tells me that the difference is almost imperceptible. The most common wooden washbacks are made from Oregon pine, but you will also see Douglas fir (also a type of pine) and larch. American whisky fermenters can be made from steel, or wood, such as the Cypress wood vats at Four Roses Distillery. Bourbon distilleries often have a larger steel vat called a beer well, which is constantly topped up from the

SOUR MASH

Sour-mashing, sometimes known as 'set-back', is a process used in the production of many American whiskies. It is often mistaken as a proprietary technique of the Jack Daniel's brand, but, in fact, almost all of the bourbon producers in America conduct sour-mashing. It works in much the same way as sourdough bread, in that a portion of old mash (previously fermented beer) is added to fresh mash that is ready for fermentation. The old mash is actually taken from the leftovers of distillation, where the spent cereal solids are removed and drained of their sour liquid. The sourness is a result of lactic bacteria growth that occurs between fermentation and distillation. All the yeast is dead at this point. Then, the bacteria are killed by heating the liquid to 100°C (212°F). The liquid is next 'inoculated' with yeast (i.e. yeast is introduced to the liquid) before it is finally added into the new mash. It's believed by many that sour-mashing is an important stage of lowering the pH of the mash, which promotes good fermentation.

Traditionally, it probably worked slightly differently, wherein a repeat visit from the yeast culture of the last fermentation batch is thought to go some way towards ensuring consistency between batches. Set-back like this would have been the only method of inoculating the next batch of mash with yeast culture, rather than using a new culture every time.

The sour part of the mash can make up over 20% of the fermented liquid, and the quantity used is strictly controlled to create a desirable pH for the yeast culture.

Below The contrast between old wooden walls and the palpable tension of of billions of yeast cells hard at work.

DISTILLATION

The art of distillation is certainly one of the more magical and esoteric parts of the whisky-making process. A juxtaposition between ancient copper kettles, the whirring of modern pumps and the steady flow of crystal-clear distillate lends a 'steampunk' feel to most distillery operations. It's fascinating to see that, despite technical advances, the alchemy of distillation has required the same amount of time and attention to detail for over 1,000 years. Even though some copper-pot distilleries now output annual bottle volumes in the tens of millions, the vast majority of distilleries in the world still use hand-made copper stills to produce their whisky, and many of them still check the strength of their spirit by floating a simple glass hydrometer.

THE FUNDAMENTALS OF DISTILLATION

Distillation does not make alcohol, but rather it concentrates it by removing many of the non-alcoholic components from an alcoholic wash. The reason that distillation works (and hence is the basis for the manufacture of all kinds of spirit) is that alcohol boils at 78.3°C (173°F), unlike water, which boils at 100°C (212°F), so the alcohol transforms into vapour before the water begins to evaporate. By heating the alcoholic wash to a very precise temperature, the alcohol vapours can be stripped out of the liquid, then cooled down and condensed into something stronger than what you started with. If the temperature is too hot, the vapour will contain too much water. If it's too cool, not enough vapour will make it through to the condenser.

So in principle, whisky distillation is quite simple – extracting ethanol out of a low-alcohol beer. Of course, the difficulty (and the exciting bit) comes with deciding which other bits, besides the alcohol, you want to take with you. Distillation is critical as it both *selects* and *creates* flavour. True, the fermentation process did a great job of that by itself, but the complex reactions don't stop there. In distillation our low-alcohol wash is finally exposed to high temperatures and phase changing – whether it be through steam coils, direct steam or direct heat. This prompts the further development of esters, aldehydes and other compounds related to oxidization.

There are a number of factors that dictate the strength of the stuff that comes out of the other end, and seemingly minor distinctions between distillation practices can have big repercussions in both the taste of the 'new-make spirit' (the final product of distillation) and the matured whisky. As we have already learned, fermentation creates numerous flavourful compounds, some of which the distiller will deem fit for the product and others that that he or she won't.

Left A casual glance inside a pot still can only hint at the true alchemy that is taking place down below and up above.

Right Three of the six 'onion'-shaped stills look out over sweeping countryside at the Royal Brackla distillery.

THE POT STILL

Of the two types of still used to distil whisky, the first is the traditional pot still and condenser used in the production of malt whisky and Irish pot-still whiskey. The pot still is always constructed entirely from copper on account of its high thermal conductivity, malleability and catalytic properties. The still normally looks like a giant teardrop-shaped kettle with a hatch for gaining access to the bottom and a pipe, called a lyne arm, that connects the top to a condenser. The contents of the still are heated by either a steam coil, pan or a direct flame; the alcohol vapours are stripped away from the liquid in the base, then they bend around the top of the still (known as a swan neck) and fall down into the condenser to be turned back into liquid form.

You would think that holding a steady 78.3°C (173°F) during the course of the run would lead to a resulting distillate comprising pure alcohol, but of course water, while not boiling at this temperature, does still produce steam. It's for this reason that no matter what you do a pot still, you'll never get close to producing pure, 100% alcohol. Irish pot-still whiskey and Scottish malt whisky producers go some way towards overcoming this through batch distillation (re-distilling the distillate), thereby increasing the alcoholic strength of the liquid with each subsequent distillation.

The first distillation for malt whisky and Irish pot-still whiskey is conducted in a wash still, where 99% of the alcohol is extracted from the beer. Even with that careful control, the resulting liquid is unlikely to be above 25% alcohol by volume (ABV) and usually around 21–22%. This is not strong enough to make whisky, so the process is repeated once more for malt whisky (there are a handful of examples of more than two distillations) and twice more for Irish pot-still whiskey. After a second or third distillation, you can expect an alcohol strength of 65–85%.

STILL SHAPE AND SIZE

The shape, size and height of the still play a part in the final product. Most of it comes down to the phenomenon of reflux (the act of alcohol vapour returning to the still for further distillation). The

Left Bulbous and heavy-looking, the stills at Lagavulin are a defining part of the character of the final spirit.

Left A big old Glenfarclas still greets visitors to the distillery, capturing snowfall too in this instance.

higher the still, the greater the range of temperature from the top of the 'swan's neck' to the base of the pan. As vapour travels up a long still, it is more likely to lose momentum from the cooler copper at the top than it would in a stocky still (like the ones at Lagavulin), which retains most of its heat throughout. For the tall still, this means that only the lightest alcohols and the most volatile can make it 'over the top' and into the condenser. In squat little stills, the heavier, oilier and more dense flavour compounds are able to make it over the top since they have less distance to cover.

In addition to this, tall stills give a spirit more interaction time (and space) with copper. Copper has a purifying effect on a distilled spirit and a greater degree of interaction removes sulphurous flavours and heightens delicate fruit and floral aromatics. This is especially so in small stills, since there is a greater surface area of copper in comparison to the volume of liquid. Of course, the effects of size vary based on how much liquid is put into the still, too.

The shape of the still also has a part to play, with the different forms encouraging a varying degree of reflux in the system. A short still can produce spirit that is reminiscent of a tall still by bulging out and pinching in at certain stages up the neck of the still. Broadly, pot stills come in three traditional flavours: lantern-shaped, onion-shaped, and boil-ball (or boil-collar) shaped. Each of the different shapes is engineered to manipulate the amount of reflux that goes on during distillation by giving the vapours a clear run, or teasing them into crevices and overhangs that lead back down to the bottom.

Dalmore Distillery in the northern Highlands goes a step further by having a water-cooled jacket halfway up the neck of the still. This further lowers the temperature of the copper in that part of the still, generating exceptional amounts of reflux and a more delicate spirit. In a similar vein to this, a handful of distilleries use a purifier system, which comprises a pipe that runs from the beginning of the condenser down to the base of the still. What the purifier does is to capture any heavy, more oily volatiles that have *already* condensed back into liquid, while the lighter volatiles float on past and into the condenser proper – destined to become liquid a little further down the line. I have yet to see a still that has water mist sprayed directly onto it, which would seem to me to be a cheap and easy-to-control measure for dictating the level of reflux inside.

The final important factor in the shape of the still is the angle of the lyne arm. Some lyne arms angle upwards (Laphroaig, for example) and they will – just like a tall still – encourage reflux, as the design is effectively extending the length of vertical copper in the apparatus. Most lyne arms run perpendicular to the neck of the still, and a few slope steeply downwards. A downward-sloping lyne arm acts as a grabbing arm for vapour that makes it up to the top of the still's neck – snatching it into the condenser before it has a chance to drop.

It's not uncommon for distillers to become fixated over the condition of their still when it can be relied upon to turn out a good product. For example, I've heard reports of dents being deliberately hammered into new copper to replicate the condition of the metal it's replacing.

This page Iconic triple pot-stills at Woodford Reserve Distillery (above); Still-shaped paraphernalia at the home of Scottish blend, Vat 69 (left).

FIRING THE STILL

Just like skinning a cat, there's more than one way to heat a pot still. The traditional manner is with an open flame, which, aside from sounding quite dangerous, has a different effect on the liquid inside when compared with an indirect heat source (more on that shortly). The alchemist Paracelsus is credited with building the first water-jacketed still, way back in 1526. This gentler approach effectively made water the 'middle man' between the direct heat source and the fragile contents of the still, which gave greater temperature control and a decreased risk of burning. These days, pot stills are heated either by direct fire or through a steam coil. The coil is the more modern of the two methods and works the same way as an electric kettle – only it is steam that heats it rather than an electrical current. Coils are easy to control and produce a consistent diffusion of heat. Scapa Distillery on Orkney is thought to have been the earliest adopter of steam-powered stills, way back in 1885 when the distillery was founded.

Direct-fired stills are heated by either oil, gas, coal or (traditionally) peat fires. In the old days, this was quite a labour-intensive job – the fires would need to be constantly monitored, stoked, raked and sometimes even hosed down to control the temperature, lest the contents boil over into the condenser. Nowadays, there are only half-a-dozen distilleries in Scotland that use direct-fired stills and all are powered by gas or coal, with the exception of Springbank, which uses a combination of oil-firing and steam coils on its wash still. There still remain a few headaches with direct firing, namely the tendency for hotspots inside the still to scald and char the liquid at the still's surface. This is far more of a problem with the wash still, since a lot more insoluble free-flowing organic matter clumps and sticks to the copper. The solution is the aptly named rummager: a long copper chain that mechanically swirls around the base of the still like a giant metal whisk.

So why all this fuss over how the damn thing is heated? You may well assume that heat is heat and that it has little bearing on the final product, but distillers are in agreement that direct firing produces a much 'heavier' spirit at the other end. In 1951, the Wine and Spirit Association of Great Britain mused that 'It is the unequal heating in parts (caused by direct firing) that develops the character and quality of Scotch whisky and brings out its special peculiarities.' It's for this reason that most distilleries resisted the transition to indirect firing right up until the 1960s. Strathisla Distillery in Speyside is unique in having both direct-fired and indirect-fired stills; the produce of both stills are then blended to create their final product. Back in the days of dramming, the stillmen would always prefer to drink the 'cleric' (the spirit just as it comes out of the still, also known as 'white dog') from the direct-fired still. But on one occasion, the men were wrongly served cleric from the indirect-fired still and there was uproar among the workers, who immediately detected the difference.

Scientifically speaking, the most likely reason for heavier distillate character in direct-fired stills is the overheating of certain compounds in contact with the hot copper. In an indirect-fired still, the copper is heated by the liquid in the still (since the steam coil is not in contact with the copper), but with direct heat, it is the copper itself that diffuses the heat. This causes complex caramelizations, Maillard reactions (the chemical reactions between amino acids and carbohydrates that give browned foods their characteristic flavour) and charring of the solid matter in the wash still, which results in the breakdown and denaturing of various compounds in the wash and the production of furfural and sulphur compounds. These, in turn, will make their way into the alcohol vapour and impart a unique flavour into the spirit.

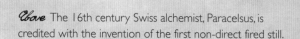

Above The 16th century Swiss alchemist, Paracelsus, is credited with the invention of the first non-direct fired still.

Right The very small and very unusual alembic-style still at Strathearn Distillery is controlled completely by hand and monitored by temperature gauges on the lyne arm and condenser.

Above In contrast to Strathearn Distillery, the towering continuous still at Four Roses Distillery, Lawrenceburg, is a powerful indicator of the volume of product that your average Kentucky distillery outputs.

THE TWO TYPES OF CONDENSER

There are two types of condensers used in the production of pot-distilled whisky – the worm tub and the shell-and-tube.

The worm tub is based on a design that has been around for almost as long as distillation itself. From the end of the lyne arm, a pipe (usually copper) snakes down into a large, typically wooden tub filled with water. The longer and narrower the pipe, the better the cooling effect of the tub. At the bottom of the tub, the pipe exits and from there, the distillate runs out in liquid form. Worm tubs are normally open-topped and located outside the distillery walls, so that the famous Scottish weather can give a regular top-up. This is not without its pitfalls however, and the temperature of the cooling water can fluctuate by up to 20°C (68°F) from winter to summer. I'm reliably told that to counteract this, stills are run slightly slower in the summer. It's also their exposure to the elements that means regular cleaning is required to prevent the build-up of silt and debris. Before the introduction of shell-and-tube condensers, the worm tub was the only option. At the time of writing, there are 14 malt distilleries in Scotland that still use a worm tub. They insist that it produces a slightly richer and meatier spirit; I agree with them.

Shell-and-tube condensers rather fittingly consist of a cylindrical 'shell' with copper tubes running through it. They work the opposite way to a worm tub, whereby the tubes have cooling water running through them and the vapour condenses on the outside of the tubes, then rolls down to the bottom of the shell. What this means is that there is a greater surface area of copper for the vapour to cling to. This increased interaction between the copper and the vapour leads to a perceivably softer spirit. The shell-and-tube system is, in effect, a heat exchanger, and some distilleries now use the warmed-up cooling water to assist in the heating in other areas of the distillery. The super-modern Roseisle (or the 'Death Star' distillery as I have dubbed it) is one such site to do this – they recycle a massive 56% of all the energy expended there.

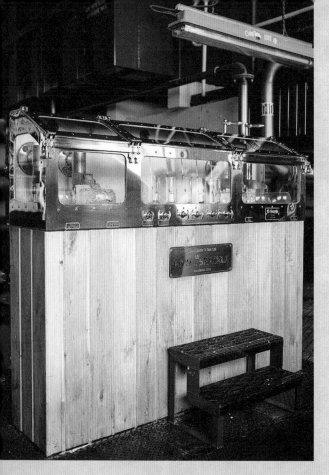

safe, and its capture can be modified by twisting the levers on the outside of the safe. Watching it always reminds me of someone manipulating radioactive material using rubber gloves attached to a sealed glass box. These days the world is a slightly more trusting place, however, and the distiller has access to the inside of the safe, but up until 1983 only the local Customs and Excise officer, who often lived at the distillery, had the key.

One distillery manager (who wishes to remain nameless) told me that once, when a thermometer inside the safe blew, he had to knock on the door of the excise officer's house to obtain the key to get inside. The thermometer was quickly replaced that day, but for a full week the distillery workers were, with expressions of sincerity on their faces, knocking on the Excise officer's door to borrow the key once more.

WASH DISTILLATION

In the first stage of distillation, the wash still is first filled about three-quarters full with preheated wort. From a 5–10% ABV wort, a distiller would expect to collect a 21–27% 'low wine' (the product of the first distillation) after a 5–8 hour distillation run. Typically, about one-third of the volume of the starting liquid will end up in low wines receiver. It's usual for the wash to froth and foam at the beginning of the distillation, which is something that can be monitored through the sight glass on the neck of the still. When this happens the heat is turned down to prevent boiling over.

Once all the low wines are collected, they're mixed with the 'foreshots' and 'feints' of the previous spirit distillation (see right). This is a curious practice that primarily aims to maintain consistency between runs and secondly to extract any additional ethyl-alcohol that may be lurking between folds of the feints.

SPIRIT DISTILLATION

The second (and in some cases, third) distillation concentrates the low wines from the first distillation

SPIRIT SAFE

The spirit safe can be found in every Scottish malt whisky distillery. It's a big brass and glass contraption with a heavy padlock on it and usually a steady flow of clear distillate running through it. The spirit safe was first trialled at Port Ellen Distillery on Islay in 1823, to coincide with the introduction of new excise duties, and was then quickly installed in all distilleries. The measure was put in place to address two conflicting issues – firstly that the distiller needed to have access to the spirit to determine when the necessary cuts and collections are made; and secondly, that the distiller was liable to steal the spirit or siphon it off to avoid payment of duties.

So what the spirit safe does, through a set of levers, is grant the stillman remote access to the flow of liquid without direct access to the liquid itself. The liquid's temperature and strength can be measured using the instruments locked inside the and hones in the character particular to the distillery. Spirit stills are often, but not always, smaller than wash stills, since they usually have much less liquid to contend with.

Unlike the first distillation, which was allowed to go about its merry way, the second distillation must be carefully monitored by the stillman so that the correct strength, quality and volume of spirit is collected. The first trickles of liquid that come through the spirit safe are known as foreshots, which are channelled from the spirit safe to the feints receiver to be re-distilled. Foreshots are made up of hard-hitting compounds such as acetone (you may recognize this as the active ingredient in nail polish remover), acetaldehyde (ethereal and fruity) and methanol (ethanol's evil sister), as well as various intensely fruity esters (essentially pleasant-smelling chemicals formed when alcohol and an organic acid are mixed). Small amounts of these chemicals can be desirable in the finished product, so it's up to the stillman to determine where the 'cut' is made (i.e. deciding which part of the distillate is collected for casking). It usually takes 5–35 minutes for the foreshots to finish coming through. Once the good stuff announces itself, the flow of liquid is redirected to the spirits receiver for collection. In the old days, the spirit would be tested by adding a splash of water; if it turned cloudy it meant that the high alcohols and acetone were still coming through. Clear meant it was safe to collect.

Exactly when the spirit collection is stopped is the choice of the distiller and a decision to be made based on the desired outcome of the product. Get too greedy and you'll be punished with a lower-strength spirit with very heavy, buttery, diesel and solvent-like aromas (these last parts of the run are known as 'feints'). Keep the collection to a minimum and the spirit will be stronger and taste lighter and more delicate... but you'll have a lot less of it.

The foreshots and feints are then ready to be mixed with low wines for the next spirit run. Now, those of you paying attention here may have noticed a slight mathematical issue with this. If the foreshots and feints from every spirit run are mixed in with the low wines for the next, surely there would be a concentration of colourful compounds building up in the feints receiver over time? Well, it turns out that this is true and it's the reason why many feints receivers are periodically stripped of the dangerously alluring alien sludge that accumulates on the walls. Recently, I was told by Russell Anderson of Highland Park that cricket-ball-sized lumps of oxidized copper also collect in the feints receiver. This was something I found quite fascinating, because the seemingly clear spirit is obviously transporting a significant amount of solid matter at either the beginning or the end of the run. The feints receiver is cleaned out completely every summer at Highland Park, and Russell told me that there were enough of these blue copper balls to fill a large bag.

Below The wash still and spirit stills at Glen Garioch Distillery, one of the oldest distilleries in the world.

Left A quick peek inside a continuous still shows one of the many 'bubble plates' that lines the column. Each bubble forms a pathway between the plate below and the airspace above, granting passage only to the lighter (stronger) vapours.

THE CONTINUOUS STILL

The second type of still used to distil whisky is the continuous still, which as the name suggests, involves an ongoing, continuous process that doesn't require all the 'stop–clean–start' frustration of batch distillation. The continuous still is sometimes referred to as a column still, patent still, or Coffey still, but they are all essentially the same piece of equipment. A quick glance at a still like this and you can immediately tell that it's very far removed from the backyard pot stills of whisky's past. Continuous stills look more like something you would find in an oil refinery than the home of your favourite whisky and are certainly a less romantic option than the pot still. They can be used to make characterless vodka, grain whisky, and are used in the production of many North American spirits, too, but what they lack in small-batch grittiness, they more than make up for in epic scale, efficiency and consistency.

The continuous still is usually made up of two towers. The first tower, known as the analyser, has a series of 'baffle plates' throughout its length, which are perforated sections that effectively each conduct their own mini distillation. Alcoholic wash is pumped into the top of the tower and allowed to flow down through apertures in the plates, while hot steam is pumped in at the bottom and rises as vapour. Where the two meet, the steam strips away the alcohol from the wash, causing it to rise up the column, too; as the steam and alcohol approach the top of the column, the heavier steam begins to lose pace and falls back down, mixed in with all the dregs of the watery wash. The strong alcohol exits the top of the column as vapour and is directed to the bottom of the next column, the rectifier. This part works like a condenser, but also does the job of separating the different alcohols. The spirit vapour rises up the column and is cooled by cold liquid running through the system. The molecules with the highest boiling point will condense first, and they are drawn off and mixed back in with the continuous flow of wash that enters the analyser. Further up the column, though, ethanol will begin to condense, and it's here that the column is tapped and the spirit extracted. Highly volatile molecules, with low boiling points, might make it all the way to the top, and they too will be mixed back in with the new wash for re-distillation.

As if all that weren't clever enough, the cool liquid that runs through the rectifier is actually new wash headed for the analyser. While it performs the task of cooling the alcohol vapour, the vapour warms it up, so little energy is wasted. The strength and purity of the resulting liquid is controlled by where on the column the alcohol is drawn off, as well as the temperature of the various parts of the system, and how hard (fast) the system is run.

Because the still doesn't need to stop (they are still cleaned and maintained intermittently) and requires very little in the way of human interaction, a column still also costs less to run. The downside, which can also be seen as an upside, is that the spirit that it produces is lighter and far less characterful. Continuous distillations tend to form fewer esters during the process, probably due to the slightly lower heat involved. They also tend to have fewer furfurals (caramel, burnt sugar flavours), fusel oils and floral qualities. This is in part due to precise selection of alcohol and in part to do with the stricter control of heat in the process. Having said that, a column still is capable of making a tasty whisky both in Scotland and in Irish and North American distilleries.

Above A large sample of 'white dog' spirit at Buffalo Trace Distillery in Frankfort, Kentucky.

DISTILLATION IN NORTH AMERICA

Now that we've ascertained the difference between a column still and a pot still, allow me to introduce you to the most commonly used still in North America, which combines both methods in one.

In a typical bourbon distillery, the unfiltered beer (or 'wash') passes into a column still, where it is typically distilled to around 60–62% ABV. Then, the low wine goes on for a second distillation in what is essentially a pot still called a 'doubler', where it comes off at about 67% ABV. Try as I did, I couldn't find a good reason why the pot still is called a 'doubler' other than that it is the second part of a double distillation. Some people put it down to the doubler actually doubling the speed of distillation by taking some of the strain away from the column. Interestingly, the use of doublers is not actually required by law in the bourbon-making process.

There are two whiskey distilleries in North America (Early Times and Bernheim) that use a type of still called a 'thumper' instead of the doubler. The thumper works in much the same way, the only difference being that the spirit is still in vapour form when it enters the thumper. The noise generated by the expanding and contracting of the thumper is where it gets its name. This kind of set-up dates back to the days of moonshining, where the thumper would have been made out of a cask. Back then, the thumper or doubler would have contained liquid (often beer) which the distillate would bubble through, extracting additional alcohol in the process.

MATURATION

The maturation of whisky in the cask is undeniably the single biggest contributor of flavour in the whisky-making process. It's at this stage that the pungent distillery characteristics of new-make spirit are, over time spent encased in wood, transformed into a more mellow and relaxed liquid through a series of complex chemical changes. By my reckoning, even in young whisky with a sturdy distillery character, the cask is responsible for 50% of the flavour of the final product. This is especially true of first-fill (i.e. previously unused) American oak casks that are used in bourbon production, and perhaps less true in heavily peated Islay whiskies, where the phenolics that are derived from the kiln-drying process still hold a firm grip on the flavour profile of the dram. In very old whisky, I think it's fair to say that the lasting influence of wood can lay claim to over 90% of the whisky's flavour profile, where almost all the nuances of the earlier process have been drowned out.

The ageing of the product is also the last significant stage in the process, a fact that in itself makes maturation the most important bit. An ugly-duckling new-make spirit can still grow into a beautiful swan if nurtured correctly by a good nose and an exceptional cask. Likewise, a new-make spirit with all the potential in the world will be destined for paint thinner if ravaged by the negative effects of a defective cask.

Below The maturation warehouse is perhaps the most exciting yet peaceful part of a distillery.

The act of placing spirit in a cask and leaving it to do its thing may seem like a simple one, and when described like that, I suppose it is. But there are a whole range of variables that can impact the outcome, from the type of oak to the size of cask, toasting or charring, climate and temperature fluctuation, and of course, time. It's for this reason that all producers of whisky will have a 'wood policy' in place, designed not around a complete understanding of the process, since that does not exist, but through knowledge of past experiences and tradition.

The resting of whisky in cask almost certainly came about through the use of wood as means of transportation and storage, rather than gastronomic pursuit. Even though wine and beer had been held in casks since at least 500 BC, the French and Dutch were probably the first to notice the positive effects that time in wood had on their *brandewijn* (brandy) as it was shipped from Cognac up to the Netherlands, back in the 15th century. And it would appear that shipping spirits over long distances is the cause for many producing regions gaining notoriety for the quality of their product. For example, Mescal made in the town of Tequila in the 18th century was stretched and squeezed though hot days and cold nights on its journey to North America. Likewise, rum barrels were shipped from the Caribbean islands to the four corners of the world.

It's likely that casks were used in the production of Scotch malt whisky at least as far back as the 17th century, where English oak would have been used by coopers, but exactly when it became the norm is not entirely clear. One of the earliest references to the positive effects of whisky in cask comes from Elizabeth Grant's *Diary of a Highland Lady*, which was written around the turn of the 19th century. She describes a cask of The Glenlivet whisky that was sent to King George III (the mad one). Ironically, The Glenlivet was an illicit, non-tax-paying operation at the time of her writing. She writes of 'whisky, long in wood, long in uncorked bottles, mild as milk, and the true contraband gout in it'. Although casks were used for moving large quantities of whisky around Scotland, most of the whisky made there in the early 19th century was for local consumption. Most of the time, whisky had little need to be stored *en masse*, especially given the comparatively small production capacity of the numerous operations. Whisky production was seasonal back then, though, so it's fairly likely that barrels were used to accumulate stock, but in most instances, the local population had no patience to wait for it, so they quite often simply ran out.

It would have been around the same time that the Americans, with their newly acquired independence, first noticed a marked improvement in the quality of their corn and rye whiskies. The landlocked states of Kentucky and Tennessee needed to move large quantities of liquor long distances to the higher-populated coastal regions. Weeks of travel by boat or over rough terrain softened the whiskey through agitation and time, improving its quality. Demand for this higher-quality whiskey increased. This is one of the benefits of having almost all of the veteran distilleries of North America situated a great distance inland – maturation was unavoidable, and with that came an improvement in whiskey character.

It wasn't until 1915, during the 'What is Whisky?' debate (see page 25), that it became compulsory for Scotch to be rested in oak barrels for a minimum of two years, extending to three years in 1916. During the early part of the 20th century, chestnut wood was as common a container as oak, and it wasn't until as late as 1990 that the British government passed an order declaring that only oak could be used. There are more than likely thousands of old chestnut casks in Scotland, which, if bottled and marketed as whisky, would actually be in breach of whisky's current legal definition!

From 1960 onwards, a change in legislation required bourbon to be aged only in new oak. This generated a sizeable surplus of perfectly good ex-bourbon casks, which were sold at rock-bottom prices to European whisky-makers. From then onwards, the use of ex-Sherry casks (which had previously been the norm) dropped off considerably. Even today, around 90% of Scotch is matured in bourbon wood and the remaining 10% in ex-Sherry and wine casks.

This page Ricks of dried timber are trimmed by hand, so that they are narrower at each end; they are then passed on to the cooper who raises a single cask every two minutes.

CONSTRUCTING CASKS

There are two main families of oak used for ageing whisky: white oak (*Quercus alba* is the most common but there are many others), and red oak (only *Quercus robur* or *Quercus sessilis*). White oak comes from America, and red oak from Europe, but America imports around a quarter of the total European oak exports and Europe its fair share of American white oak. The trees themselves resemble their cultural counterparts in some ways, too. White oak has a paler-coloured bark than red oak, but there's little difference between the colour of the cut wood. Red oak grows slowly; it twists and turns and only reaches maturation after 150 years. The resulting whisky is more tannic (a trait arising from the slow growth), peppery and spicy with, rather fittingly, flavours of red-coloured things like cherries, grapes and red apples. White oak grows much faster, and it grows straight and true because it's planted with more space, accelerating along to maturation in only 60–80 years. The result is a more 'obvious' wood influence, with plenty of vanilla and associated white-coloured things, like banana, white chocolate, buttermilk and custard.

From a visual examination of the wood alone, it's difficult to tell the difference between the two, but one way to distinguish them is by examining a cut cross-section of the wood. Both types of wood are porous along the growth lines of the wood, but the pores on the white oak are actually filled with tylose (a kind of natural wood-filler), whereas red oak pores are open. The *tylose* in the white oak actually makes the wood slightly more watertight than red oak. Sometimes it's easier to feel the difference with your fingers when looking for the pores, with red oak feeling a little less smooth than the white oak. Another way of telling the difference is by examining the medullary rays on the grain of the wood. These rays are small, dark pencil dashes that run with the grain of the wood, and on red oak they tend to be under 10mm/⅓ inch in length, while on white oak, they tend to be around 20mm/¾ inch in length. Since the medullary rays are considered to be completely impervious to liquids, it is yet another point in favour of white oak as the better container. White oak is also straighter and more malleable. Red oak, grown mostly in the forests of northern Spain and France, is naturally inferior at all of the same things and it takes longer to accomplish it. But red oak

does have the advantage of being slightly longer-lasting than white, and it is highly regarded by some for the flavour that it imparts in whisky.

Also becoming more common are the French oak (*Quercus petraea*), which is much-loved by the Cognac industry, and *Quercus mongolica*, an expensive oak revered by the Japanese and prized for its tropical fruit and heady incense aromatics.

After felling, the wood is first dried for up to a year, in log form. Next it is sliced into quarters, like batons of a carrot, then cut down to stave billets that follow the grain of the wood. Bourbon barrels are usually cut with a slightly curved saw that traces the curvature of the barrel along the width of the stave. European cuts are normally straight and the wood is later trimmed to form flush joints between staves. There's significant wastage from the tree, comprising bits of wood too small to be made into staves, but some coopers use the waste to fuel the fires used in the toasting or charring stages later.

Only the inner 80% of the log, known as the heartwood, is used since the outer sapwood, which sits directly behind the bark, is too porous. Most American oak staves that are destined for American whiskey maturation are traditionally kiln-dried for about 30 days at this stage. This takes its moisture

level down from 50% to 12% and the wood is then ready to be coopered into a cask. Oak used by the Sherry industry in Europe, on the other hand, is yard-dried in stages for a further nine months to three years; typically, this brings the moisture content down to around 14%. Some bourbon producers are now experimenting with yard-drying their wood in the pursuit of better flavour release; Woodford Reserve even released a 'Seasoned Oak-finished' expression that saw aged bourbon infused with five-year-dried oak.

What's the difference, you may ask? Well, if you'd asked 20 years ago, the answer may have been *nothing*. But kiln-drying is quite an aggressive process, and recent studies suggest that the kiln-dried wood skips an important stage of fungal growth that assists in the conversion and liberation of flavoursome compounds in the wood. By contrast, yard-dried wood plays host to a succession of travelling microscopic fungi during its seasoning period, which 'acupuncture' hydrogen peroxide into the surface of the wood, softening and relaxing the harder structure of the wood, and therefore allowing better penetration from the spirit. The fungi, along with rainfall, are also thought to assist in the removal of tannins, even leaving behind a

This page The various components of a barrel's life, from preparation for dumping (bottom left) to the charring of its inner surfaces (top left) and finally the cooper's tools (bottom right).

visible tea-stain of tannin on the ground where the wood had been placed.

Staves are born straight, so to form the familiar barrel shape they must be trimmed down and bent into submission. The stave is cut so that it tapers in at either end – a necessary step to form the bulge in the barrel. The bulge is an essential feature that physically helps to hold the barrel together and aids in the manoeuvrability of the barrel by hand. The bulge allows the barrel to be easily rocked and rolled about the place, despite weighing in excess of 400kg/880 lbs. A 180-litre/190-quart bourbon cask is constructed from roughly 30 finished staves, which are placed in hoops, then heated by steam and forced together mechanically. A 500-litre/528-quart cask (or 'butt') needs approximately 50 staves. They are formed in a similar way, but usually warmed with an open flame and water (to prevent cracking) before being bent into shape.

The circular barrel ends are made from shorter stave cuts that are drilled out and pinned together with dowel rods (solid, cylindrical pins used to fasten two staves together) to form a square. They are then sawn into a circle and sent on for toasting or charring along with the barrel shell.

Toasting and charring are not interchangeable terms, although they might sound the same. Charring is an all-out flamethrower assault on the interior surfaces of the barrel, as ruthless licks of heat blast the wood for up to 30 seconds, causing the surface to bubble and writhe as it catches fire. One legend describes how the charring process was introduced by the Reverend Elijah Craig (the dubiously proclaimed inventor of bourbon), who wanted to store his whiskey in oak casks that had previously held fish (other reports state that they formerly contained nails), so he aggressively charred the inside to remove the fishy flavour. Whether it was Craig or not, I'd say that there's a good chance that the man or woman who did first char a cask was intending to overcome a similar problem.

When a cask is toasted, the heat is applied more gently, sometimes through convection rather than direct flame, and over a longer period of time – up to and around six minutes. Toasting is kind of like roasting a sausage slowly, whereas charring is something akin to barbecuing a sausage quickly.

Visually, there is a similar contrast, too. Charred barrels look as if they have (barely) survived a pirate-ship battle, with blackened scabs and brittle blisters. A light char is the colour of graphite and a heavy char is as black as coke. The colour of the internal surfaces of a toasted cask on the other hand can range from vanilla fudge through to dark coffee. The toast level is controlled during the process and categorized as either light, medium, medium+, or dark. The general rule of thumb is that barrels intended for the bourbon industry (which are always white oak) are charred, and barrels intended for Sherry, Madeira, Port, or other types of wine are toasted. The Brown-Forman Cooperage in Kentucky, which produces casks for Woodford Reserve and Jack Daniel's, among others, actually toasts its casks before charring, in a kind of why-do-one-when-you-can-do-both approach. The Independent Stave Company, which makes barrels for most of the rest of the American whiskey industry, offers a computer-controlled barrel-profiling service, where its customers can request specific flavours and the cask is charred to a unique heat curve – like roasting coffee to liberate a distinct aroma.

Whether by toasting or charring, the heat treatment of these casks is a critical step in the influence of flavour in whisky. Indeed, the impact that the cask's toast or char has over the final whisky cannot be overstated. Grilling the barrel like this achieves three functions – the degradation of wood polymers into flavoursome compounds, the destruction of unpleasant resinous compounds in the wood, and in the case of charring, the forming of a thin layer of active carbon. I would also propose that the char or toast assists in fusing the spirit to the wood by absorbing the liquid and holding it close to the adjacent wood surface – kind of like pressing a wet sponge against your skin.

In the final stage of production, the barrel ends are securely fitted and wax-sealed, then the bung hole is drilled. The container is then tested for leaks and filled with a splash of water to prevent it from drying out before filling. The process is now complete. Now the cask is a giant teabag in reverse; a potent package of densely clustered compounds, ready to reap slow, sapid domination on any liquid fortunate enough to be imprisoned within its walls.

PUTTING CASKS TO USE

In the production of American straight whiskey and bourbon, the liquid must be aged in charred new white oak barrels, which imparts a lot of colour and associated wood characteristics into the spirit in a very short time. The combination of fresh wood and warm climate means that bourbon matures quickly. The minimum age required is two years and many products available are little more than four years old. The characteristics we associate with bourbon are largely derived from this wood policy.

Once bourbon casks have been used, they cannot be regenerated or re-used again for American whiskey (with the exception of corn whiskey – see page 99). It's not a problem, though, as there's plenty of demand for casks from tequila and rum producers, as well as other whisky producers around the world. The bourbon casks are either broken down into staves for shipment, or, as is often the case more recently, left in barrel form and sent off to their new homes. Irish, Canadian, Japanese and Scotch whisk(e)y producers all use ex-bourbon casks to age the majority of their whiskies, where it's common practice to cooper ex-bourbon casks (with capacities of 180 litres/190 quarts) into slightly larger hogshead casks (250 litres/264 quarts by slipping in a few extra staves.

You may wonder why the Scotch whisky industry would use American cast-offs. Why not build casks intended solely for malt whisky maturation? Well, the answer to this lies in the requirements of two styles of whisky. Two of my younger brothers used to share boiled eggs at breakfast-time. One of them liked the egg white, and the other the yolk. It was a simple arrangement,

the first brother would peel the whites off and eat them, then he would pass the yolks on to the other. Bourbon barrels are the same deal. American whiskey producers demand the initial flavours of coconut ice cream, hard toffee and cream soda, which can only be provided by charred new American oak. Conveniently, these are the flavours that other whisky-makers wish to avoid. Essentially, the bourbon industry gets exactly what it wants from the cask before passing it on to the next guy, who can be confident that the cask has been sufficiently depleted of the bits he doesn't want.

And it's the same situation with the wine industry in Europe. While the flavours may be slightly different in the initial hit of a toasted oak cask, the extraction of them into Sherry and other wines remains an important step towards a cask that is fitting for malt whisky maturation.

So the first liquid to enter a new cask knocks out the high notes of the wood, but what of the liquid's impression on the cask? Can you detect whether an oak cask previously held Sherry or Madeira? A typical Sherry butt is thought to 'in-drink' somewhere around 10 litres/10.5 quarts of Sherry over a two-year period, but many casks have water added to them in the interim period to draw out the wine – so the question is whether you might be able to detect a few litres of Sherry added to 500 litres/528 quarts of whisky. This is a matter that is open to debate, and I know of some who claim that it is impossible to detect the difference between different wines that the cask held in previous fills, yet many producers place great emphasis on the past affairs of their wooden barrels. I personally think that the effect of the previous fill is increased over time; having tried some very old (50+ years) Sherry-cask single malts, I can certainly testify to considerable (to the point of incredible) Sherry influence. Perhaps, like many of us, it just takes a while for past relationships to eke out of the system.

This leads us on to the topic of finishing, whereby a whisky that is considered to be aged sufficiently is 'finished' in a cask of a different type in an effort to imbue the spirit with further complexity and character. This is a much more common practice in malt whisky, but there are some examples of bourbons, such as the Angel's Envy, that

spend a short time in ruby Port casks, and Maker's 46, which has (new) French oak staves introduced during its maturation.

In the case of finishing in malt whisky, there are examples of Port, Madeira, oloroso, fino, Pedro Ximénez (PX), Bordeaux, Burgundy, Muscat and many other types of casks used in finishing whisky today. The question is, though, how apparent is the flavour of the previous inhabitant when finishing is typically only six to 24 months? Not much, in my opinion. Sure, if your whisky squats in a PX cask for a couple of years, with all its sultana/golden raisin and black cherry sweetness, there will be some noticeable influence; Lagavulin Distillers Edition is a great example of this (see pages 120–121) – but to differentiate between different sherries and wines, I think is a stretch.

Interestingly, there are no official rules around the use of the term 'Sherry cask' in Scotch whisky production. This means that the cask could be a cheaper, ex-bourbon cask, that has had only the most fleeting of brief encounters with Sherry, or a new cask that has only been briefly seasoned with Sherry. The neglect to tackle this point has left the door open for producers to 'rejuvenate' dead or drying casks by seasoning them with Paxarete, a type of very sweet wine. A small quantity of the concentrated wine is added to a cask, and the vessel is sealed and pressurized, causing the wine to percolate into the wood. Any excess wine is drained from the barrel and is then sent off for filling with whisky. I should say that this practice is thought to be far less common today, but it strikes me as odd that even though it's illegal to adulterate Scotch whisky with flavourings, it's not illegal to adjust the flavouring of the vessels that it is stored in.

TIME AND TEMPERATURE

Time is the most obvious variable in the maturation process. We're all familiar with gauging maturation characteristics by looking for a number on a bottle, and all-too-often placing our faith in it as a marker of quality. Sadly, the maturation process is not as simple as 'the longer you leave it, the more woody it gets', and certainly not as simple as the older the whisky, the better it tastes. An age statement can be useful, but only really becomes relevant if the other

Above Quality control on the production line at the Brown-Forman cooperage in Lousiville, Kentucky.

variables are made aware to us. And even today that scarcely happens. Without information like the type of cask and its condition, char/toast level and warehouse conditions, the age statement becomes an arbitrary figure and you're better-off assessing the whisky on the quality of the box it comes in and the size of the distiller's shoes.

The best wood that money can buy will be no use if warehouse conditions are not taken into account. Temperature and humidity of the maturation environment both play critical roles in the rate of ageing as well as the inevitable loss of product through evaporation.

The size of the cask also has a bearing on maturation speed. Larger casks have a higher surface-area-to-volume ratio, meaning that there are fewer square centimetres/inches of wood per millilitre/fluid ounce of liquid. Small casks have a lower surface-area-to-volume ratio, meaning that there's more wood to go around per millilitre/fluid ounce of spirit. You might think that this means faster ageing for smaller casks, and to an extent this

is true. Wood extractives are found in higher concentrations in smaller casks, but there's no substitute for time. Because some of the job is done much quicker in small casks, there is a risk of too much wood character being imparted, so the whisky is removed. The flip side to this, though, is that other important oxidative and ester-creating reactions that can take longer have had too little time to make an impact. The result? In my experience, small casks impart a kind of pseudo-maturation; while many of the familiar markers are there, it somehow seems rushed and immature. You can dress a baby in a man's clothes, but underneath the bow tie and sharp suit, it's still a baby.

And then there's the alcoholic strength of the liquid in the cask to consider. Most of the Scotch whisky industry fills its casks at 63.5% ABV which, through trial and error over the years, has been deemed the optimum mix for a neat and even extraction from the cask. Within the realms of sensible fill strengths, the following rules generally

This page A traditional 'dunnage' warehouse at the Balblair distillery in the Scottish Highlands.

apply: lower-strength (more watery) liquids extract more tannin and sugar, whereas higher strength spirits extract more lactones (think coconut and butter) and, rather surprisingly, less colour, but also make more sugars available by breaking down hemicellulose and lignin. Tests show that raising the fill strength from 55%–75% ABV can cut sugar levels by half over typical maturation periods.

Some malt whisky distilleries do fill higher than 63.5% ABV, with one obvious benefit being that fewer casks are required. Scotch grain whisky is commonly put to cask at 67–68% ABV. Irish whiskey is commonly filled at 71% ABV, but there are no legal limits regulating it. In America, whiskeys that are destined to be sold as 'straight' or as bourbon cannot enter the cask at over 62.5%

ABV, and from what I can tell, most producers fill at the legal limit. Canadian whisky usually sits between 68–72% ABV, but can be anywhere up to 78% ABV, as per Hiram Walker.

Local climate has always been a contributing factor in how a whisky tastes and feels. Cold, wet winters and mild, humid summers in Scotland slow things down to a snail's pace, whereas the racked warehouses in Kentucky can reach in excess of 60°C (140°F) in the dry summer heat. Japan's first whisky distillery, Yamazaki, was specifically located in the misty hills around Kyoto on account of its climatic similarity to the Scottish Highlands.

Warehouses come in two types: traditional dunnage warehouses, where casks are laid on a floor in rows, called stows, stacked two, three, or four levels high; and the more modern equivalent (popular in the US), of a racked warehouse, where floor-to-ceiling shelves hold the casks. Aesthetically, the dunnage warehouses are more pleasing, because there's a timeless feel about them, but there are other things at work here besides looking pretty. In a tall, racked warehouse the temperature can vary by as much as much as 40°C (104°F) from the bottom to the top. This means that casks at the top will mature in a different way to those at the bottom, an effect that is combatted by a constant rotation of stock.

This brings into question the matter of humidity. Some loss of liquid (the 'angel's share') is inevitable when maturing spirits. In Scotland, Ireland and Japan, this tends to be around 2% of the liquid in the barrel every year, the larger proportion of which is alcohol. In hotter climates like Kentucky and Tennessee, it can be up to 5%, but it depends on the position and temperature of the warehouse. Big brands have gone to great lengths to reduce the angel's share, since it is effectively their profits that are disappearing into the ether. One large corporation even conducted trials of cling-filmed/plastic-wrapped casks, but the experiment failed. Two-way interaction betwen the barrel and the world outside is essential; the angel's share is simply the lesser of two evils.

In high-humidity environments, the ethanol (alcohol) depletes at a quicker pace than the water, meaning that the ABV of the liquid lowers over time – this is the way of things in Scotland. In very dry conditions, the water will evaporate faster than the alcohol, as is often the case in Kentucky, especially near the roof of a racked warehouse. This explains why some cask-strength bourbons are often many degrees higher than permissible.

THE IMPACT OF OAK

Much of what goes on in the perpetual twilight of a warehouse is unpredictable without the analysis of every stave of wood that makes up every cask and every drop of liquid that goes into it. The impracticality of this is obvious, so a whisky 'nose' relies on experience, senses and, of course a little science to gauge the quality of a cask and the optimum time that a whisky should spend in it. Besides systematic testing and tasting, the ageing process is most often a simple guarding of treasure that has yet to achieve its full worth. The changes that take effect in the murky realms of the vessel are even today being scrutinized and tested to better understand the effects of the barrel and the optimum maturation conditions for the whisky. Below I've given a pitifully brief explanation of the goings-on inside a cask. Having said that, it's likely that you will encounter some unfamiliar words and terms, so wherever possible I have tried to relate them to the ultimate reason for all of this: flavour.

Oak itself contains over 100 volatile opponents capable of contributing flavour in a whisky. Additionally, there are other compounds formed through the oxidation of wood extracts and compounds already present in the new-make spirit. Finally, there are certain subtractive effects caused by the char layer of a bourbon cask. Think of maturation like building a house brick-by-brick, the only difference being that your bricks can appear and morph in size at will, walls are prone to disappear in their entirety, and you have virtually no control over the shapes and sizes of the rooms!

The additive effects of the wood come from four potential sources that make up much of the composition of oak: lignin, hemicellulose, extractives, and oak tannins.

Lignin makes up around 25% of the oak, and it's this stuff that provides much of the aromatic qualities of woodsmoke, as well as some very important acids, phenols and aldehydes that influence whisky flavour. One example of a compound, derived from the heating of lignin during toasting or charring, is guaiacol, an aromatic oil that contributes roasted qualities reminiscent of coffee or toast to the liquid. Guaiacol is also a precursor to other flavourful compounds, like vanillin, which gives us caramel, chocolate, toffee, cream and vanilla aromatics; and eugenol (see below). Lignin is broken down more or less linearly as maturation continues, so expect these flavours to increase over time.

Hemicellulose is the breeze block of oak's secondary cell walls, and is thought to react with complex acids in the spirit, causing the extraction of simple wood sugars (around 200 different types) that provide body and smoothness to the liquid. The treatment of the wood during coopering causes some of these sugars to undergo caramelization, too. The sugars provide little in the way of actual sweetness, but they are thought to knock back some undesirables, and the caramelized sugars can give plenty of associated aromatic sweetness. This includes compounds like furfural (an aldehyde formed from the sugar xylose), which has a nutty aroma, and cyclotene, with its distinctive maple syrup and liquorice/licorice flavours.

Extractives are free-running compounds that are 'washed' out of the wood. Important extractives include eugenol, which encompasses a whole family of dry, spicy flavours like nutmeg and cinnamon. Also attending the party are oak lactones (coconut aroma); then there's a whole range of other unpronounceables that give us subtle, grassy, baked, wood-sap, peachy, floral and even greasy aromas.

Wood tannin gives the familiar drying sensation

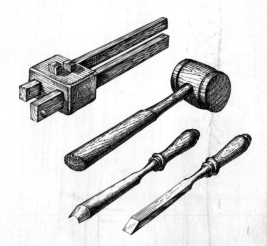

on the palate, and when managed correctly, it adds balance and grip to an otherwise flabby spirit. Tannins also help to combat a sulphury character in young whiskies, and act as a crude marker of overall wood influence by stabilizing colour. Tannins, although odourless, are also catalysts for oxidative reactions, so they do indirectly affect whisky aroma. It's thought that differences in the levels of tannins and extractives between white oak and red oak is the main defining factor in the character of the whisky that they each produce.

In addition to the additive effects of the wood, the charred layer of carbon on the inside of the bourbon cask adds a different slant to the process when compared to the toasted European cask. It's thought that the thin layer of active carbon acts as a kind of filtration system by locking down undesirable compounds that may be present in the whisky, like dimethyl sulphide (DMS), which asserts a cabbage-like aroma on white dog and new-make whisky. In effect, this carbonic layer further accelerates the maturation process by stripping distillery character, while the cask goes to work on adding new stuff.

Finally, there is colour, on which I think too much emphasis is placed. Although colour plays an important part in flavour perception, bending our better judgement towards grass, fresh fruit and heather when a whisky has a green tinge, and plums, florals and jam when the whisky is red – it is in truth little more than an indicator of cask type and condition. I have tasted 40-year-old malt whiskies with only a soft straw colour, and I have tasted three-year-old bourbons the colour of orange Fanta. Likewise, I have a 1981 bottle of Karuizawa on my shelf that is the colour of molasses. Perhaps some approximate forecasting can be made of a whisky's flavour-profile based on the assessment of colour alone (dark hues are sometimes an indication of tannin), but how much of this is our mind's curious ability to make red things taste 'red', I do not know. It's far better to drink it than to look at it, in this author's opinion.

Extraction of colour is for the most part a linear process – the longer the time in cask, the darker the colour gets. The exception to this is the first 6–12 months of ageing, especially in new-oak casks, (particularly applicable to the American whiskey industry). During the early stages of maturation, the spirit will take on an increased initial splash of gold, as free extractives invade the liquor. Once these 'easy-pickings' compounds are exhausted it's back to the usual breakdown of lignin and other colour-contributing wood components over time.

Last, but certainly not least, is the chemical degradation of the liquid through oxidation. Besides ethanol, there are numerous other trace alcohols present in the spirit. Each alcohol has its own style and is subject to the effects of oxidation, resulting in the formation of aldehydes and acids. For example, the oxidation of the ethanol (alcohol) in the cask forms acetaldehyde and acetic acid. Aldehydes play an important role in whisky aroma, like benzaldehyde (created through the oxidation of benzyl alcohol), which smells like almond.

Acetic acid, along with other oxoacids, is crucial for the formation of esters. Esterification is where an acid reacts with an alcohol and creates a new, highly aromatic compound. Isoamyl acetate, which provides the banana aroma that is prevalent in Jack Daniel's, is formed when isoamyl alcohol reacts with acetic acid. Esters provide all of the fruity and floral top notes in whisky aroma, everything from geranium or jasmine right through to apple, sage, pineapple and strawberry.

REFILLING AND REJUVENATING

Just because a cask has been (re)filled once, it doesn't mean it's going straight to the knacker's yard/slaughterhouse to be turned into a plant pot. At the time of writing, a new bourbon cask costs about £250/$420 and gets sold on after its first fill for around £150/$250. An ex-Sherry butt costs about £700/$1,175. For non-bourbon producers, the cost works out to be just over £1/$1.70 per litre/quart of whisky that the cask will hold, which makes wood the most expensive raw ingredient (and it is an ingredient) in the bottle. The canny Scotsman always has an eye on his wallet, so it should come as no surprise that it's common practice to refill casks, sometimes two or three times, in an effort to get your money's worth.

Refilling is not as simple a practice as it may sound, though, because, as previously mentioned, the cask will not necessarily continue in the same

Above Most coopers have to repair their own tools these days, because it's very difficult to buy new ones!

manner that it started. All of the contributing compounds in oak play a part, but some are exhausted in a matter of weeks, and for others it may take decades. Some readily soluble compounds will diminish after the first fill and others will continue to influence subsequent fills; like reusing coffee grounds, the effect is not only a lighter influence but disparity in balance, too.

Once a cask becomes 'inactive', efforts to extract anything worthwhile will be mostly fruitless. Rejuvenation is a potential solution. A little like sanding down a floor and reapplying the varnish, it involves mechanically scraping the inside of the cask to remove the char or toast, as well as the surface directly behind it, then re-charring or re-toasting the cask to bring it back to life again.

BLENDING

Blending is art of combining whiskies of different ages, from different distilleries, with the aim of making a product of a specific style and price. Most blended whisky is a combination of grain whisky and malt whisky, but there are also blended (or vatted) malts available, which are literally a mixture of different malt whiskies. Blending achieves a number of different things but, more than anything, it offers whisky a more competitive price than the costly-to-produce single malts. Having said that, there are some very expensive blends out there, too, which is a subject that I will tackle a little later on.

Blends also traditionally offer a more consistent product, since in the past malts tended to be a little inconsistent. However, malt producers have done a good job at smoothing over bumps in the road in recent years, and I see little reason to avoid drinking a malt for fear of it not tallying with your memory of it. Finally, blends are balanced. For the same reason that we blend tea, coffee, fragrances, paint and spices, it allows us to take disjointed or unexceptional elements and combine them into something greater and perhaps unachievable were it not for the careful mixing of components.

I like to think of a blend like a piece of music, where the instruments represent the various sections of an orchestra. Some malt whiskies are best compared to light and delicate string instruments, and others are more like the brass or percussion section. The blender is the composer, selecting whiskies based on what they bring to the piece. The difficulty comes when re-creating that composition time and time again. In an orchestra you would find the best musicians of their time to play the piece, but as any concert-goer knows, there will always be subtle changes to the arrangement in each subsequent performance. The blender (or conductor) has similar challenges in the form of differences between casks and the longer-term evolution of a distillery's character.

One way of getting around this is by diversifying the blend. A blend doesn't need to contain more than two whiskies. However, if one member of a two-man band drops dead, the music will not sound the same. But one fewer violinist in a symphony orchestra is more difficult to detect. The art of blending is about fine balance, and about ensuring that sufficient stocks are available to produce the same results year-on-year. The raspberry jam nuance that came from a set of Glenfarclas casks last year might herald Glen Elgin the following year. Hedging your bets on many distilleries grants a kind of insurance policy on the longevity of the flavour profile of the blend.

But with a great number of barrels comes a great responsibility. Managing a blending program is one of the most complex tasks in the industry, since the style and quality of future stocks is difficult to guarantee. The formula for any given blend must be constantly adjusted to accommodate a fluctuation in character of the component single malts. It's like continually proposing new questions to an answer that must remain the same. It's the job of the master blender to smooth out any surprises that might come out of the casks of the component malts and to ensure that those malts play nicely together.

Aeneas MacDonald wrote of blending in 1930:

'Whiskies are capricious, sensitive creatures; they are not to be flung at one another like goats. Rather are they to be compared to fillies which are highly likely to land iron heels in the belly of the too-forward stallion. They must grow accustomed to one another and, unless they have been carefully chosen, no amount of time will persuade them to live together in amity.'

The grain-whisky component of a blend typically makes up 20–60% of the liquid. It's this light canvas that acts as a playground for the more boisterous malt whiskies to mingle. All of the big blending houses are owned by large corporations, whose empires may span multiple grain-whisky distilleries

– factories, in essence, that pump out the necessary grain whisky to fulfil the blender's need. There's nothing particularly wrong with grain whisky, but hardly any of it finds its way into a bottle, and when it does, it's usually an independent merchant. The same big companies will also have investments in malt whisky distilleries, which also helps to guarantee the longevity of the blend by controlling quality right from the start of the process. It's easy to forget nowadays, with all the romance and intrigue of single malt whisky, that over 90% of the whisky consumed in the world is blended. Indeed, even the most prestigious of distilleries in Scotland will usually make some contribution towards blends that are owned by their parent company. Diageo, for example, at the time of writing owns and operates around 28 malt distilleries in Scotland, and all except one (Oban) contribute whisky to the Diageo blend portfolio. Oban is a very popular whisky in the US and has a relatively small production run, so all stock is bottled as malt whisky. But even some of Diageo's most prestigious malts (Lagavulin, Talisker and Clynelish) will still roll up their sleeves and help tow the blending line. Around one-third of Diageo's malt distilleries don't even have official malt whisky bottlings – almost all of their product is used in the Johnnie Walker, J&B and Bell's blends.

A big part of managing a warehouse of stock is tapping casks for samples and sending them to the lab for testing and tasting. A blender's room is full of such samples, and they act like stethoscopes, probing the lifeblood of each cask and monitoring its progress to perfect maturation. The decisions made in blending rooms are then escalated up to huge proportions, where tiny quantities of this and that may become many hundreds of thousands of litres/quarts in the large-scale composition of the whisky. This is why it is said that the blender's nose is the most valuable asset Scotch whisky possesses, because it is that one single organ that determines the bottle contents of millions of bottles across the world.

Blending is common practice in Canada, and if you were to go back 20 years, you'd find that

almost all of the whisky there was blended. Although they are not awarded a reputation for it, the Canadian blenders are some of the best blenders in the game. I think they deserve this accolade because they blend not just different-aged whiskies, but also different new-make whiskies *prior* to ageing. This amounts to what I can only describe as blending in 3D, where proportions must be calculated both before and after maturation, forcing the blender to pre-empt flavour characteristics before they come in to existence – like predicting that a group of children will be friends before some of them have even been born.

Right This blended Scotch is a recreation of abandoned cases of whisky shipped to Antarctica in 1907 by the explorer Ernest Shackleton to fortify his 'Nimrod' expedition.

Filtering, Colouring & Strength

Filtering

All whisky will undergo some kind of filtration before being bottled. It can be as simple as a mechanical filter (steel, cellulose or nylon mesh) to remove small pieces of wood particles that might have detached themselves from the inside of the cask. Other methods of filtration are also sometimes incorporated to do a more rigorous job.

Some whiskies are charcoal-filtered using 'activated' charcoal, which is carbon that has been treated with oxygen. These lightweight black granules are unique and unrivalled in their surface-area-to-mass ratio – a single gram can have a surface area in excess of 500 square meters (5,382 square feet)! The more surface, the better the chance that large impure molecules hold on or 'adsorb' to the mass of the charcoal. This can be a good or bad thing, since charcoal is not great at discriminating between 'bad' and 'good' flavour molecules. Either way, it has been used in spirits' production for over two centuries, and is especially important for vodka, where flavour-free is often the goal.

Tennessee whiskies are known for their use of the Lincoln County Process, which sees the white-dog whisky filtered through sugar maple charcoal before ageing. The idea here is that the filtering removes impurities present in the distillate but retains the cask flavour, since no aggressive filtering takes place after ageing (the exception to this rule is Jack Daniel's Gentleman Jack, which undergoes filtering both before and after ageing – see page 183). Incidentally, the Prichard's Distillery in Tennessee does not conform to the Lincoln County Process (see page 185).

Many whiskies undergo additional filtering to remove impurities that might affect the clarity of

the product. A cloudiness or haze can form in bottled whisky if it is subjected to particularly cold storage conditions, or if served over ice or from the freezer. This is caused by big fatty acids and long-chain esters that come out of solution when the liquid becomes too cold – like covert jellyfish emerging from the ether. The same effect can be seen when pastis or absinthe are diluted with water: suddenly the oils that were previously hidden emerge from suspension.

Cloudiness can also be a sign of a potentially dangerous product, but assuming you are assured of the provenance of the bottle, it's absolutely nothing to worry about. Most of the time the haze will disappear when the bottle is transferred to a warm environment, and it doesn't occur at all in spirits above 46% ABV.

Many producers choose to chill-filter their product before bottling to remove haze-causing particles, deemed to be off-putting to consumers. As the name implies, the whisky is chilled down below 0°C (32°F) (and sometimes as low as -12°C [10°F]) before passing through a mechanical filter, which removes the guilty particles and leaves the whisky perfectly bright and clear.

Not everyone agrees that chill-filtering has a positive impact on quality, however. While it may be a good way of removing haze, many producers label their product as non-chill-filtered, believing that process removes mouthfeel as well as precious flavour-giving components of the whisky. These tend to be single malt whiskies from Scotland and Japan, but there are a few barrel-proof bourbons that forego filtering, too.

Colouring

For most of you, I'm sure the idea of colouring a whisky seems absurd. Indeed, if you're brave enough to broach the subject of *artificial* (I'll come

Left Dumping mature bourbon at the Jim Beam Distillery. The breather pipe is inserted into the bung hole so that air can enter the cask and the spirit can flow more freely.

back to why I've chosen to put the word in italics shortly) colouring with whisky aficionados, your best bet is to scope out the exits. After all, adding colouring to good-quality single malt, expensive blended whisky, or even Irish pot-still whiskey is hardly necessary, right?

Distiller's caramel, or E150a, as it is also known, is used widely to keep the colour of whiskies consistent and to assist with grading colour according to the age statement of different expressions. This may not seem important to all of us, but to a lot of consumers there is still an association between colour, age and quality. It's a difficult association to overcome for the best of us, and I think that many of us, while perhaps not deeming it a fault, will find something to talk about when a 30-year-old single malt is paler in colour than a 25-year-old expression. Given the fickle nature of wood, this sort of thing is not only possible, but commonplace.

Above So many choices. In this blender's paradise we see numerous cask samples that can be assessed, blended, and then mixed on a larger scale to create something delicious.

E150a sounds a lot worse than it actually is. By definition, it is caramel colouring obtained through the heating and caramelization of carbohydrates (sugar). So it is, in fact, just caramel. E150a has no sweetness to it, though, since the process is carefully controlled so as to caramelize all of the available sugars, resulting in a very thick black syrup. By itself the flavour is bitter, if anything, and a little goes a very long way here. A pin-prick of caramel is enough to muddy a sink-full of water. For those who believe it can be detected on the tongue, I would happily challenge them. There have been a good number of tests conducted in the past where E150a has been added to water, and only in higher concentrations could it be detected – and that's water we're talking about, not whisky.

I am personally not against the use of caramel for the purpose of uniformity. I do believe it should be stipulated on the bottle, however. What does interest me is the effect that darkening a liquid, with no detectable change to its taste, might have on our flavour perception of the whisky. In other words, do darker whiskies taste of darker things through the power of association alone? In the past, some blenders have broken the trust of the magic circle and revealed caramel as the secret to 'bringing together' a blend. Perhaps it's a darker hue that, in part, cements the relationship between some whiskies.

Oh, and by the way, no colouring is permissible in American whiskey.

STRENGTH

One final consideration, and it's an important one, is the strength at which the product is bottled. I always looked upon the strength of a whisky as a gauge of how much enjoyment I was likely to get from the bottle (higher is better by the way), and how distorted my face would become when I sipped it. Stupid as it sounds, both factors are pertinent, if perhaps not for those reasons.

Cask-strength whisky provides a stronger connection to the production process of the whisky by removing additional (unnecessary some would argue) steps. It also allows the end user (you) a greater control over how the whisky is consumed, by giving you the freedom to dilute it as you see fit... or not at all. Some cask-strength single malt whiskies can top 60% ABV, which is half as strong again as a typical bottle of blended whisky; a 50ml (1¾ fl. oz.) dram of Glenfarclas 105, for example, would require 25ml (1 fl. oz) of water to take the dram down to 40%. Some bourbons are known to top 70% ABV, an achievement only possible through racked warehousing, or through strict humidity control. The sought-after George T. Stagg release from Buffalo Trace Distillery is one of the strongest that I have come across; the 2007 vintage weighed in at 72.4% ABV – you don't want to see the face that I make at that stage.

How and when whisky is diluted prior to bottling is likely to affect the final flavour of the product. Logic tells us that adding a flavourless liquid to a flavoursome liquid would result in a linear curtailing of flavour in the flavoursome liquid. Exothermic reactions take place when water and alcohol are mixed, and it's likely that there are some changes in perception of sugar and esters based on whether the product was diluted before bottling or during bottling.

There is, like it or not, a certain association between strength and quality. This goes back some years, and the cynic in me would argue that as long as there have been distilled spirits, there has been someone lurking in the shadows with a jug of water eager to dilute the quality and line their pocket. I have seen evidence of one possible Scottish tradition, similar to the famous 'tequila worm' (which is actually neither a worm nor found in tequila) whereby a fledgling distillery would bottle a small snake with their first run of liquor – the idea being that the successful preservation of the reptile gave assurances to would be buyers of the product's fortitude. The practice reminds me of something that W. C. Fields once said: 'Always carry a small flagon of whisky in case of a snakebite... and furthermore always carry a small snake.'

Some will find high-strength whisky enjoyable and others will recoil at the thought of it – the decision is yours. But more than that, the bottling strength of a whisky can have a big impact on the flavour, too. Alcohol does strange things to our sensory equipment, even though it has little flavour itself. An increase of only 1–2% can be the difference between dark chocolate and milk chocolate flavours, or marzipan and bitter almonds. Higher-strength bottlings offer more scope to play around with this kind of thing by exploring a whisky through different degrees of hydration.

The final factor to consider is price. With a high alcohol percentage comes a high price tag, since it costs the producer more to make it and in most countries it is subject to higher rates of tax. It's easy to forget this when looking at the lofty price tags of some whiskies, and if you're the kind of person who cuts your whisky back with a good splash of water, it's sometimes nice to look at that 70cl (24 fl. oz.) bottle as 170cl (57 fl. oz.) instead – it makes parting with your money that little bit easier!

CATEGORIZING WHISKIES

AMERICAN

On the face of it, the classification of American whiskey seems like a simple affair, but delve a little deeper, and you'll find that it's not the case. Each category has its own subtle differences and it's only once you start to list them all down (American, Straight, Bourbon, Straight Bourbon, Kentucky Straight Bourbon... the list goes on), that you begin to realize how complex it really is. The problem is compounded by slightly different laws on labelling between the USA and Europe. For the sake of simplicity, and my own sanity, I have chosen the American take on things in the following sections.

The trick to understanding the American whiskey categories is to understand the hierarchy of terms, and to remember that as the category is further refined, it continues to incorporate the requirements of its parent. For example, *Kentucky Straight Bourbon* needs to meet certain requirements, as well as the requirements of *Straight Bourbon*, *Bourbon* and *Whiskey* itself.

To be sold as *Whiskey* in the USA, the spirit must be made from grain and must be distilled to no more than 95% ABV. It must also have been aged in oak containers, but there is no minimum time restriction for this, or guidance on barrel size and charring or toasting. You could simply give the spirit a swirl in an oak egg cup and call it Bourbon Whiskey.

No additives, including caramel colouring, may be added to whiskey made in America, with Blended American Whiskey being the exception to the rule. The label must list the state in which the product was made.

BOURBON WHISKEY

Bourbon can be made anywhere in the USA, but most common is Kentucky Bourbon (typically *Straight*). Bourbon has no minimum ageing requirements, but it must be aged in charred new American oak containers with the spirit entering the cask at no more than 62.5% ABV.

All Bourbon whiskey must be made from a minimum of 51% corn in its mash bill and distilled to no higher than 160 proof (80% ABV). Many feature mash bills of up to 80% corn, however, with the remainder of the space being inhabited by rye and/or wheat and malted barley. Bourbon is not permitted to be distilled above 80% ABV: a measure put in place to retain the character of the cereals.

Bourbon aged for under three years may not be called Bourbon whiskey in the EU, but can be called simply 'Whiskey'.

Left Jim Beam White Label is a Kentucky Straight Bourbon Whiskey, which means it meets the minimum requirements of a whiskey, as well as those of the sub-categories, 'straight', 'bourbon' and 'Kentucky'.

RYE, WHEAT & MALT

Rye follows exactly the same rules as Bourbon except that it must be derived from a mash bill comprising a minimum of 51% rye cereal. There are currently six Straight Rye distilleries, including Anchor, which uses 100% malted rye. Wheat whiskey follows exactly the same rules as rye, in that the product must be made from a minimum of 51% wheat. Rather interestingly, malt whiskey (like rye and wheat) needs only to be made from 51% malted barley, or more.

CORN

Corn whiskey must be made from a minimum of 80% corn and distilled to no more than 160 proof (80% ABV). No ageing is required, but if the product is aged, it must be in either uncharred casks or, as is more common, refill casks. This prevents the product from sitting in both the *Bourbon* and *Corn* categories at the same time.

STRAIGHT

Whiskey labelled as 'Straight' must be aged for a minimum of two years in oak barrels. The 'Straight' designation is usually, but not exclusively, coupled with a parent category, i.e. *Kentucky Straight Bourbon*, or *Straight Rye*.

Where *Straight* is applied, and the whiskey is aged for under four years, it must display its age on the bottle; if it's aged above four years, it is optional. It's a good incentive for producers to hit the four-year mark and avoid having to own up to only being 36 months old in the small print. There is one exception to the Straight classification – when applied to corn whiskey, uncharred casks can be used for the usual minimum ageing time of two years.

Right George Dickel choose to spell whisky with no 'e', which, interestingly, is the chosen spelling as set out in the US FDA whisky regulations. Whisky and Whiskey are both permitted, however.

Right Note that this White Dog from Buffalo Trace Distillery does use the word 'whiskey' in the small print, which means it must have been matured, if only for a brief moment, in an oak container.

BUFFALO TRACE
DISTILLERY

WHITE DOG

MASH #1

Corn, Rye and Malted Barley Recipe
62.5% Alcohol by Volume [125 Proof]

WHISKEY · DISTILLED & BOTTLED BY BUFFALO TRACE DISTILLERY
FRANKFORT, KENTUCKY · 375 ML.

Above The term 'sour mash', as made famous by the Jack Daniel's brand, is neither a legally recognised term nor a process unique to the Jack Daniel's brand.

Left & above Beam's Eight Star looks similar to Four Roses at first glance, but closer inspection tells us that Beam's is in fact a blend of only 20–50% straight whiskies, and neutral grain spirit.

KENTUCKY WHISKEY

Obviously this stuff needs to be produced in Kentucky, but other than that, it needs only to adhere to the requirements of an American whiskey. Almost all whiskies produced in Kentucky are Straight Bourbons, however, and even the ones that aren't, usually adhere to the Bourbon rules, if not the Straight.

TENNESSEE WHISKEY

Tennessee is essentially a Straight Bourbon, but two things make it distinct. Firstly, the fact that it is made in Tennessee (which in itself does not prohibit it from being a Bourbon), and secondly, that it is filtered through 10 feet (3 metres) of maple sugar charcoal before ageing, also known as the Lincoln County Process. It's this process that makes it a Tennessee Whiskey and prevents it from being either Straight, or Bourbon. The exception to this rule is Prichard's Tennessee Whiskey, which does not conduct the Lincoln County Process after being granted a legal exemption (see page 185).

BOTTLED IN BOND

Bottled in Bond is a term that crops up from time to time in American whiskey. It's a little like the single malt of the whiskey world.

Federal regulations state that a Bottled-in-Bond Whiskey must be the product of one distillation season in one distillery. It also must be aged for a minimum of four years and bottled at a minimum of 50% ABV. Otherwise, Bottled-in-Bond Whiskey follows the same barrel and distillate strength regulations as Straight Whiskey.

AMERICAN BLENDED

Whisky designated as *blended in the US* must contain a minimum of 20% *Straight Whiskey* (blended or otherwise). Other than that, you can add neutral spirits or younger whiskies to the mix. If the product has Bourbon, Rye, Wheat or Malt in its name, it must then contain a minimum of 51% of that particular designation of whiskey. This does not mean the cumulative mash bill is made up of 51% rye – in a *Blended Rye*, for example, it could be as low as 26%.

SCOTCH

The term *Scotch Whisky* by itself is a bit useless, since any given product must reside in one of the sub-categories listed below. But broadly speaking, Scotch whisky must abide by the following rules (according to the Scotch Whisky Regulations 2009: it must be made in Scotland from water, cereal and yeast only, whereby sugars are obtained through malt enzymes (diastase). Mashing, fermentation and distillation must take place in the distillery and it must be distilled to less than 94.8% ABV. It must then be aged in oak casks no bigger than 700 litres/739 quarts, for a minimum of three years. Before the three years are up, it is known simply as 'British New-Make Spirit'. Plain caramel colouring may be added.

SCOTCH SINGLE MALT WHISKY

Single Malt Whisky must be made from 100% malted barley, but the barley can be grown and malted anywhere in the world. It must be distilled a minimum of two times in a copper pot still; you can distill three times (like Auchentoshan), or even more, but it's not all that common. As with all Scotch Whisky, the maximum permitted distillate strength is 94.8% ABV, but most Single Malt Whiskies run off at 65–75% ABV.

Ageing must take place in Scotland, but not necessarily on the site of the distillery. Obviously most bottlings are much older than the required three years, but it is possible to get young whiskies that exhibit a lot more distillery character than the 12-year+ drams most of us are familiar with. During the period in which the whisky is kept in barrels, it's stored in a government-bonded warehouse.

As with all types of Scotch, the age statement on the bottle must refer to the youngest whisky in the bottle. Vintage Single Malt Whisky poses another challenge, as it can be a little confusing when deciphering its age. These whiskies are permitted to list only one year on the label, and it can be either the 'distilled on', or 'bottled on' date, accompanied by an age statement. As of 2009, all Single Malt Whisky must be bottled in Scotland.

Above & left Single malt Scotch whisky, such as Caol Ila 12 and Glenfiddich – the best-selling Single Malt Scotch in the world – must conform to a long list of standards, as set out by its governing body, the Scotch Whisky Association.

Right & below Age statements aren't essential for Scotch whisky, but without one the consumer can only be assured that the whisky is at least 3 years old.

SCOTCH BLENDED MALT WHISKY

As the name eloquently suggests, this type of whisky is a blend of two or more single Malt Whiskies. In the past, Blended Malt has gone by the title 'Vatted Malt' and 'Pure Malt', but 2009 legislation put a stop to that. This type of whisky is usually big, bold and not all that often seen, since most people would rather drink a Blended Scotch or a Single Malt rather than something in-between. As is the norm, the age statement on a Blended Malt refers to the youngest whisky. Johnnie Walker Green Label is a great example of a smoky Blended Malt (partly down to the inclusion of both Talisker and Caol Isla in the blend), and I also love Compass Box's Spice Tree, which controversially spent a brief spell out of production over a dispute with the Scotch Whisky Association.

SINGLE GRAIN SCOTCH WHISKY

Like Single Malt, Single Grain must be the product of one single distillery, but it can be made from any combination of malted barley and other un-malted cereals (but not other malted cereals). It is typically produced in a column still, which produces a much lighter spirit than a pot still. Single Grain Whisky is seldom bottled for consumption on its own, and almost all of the Single Grain Whisky in Scotland is used in blends.

If you are in the market for a bottle, check out Cameron Brig, which makes up the backbone of many famous blends.

BLENDED SCOTCH WHISKY

Despite the growing demand for Single Malt in the past 20 years, blended Scotch makes up over 90% of the global Scotch Whisky sales today. It must be made from at least one Single Malt and one Single Grain Whisky. As far as I am aware, there are no blends that contain more than one Single Grain Whisky, but many contain over 30 Single Malts.

Left & below Johnnie Walker 'Pure Malt', also known as 'Green Label' is a rarity now; unlike the ubiquitous Black Label, it was a blend of malt whiskies only.

IRISH

The rules that govern Irish Whiskey are much broader than those of Scotch or American. The Irish Whiskey Act of 1980 set out three basic requirements for Irish Whiskey: firstly, Irish Whiskey can be made from any combination of cereal so long as it is 'saccharified by the diastase of malt' (i.e. there must be some malt used); secondly, it must be distilled to an alcoholic strength of less than 94.8% ABV; and thirdly, it must be aged for a minimum of three years in wooden casks.

The broad scope of this law means that any additional information on the label, such as 'Pot Still', 'Single Malt', or 'Single Grain', are in fact meaningless, since their definition is covered by the act. These terms are, of course, familiar in the world of Scotch Whisky, and one can only trust that they are in reference to similar quality standards when used on Irish labels.

CANADIAN

There is a common perception harboured by aficionados that Canadian whisky is largely unregulated and that the kids are essentially left to run amok. On the face of it, Canadian whisky follows similar rules to that of Scotch Grain Whisky, besides the obvious fact that it must be made in Canada, that is. According to the Canadian Whisky (Food and Drugs Act 1985), Canadian Whisky must be made from the diastase (enzymes) of malt. It cannot be distilled above 94% ABV; colouring is permitted; and it must be aged in 'small wood' containers (maximum of 700 litres/740 quarts) for no fewer than three years. Where Canadian Whisky differs from other styles is in the sanction of up to 9.09% 'flavouring' that may be added to it, which can be in the form of Sherry, Port, wine, or even other spirits. The exacting figure of 9.09% is equal to one part out of 11, or one part flavouring for every 10 parts whisky (see pages 204–205).

Above The loose and liberal. Irish whiskey rules are set to change in the near future, while Canadian whisky regulations still permit the use of flavourings, even though most new distilleries take no advantage of it.

It would be frowned upon, however, if you slopped a load of melted chocolate into the vat. Regardless of flavouring, the product must 'possess the aroma, taste and character generally attributed to Canadian Whisky'.

RYE

Whiskies labelled as 'Rye' in Canada contain a proportion of rye in their mash bill, but typically only 5–15%. If they are to be exported to the USA, the 'rye' must be removed from the label, unless the product meets the minimum (51%) rye requirements required by US law.

PART THREE
THE WHISKY TOUR

THE SCIENCE OF WHISKY FLAVOUR

To understand where a whisky's flavour is derived from is an understanding of whisky-making itself. I am quite persistent when it comes to discovering the inner workings of a problem, but I think of it as a wonderful thing that, even given the extraordinary technological advances, we are essentially shooting in the dark when it comes to building a whisky recipe with the aim of a specific result. There are of course stages of production that we can manipulate to affect certain outcomes, and these are covered in the production sections. But the act of truly picking and choosing a highly specific flavour profile of a whisky remains in the hands of whisky blenders – and it's a likely contributor to the success of blended whiskies. Those people in the past who have established a new distillery from scratch have all faced a uniquely daunting prospect – limited control over the final outcome of the product and no guarantee that it will even be to their own tastes. The good news comes in the shape of hindsight. Even though we lack the ability to truly control flavour, we do have the luxury of looking back on it, acknowledging it, and working out where it came from.

SUBJECTIVE FLAVOUR

We are all born with more or less the same sensory apparatus. Women tend to have a slightly better sense of smell than men, and some people have a better or worse sense of taste than others, which can be distinguished by the concentration of papillae on the surface of the tongue. Don't fret just yet if you believe yourself to be near the bottom of the sensory gene pool – a huge chunk of our ability to detect flavour comes from developing a good flavour dictionary. Your flavour dictionary is like a reference manual for everything that you taste and smell, but it also behaves like a thesaurus by matching some flavours with others and building up associations. The flavour dictionary is set in stone; for example, raspberry tastes likes raspberry because it contains naturally

occurring esters, aldehydes, sugars and acids that make up the raspberry flavour. The flavor thesaurus, on the other hand, is an ever-evolving entity, edited and rewritten according to the things that we eat and drink together. If you fed me raspberries and mushrooms together every day for a year, it's fair to say that I would establish an association between the two that is unique to me (since it's doubtful anyone else would pair the two). Some of us have bigger dictionaries than others and we all possess a different copy of the thesaurus – remember that.

Having the dictionary alone is great for appreciating flavour, but to share your joy in flavor, you also need the necessary experience to articulate it. Describing flavour to another person can often feel like describing a piece of music. It's hardly surprising, since both music and flavour are, to an extent, subjective to the individual; I would struggle to describe a piece of classical music accurately to an orchestra conductor, since that person possesses a wealth of musical awareness that is absent to me. I simply lack the hard-earned tools to pick it apart and convey my meaning.

You may hear experts sometimes describe aromas with fantastical language that makes no real sense – marshmallow oil, bee farts, and rainbow fur randomly spring to mind – but imaginary smells and creative language are some of the most enjoyable things about discovering flavour, and specifically flavour in whisky. Importantly, these seemingly fanciful descriptions say something about the emotional and spiritual impact of the spirit, alongside that of flavour. Communicating it is a big part of it. Practice is the key to nailing your own communication – not such a bad thing when it comes to delicious whisky! It's through practice and continuous referral to our ever-growing flavour dictionary that we can begin to communicate our findings about individual liquids.

Given the breadth of flavours out there and the infinitely complex associations that are strung together in our minds, it should come as no surprise when I tell you that people, even experts, often disagree on flavour. It's not down to stubbornness or arrogance that this happens (generally), but rather an inconsistency between our flavour thesauruses and the vocabulary we use to express them.

The point is: don't worry if you find it difficult to express your opinion on a whisky, and don't worry if your experience is different to that of someone else around you. You are unique, and like everyone else in the world, you are furnished with a multitude of flavour-detecting mechanisms that have been tuned to a rare state of perfection.

THE FLAVOUR OF WHISKY

The range of flavours in whisky is broad, and even though this book uses hundreds of different words to describe whisky flavour, the category itself is for the most part confined to a few key flavour groups. An example of this would be the aroma of smoke, which is prevalent in some single malt whiskies. Anyone who has ever smelled smoke, be it on a barbecue, bonfire, or even a burning building, should be able to detect the aroma of smoke in a whisky from the Laphroaig Distillery on Islay. An example of a less-common aroma would be vegetal, which could possibly feature in a particularly sulphurous whisky, but is less likely to feature in the vocabulary of this book.

Broadly speaking, we can separate whisky flavour into ten groups: fruity, floral, cereal, sulphury, vanilla, nutty, musty, woody, spicy and smoky. Later, we will tackle the subject of which stage in the whisky-making process these different families of flavours are derived from. First, let us discuss how these families interact with each other to create a flavour image.

In some whiskies you may find a distinct representation of one these 10 flavour camps: a strong generic fruity smell, for example. It could be that the fruitiness is more specific, like apples or pears. It even be that you can distinguish the type of apple, or its condition, be it freshly cut and green, or baked and red. In others, there may be a broader representation of five or more flavour camps and it's here that it often becomes tricky to differentiate between flavours.

Above The flavour of Japanese whisky regularly walks a fine line between powerful distinction and subtle nuance.

I like to think of distinguishing flavour like having multiple stories read to you at the same time. If you only have one story to follow it is easy to focus on the plot and to understand it. But if you have three, or five, or 10 books being read to you simultaneously, perhaps different volumes, it is impossible to keep track of all of them at once. This is often the case with a complex whisky. You can recognize that there are multiple interweaving stories that are being told in the glass and the overall perception is that of rich and varied information, but only when you focus on one flavour plot at a time can you begin to distinguish the subtleties of the tale. The situation can become even more complex when you realize that some characters can appear in multiple stories. In flavour terms, this means that many aromatic molecules crop up in multiple flavour camps. An example would be benzaldehyde, which is most strongly

Left The rigorous recording of every production stage is the best way to understand where flavour in the final product is likely to have come from.

merely works with the sugars, salts and acids already present in the wort to create new weird and wonderful molecules. In a sense, yeast is no more an ingredient than a mash tun is.

The distillation process further develops these flavours and then goes on to select them through the type of still used and the way that it is managed. Finally the barrel mellows and flavours the liquid through oxidation, through the extraction of harsher flavours and through the infusion of its own. Below I have listed the ingredients and equipment used to make whisky, and how much I believe they contribute towards flavour.

Water

No affect on whisky flavour other than in the quality used to cut spirit to bottling strength.

Variety of barley

Negligible effect on flavour.

Steeping, malting and kilning

The exact timing and subsequent kilning after germination can affect the build-up of enzymes and carbonyls that can hang around and affect flavour later down the line.

Peat

Peat is potentially a big portion of flavour contribution, depending on the level to which the barley is peated. Smokiness from peat-drying can be transmitted in various ways into the final product, from phenolic iodine, almost medicinal smoke, through to sweet BBQ, roasted meat, sooty chimney and grilled fish.

Mashing

More likely to affect flavour based on how the barley is agitated during mashing and how the wort is filtered out afterwards. Traces of insoluble organic compounds can go on to affect fermentation and distillation character.

represented by the aroma of almonds, but is also present in apples, apricots and cherries.

Whatever form the aromas take, it comes down to your own personal preference as to whether the positive characteristics combine to significantly outweigh the negative (if any). Many books and magazines put a great emphasis on the grading of whisky through quantitative tastings. While I don't agree with these practices, it's fine to do that if the end goal is a long list of numbers. For me, my assessment of a whisky is done on a drink-by-drink basis and relies on my enjoyment of the liquid at that time, for whatever reason I deem fit.

Where the Flavour Comes From

Here is yet another subject that is open to debate – where exactly does the flavour of whisky come from? On the face of it, the answer is simple, as it comes from the three ingredients used to make it: grain, water and wood. Some people may also wish to include yeast as one of whisky's ingredients, especially given all the flavourful compounds that we associate with fermentation. But yeast imparts no direct flavour into whisky; it

Yeast and fermentation

Critical in the formation of higher alcohols, fatty acids, aldehydes and esters, which all play a critical role in the character of the new-make spirit and beyond. The yeast strain, temperature and pH of the wash will all affect the outcome.

Shape of the still, the condenser and the method of firing

Direct-firing affects density of the resulting new make and the potential formation of other flavours during distillation through caramelization and Maillard reactions. The use of a worm tub over a shell-and-tube condenser will make for a more sulphurous and meaty spirit. The shape of the still and the degree of reflux will determine how much of copper's catalyzing affects are leveraged into the new make. Greater levels of reflux are the catalyst for further breakdown of heavier compounds.

How the still is run and the spirit cut

How rapidly or gently the still is run can affect the heaviness of the spirit, again in relation to reflux. The cut will determine exactly which flavour components that have been generated thus far make it on the next stage, so is also an important factor.

Barrel ageing and finishing

Naturally, ageing has a far greater effect the longer the spirit spends in cask. The type of wood, condition of wood, size of cask, charring or toasting level, temperature of storage and many other factors will play a part, however. Oxidative effects convert alcohols into aldehydes, which in turn convert to fruit esters. Extractive effects cause reactions between hemicellulose in the wood and fatty acids in the spirit, softening and integrating the product. Infusion adds vanillin, tannin, spice and nutty flavours (from lignin) in various degrees to barrel-aged spirits.

Below Measuring the gravity of new-make spirit in the spirit safe. The precise timings of the spirit 'cut' will guide the weight and character of the spirit.

SCOTLAND
* ISLAY *

Islay is the spiritual home of malt whisky in Scotland. It is the most southern island of the Inner Hebrides, which lie off the west coast of mainland Scotland. It has a footprint of only 34 x 27 km (21 x 17 miles), shaped like a kind of smudged version of the British Isles. On this basis you could say that Laphroaig, Lagavulin and Ardbeg are Southampton, Brighton and Dover. Bowmore is Liverpool, Caol Ila is Edinburgh and Bunnahabhain Aberdeen. Bruichladdich is Dublin and Kilchoman would be Galway.

Don't let Islay's diminutive form fool you; with eight active distilleries and a ninth in the pipeline, the 3,500-or-so people who call Islay home are sat on an industry that would probably make every one of them a millionaire, were Islay to be an independent state. Unlikely as it may sound, once upon a time Islay and many of the other Western isles were ruled as separate kingdoms, and it was the kings of those lands, who in 843, founded the Royal House of Scotland. Even today 'The Queen of the Hebrides' has that feeling of something epic, ancient and wild, weathered by old winds and relentless sea.

It was on Islay that the first Scottish whiskies were probably made. Once the know-how sailed over the short 31-km (19-mile) crossing from Ireland, thirsty lords set their minions to task

creating *aqua vitae*. And Islay was ready for it, thanks to its water and fertile soil, not to mention the fact that around the third of the island is peat bog that could be used to fire the stills.

During the late 18th century, illicit farmyard distilling was endemic and continued well into the 1800s. As Alfred Barnard put it in 1887, 'In those days every smuggler could clear at least 10 shillings a day, and keep a horse and cow.' Many legitimate operations were also registered during this period, but most failed the test of time, or were swallowed up by the more familiar names that still stand today. A church minister from Port Ellen wrote in 1794 that 'The quantity of whisky made here is very great' and 'the evil that follows drinking to excess is very apparent on this island.' A few years later, a small armed force was sent to Islay to deal with the issue of illicit distilling. Excisemen were too scared to police the island, regarding the locals as 'wild and barbarous people'.

Whatever their temperament, it didn't take away from their thirst for making and drinking a good dram. By the middle of the 19th century, Islay whiskies were held in high esteem, with even the Royal Family placing orders for 'a cask of best Islay Mountain Dew' in 1841. As the time of blends drew closer, though, Islay malt whiskies became more of

SCOTLAND

Islay

Above It's hard to ignore the coastal influence present in most Islay drams. It would appear that the whiskies made here have somehow distilled the nature of the island.

a rarity, with almost all of the spirit being sucked up by blenders such as Johnnie Walker, Black Horse, Dewar's and Bell's.

Nowadays, Islay whisky draws in a big crowd in its own right. It's the end of the journey, the final piece in the puzzle, and the huge rough-cut jewel in the crown. Islay whiskies to me are the raggedy blueprint for Scotch as a whole.

A visit to Islay today can be made either by ferry from the Scottish mainland, which takes about two hours, or on a short flight from Glasgow Airport. The island is like an unofficial whisky theme park, colour-washed and wind-battered by the fierce climate. Nearly all of its inhabitants are employed by

whisky in one shape or another, whether it be as a hotelier providing accommodation for the droves of notepad-clad visitors; or a lorry driver, shifting the 1,500 tons of barley that move around Islay every week; or a distillery worker.

Laphroaig, Bowmore and newcomer Kilchoman all conduct their own floor malting on site, but they and the others also buy in from commercial maltings, too. Port Ellen is the principal malting on the island, and back in its days as a distillery, it was the first to trial a 'spirit safe' (see page 76).

Below The landscape of Islay, fittingly known as the 'Queen of the Hebrides' is simply spectacular.

CAOL ILA

When we think of Islay whiskies, it's usually the big names like Laphroaig, Bowmore and Ardbeg that spring to mind. But Caol Ila, or 'Sound of Islay' as it translates to, is the sleepy giant of the island that quietly churns out more whisky than any other producer. In the past, most of the spirit made at this distillery was used in blends like Johnnie Walker, and much of it still is. Indeed, were it not for Johnnie Walker and J&B's thirsty need for something peated, you would have to question where 324 tons of barley that gets delivered to Caol Ila every week actually goes. But Caol Ila has emerged as a competitive stand-alone malt in recent years – rightly so, in my opinion, as some of the special releases in particular have been absolutely mind-blowing.

From the outside, the beautiful old warehouse, which dates back to the distillery's founding in 1846, is contrasted by a much newer production building that replaced the old one in 1970. Sadly the newer building looks, by all accounts, more like a Soviet detention centre than the home of one of my favourite peated whiskies. Inside looking out is a different story, however. The stillhouse overlooks the thin stretch of water that is known as 'the sound' to the rising 'paps' of Jura. This is a view that would challenge any distillery for sheer breathtaking magnificence and is made all the more epic by the four gigantic stills that pump out 6.5 million litres (6.9 million quarts) of new-make spirit a year.

Caol Ila is a 24-hour operation, manned by only one person at a time. The stills are only 50% filled, giving prolonged conversation with the copper. This integrates the peat nicely into a citrus-driven dram. Here, it's not an all-out domination of peat, but a controlled melody of smoke that wafts and wavers through the dram, plucking out other interesting facets as it goes and leaving behind a taste of Islay in its wake.

Production increased in 2011. 'It was the washbacks that were holding things back,' Billy Stitchell, the now-retired distillery manager, told me. Another two washbacks were added to make six in total and it effectively doubled the output of the distillery. The washbacks here are different than most in that they are vented and the carbon dioxide that is produced by the fermentation process is pumped out of the massive Canadian larch containers. This makes for a spookily empty experience when you dip your head in the airspace and your nose is greeted by a soft breeze, rather than the usual pungent sting of fermentation.

Billy Stitchell oversaw operations at Caol Ila for nearly 40 years until he retired at the end of 2013. This marked the end of the Stitchell family legacy at Caol Ila, who have acted as regent for the distillery for four straight generations. His exit was marked by the special release of Caol Ila unpeated, entitled 'Stitchell Reserve'.

Left The huge stills at Caol Ila are awarded a fantastic view across the Sound of Islay to the 'Paps' of Jura.

CAOL ILA 12-YEAR-OLD

Smoke is the first thing you notice in the aroma of Caol Ila 12-year-old. It's both sooty and clean at the same time, refreshed by a blast of salty sea air. The palate is oily and full, the malt tastes almost mechanical, steely and hard-working.

CAOL ILA MOCH

Caol Ila Moch begins with fruit: figs, apricots, lemon... lots of lemon. Yes, there is smoke, but it's not terrifying and certainly this is a lighter dram compared to the 12-year-old. The flavour absolutely fills the palate, touching base on all the necessary sections. Smoke is unleashed, but it's tempered by the lemon, slipping around the place like a greased bullet. The finish is sweet and sooty, like the aftermath of a good bonfire party.

CAOL ILA UNPEATED

After experiments dating back to 1999, Caol Ila Unpeated has been released in successive years (and age statements), starting in 2006 with an 8-year-old and usually in batches of 6,000 bottles. It's difficult to get hold of, but worth the effort if you can, as it's like seeing your favourite rock band perform a ballad. The eighth release of this expression is subtitled 'Stitchell Reserve' as a mark of respect to the long-serving distillery manager Billy Stitchell.

CAOL ILA 25-YEAR-OLD

Caol Ila 25 year old is massive. An invisible bubble of polished rosewood and plump candyfloss fill the nose, but that's just to lull you into a false sense of security. Smoke appears, soft at first, but building in intensity until kept in check by candied pear, honey and even melon. The taste is, needless to say, full. It builds almost as slowly as it drifts away, with incredible, almost Cognac-esque levels of refinement. The list of flavours goes on: dessert apple, cherry gum, bitter almonds, peppered mackerel oiliness, and of course, peat, which is well integrated and manages not to steal the limelight.

CAOL ILA 59.6% CASK STRENGTH

The bottle I have was distilled in 1991 and bottled in 2000. It has serious acetone notes on my initial sniff, with lots of lovely fruit esters coming through, cantaloupe melon in particular, but there's

Above Not the most picturesque of distilleries, but it more than makes up for it in the quality of the whiskies it produces.

a hint of peach there as well. There is only a whiff of smoke at this stage, but when water is added the smoke comes to life, crushing but not destroying the weaker aromatics. There is unprecedented sweetness on this one (where is that sweetness coming from?), which only amplifies those lovely fruit notes that were on the nose. It's the texture, too: thick and gooey on the palate. Smoke comes through 1–2 minutes later; then it simply hangs around for another 20 minutes after. Sublime.

CAOL ILA 24-YEAR-OLD 100% SHERRY CASK

When I was at Caol Ila, I was lucky enough to taste a rare cask sample that was apparently an accident. Caol Ila 24-year-old 100% Sherry Cask was a lost cask until it was discovered a couple of years back. It is not common to see whiskies that have spent so long in Sherry wood, as it tends to dominate the distillery character. It's even rarer to see an Islay malt treated this way.

'Progressive Hebridean Distillers' it says on the tin. You would have to agree with them as well. Indeed, Ardbeg is the only other distillery on the island that has come close to challenging the innovative, ostentatious and, at times, brazen approach to modern Islay whisky distilling. With an ever-increasing range of product lines, about 10 separate new makes, and more special releases than you can shake a malting shiel at, Bruichladdich's approach seems to be that of throwing peat at a wall and seeing what sticks. This strategy can sometimes weaken a brand, but not so with Bruichladdich, as pretty much everything it makes tastes great.

So it's easy to see why the distillery was recently sold to drinks giant Rémy Cointreau for the princely sum of £58 million ($99 million). Mind you, it wouldn't have been so easy to imagine this happening a mere 15 years ago. Like many others, Bruichladdich had it rough in the 1980s and 1990s, changing hands a couple of times and finally being mothballed in 1995. Five years later it was purchased by independent whisky bottler Murray McDavid for less than £7 million ($11.8 million). That might seem like a bargain, but the warehouses were apparently in a sorry state, housing an array of miserable old casks that should have been wheeled out to the dump a few decades previously.

Murray McDavid appointed Jim McEwan as Bruichladdich's production director. Jim, by my reckoning, is one of the greatest talents in the Scotch whisky industry. In fact, it's fair to say that he's a bit of a hero of mine. He joined the industry at the tender age of 14, as an apprentice cooper at Bowmore. By the age of 22, he was the cellar master for Bowmore (it's still only 1971 at this point) and he later went on to work in blending and eventually became the distillery manager at Bowmore. When he joined Bruichladdich in 2000, he set about replacing all the old casks and plugging the production gaps through clever use of wood and blending. The warehouses now contain a huge spectrum of timber, coming from Sherry industries, bourbon and right through to first-growth Bordeaux casks, some of which are used to make the fantastic Black Art expression. Along with Kilchoman, Bruichladdich is the only distillery that matures and bottles every drop of its whisky on Islay.

With wood ticked off the list, the other great focal points of the distillery are barley and terroir. Up until the distillery's recent sale, this has been driven largely by Mark Reynier of Murray McDavid. His background before whisky was in wine, so terroir comes naturally, and he believes that the 28-or-so farms on Islay that supply over 40% of Bruichladdich's requirements each have an identity marker in the new-make spirit. Mark once even conducted a tasting with the farmers on the island as a means of determining how and why their crops produced a different-tasting spirit – an exercise that no doubt quickly descended into anarchy.

Once malted at Port Ellen, the barley is in for a real treat when it arrives at the distillery as the original 1881 belt-driven mill is still in working order. As someone who has toured over 40 malt distilleries in Scotland, I can tell you that it doesn't get much more boring than mills. Not so at Bruichladdich, where there is a genuine functional antique. In fact, the whole distillery is operated largely by Victorian-era equipment.

A final mention must be given to Octomore (see right), the peatiest whisky available today.

SCOTTISH BARLEY

At first there's a pungent lime-oil note that then takes a step back to reveal rice pudding, brown sugar and coconut. It has an excellent grip on the palate, through a combination of tannin, dryness and a good blob of sugar. There's little in the way of fruit here; it's all about vanillin and cereal, with a pebbledash of malt drying up the finish nicely.

ISLAY BARLEY – ROCKSIDE FARM
Distilled 2007

Earth and sea clash, from dry brown leaves through to sea mist. On the second sniff, the aroma becomes more full and spicy; golden grapefruit, dried ginger, fenugreek and clove make an appearance. Also, despite being unpeated, there's smoke here, too. Big

Right The lasting influence of a good dram has inspired many a poet and artist. Islay resident Jane Taylor is one such individual, who created this fantastic illustration, entitled 'The Hill on the Shore', depicting the Bruichladdich Distillery gate, still and pagoda-style roof, among other buildings.

spice and heat on the tongue, are softened by coconut, crème anglaise and hard toffee. The finish drys up nicely, leaving a mouth-coating tingle.

PORT CHARLOTTE HEAVILY PEATED

Roast-beef crust, fennel seed and mustard attack the nose. This leads into a softer, more sooty smoke, with aromas of banknote and underlying aniseed. Powerful yet elegant. Smouldering coals, Lapsang Souchong tea and wood sap linger on the palate.

BLACK ART 4.1 RELEASE

There's a waxy quality here that's rare to find. A slow drizzle of liquid amber, soft candle. It's thick and docile on the palate in a good way – almost as

if it's slow to come to terms with its fate! It has a massively concentrated flavour of fig, plum and plenty of wine tannins and European oak. A long, polished fruit finish fades to sweet almonds and dates. This is a truly fantastic dram.

OCTOMORE 06.02

Sweet BBQ sauce, smoked paprika, even tomato ketchup drift into a heavier peat reek, coal scuttle and wet wood. Alternating between sweet and dry on the palate, but never quite making up its mind. There's no question about the smokiness, but there's an inky darkness to the flavour, too. Water brings the sweetness to the forefront, reverting to sickly BBQ sauce, gamey meat and burnt green wood. Smoooooooooke.

BUNNAHABHAIN

Islay's red-herring distillery is perched on the north-east coast just above Caol Isla, and is notable from the outset for being one of the few Scottish distilleries that truly warrants a phonetic spelling – BUN-eh-HAV-in. I usually find it best to fall back on the local abbreviation of 'Bunny'.

Production potential at Bunnahabhain is massive and it was during that period of great optimism in the early 1960s that the capacity was increased to its current bloated state – solely to fulfil the requirements of the Black Bottle blend to which Bunnahabhain is an important contributor. The six washbacks are some of the largest I know of, and at 110,000 litres (116,236 quarts) each they are more like small swimming pools than fermenters. Bunnahabhain is still the core of the Black Bottle blend of whisky, which was recently relaunched in an actual black bottle (it used to be green) – which must make the life of the marketing department a little easier.

I refer to Bunny as a red herring because, up until quite recently, it produced no peated whisky whatsoever. For an Islay distillery this is a highly unusual situation, but it would appear that in the latter half of the 20th century, peated malt simply wasn't required to fit the needs of a blend intended to be mixed with soda. Go back to 1881, though, when the distillery was first built (complete with an entire village and village hall) and the spirit would almost certainly have stunk of peat – some of the recent releases are a testament to that time. Jump forward 101 years (stick with me) to 1982 and the whisky industry was crashing, the distillery was mothballed and was only in operation sporadically over the following 20 years.

Things are back on track now, however. The core range remains unpeated and proud of it, but the first peated release came in 2004 in the form of a 6-year-old *Mòine* (Gaelic for 'peat'), a reflex action to the increased demand for peated Islay drams in the late 1990s and early 2000s. Since then, the delicious *Toiteach* (Gaelic for 'smoke') has become a permanent member of the Bunny stock. As a general rule, if it has an age statement, it isn't peated.

Below The picturesque village of Bunnahabhain was founded to house the distillery's workers.

BUNNAHABHAIN 12

Apple compote, raisins and porridge/oatmeal on the nose, with plenty of sweet barley notes penetrating. Peppery, dry and spicy on the palate, an effect that continues into the finish. This is a curled-up, tense package of a dram.

BUNNAHABHAIN 18

A crunch of shiny red apple (think Snow White), nougat, along with a touch of preserved ginger and bags of vanilla sugar. The spice drops off more quickly than the 12 with a pounding dryness, red-apple bruise and macadamia cookie, all contained within a well-formed structure of mouthfeel.

BUNNAHABHAIN 25

This has a honeyed, rum-like aroma and plenty of cask character giving chocolate and caramel shortbread, yellow custard, vanilla yogurt; and then the fruit kicks in... preserved cherry, fig jam and candied pear. It has a honeyed finesse in the mouth: luxurious and soft to begin with, but giving way to dryness, oxidized Sherry characteristics, tannin and a long, wood-spiced finish.

BUNNAHABHAIN 40

A veritable sweet/candy shop! Zingy fruit esters give

Above There's no better place to enjoy a glass of Bunnahabhain than at the distillery itself!

cough candy, orange sherbet, mango nectar and candyfloss/cotton candy. A restrained wood influence contributes a hint of warm leather and hazelnut praline. After a false start, the flavour develops into wine gums, soft milk chocolate and mixed spices; spice is back in the long finish.

TOITEACH

Barbecued banana gets in there early, leading to smoked orange and 'bacon bits' with just a touch of sun-dried tomato. The taste is a fruity barbecue sauce, orange oil, fennel seeds, bitter almonds, settling on dry spice.

KILCHOMAN

Kilchoman is by far the youngest distillery on Islay – by a full 124 years in fact. For me, it's the youth that shines through in the whisky produced here. It would do, of course, since the first spirit runs came through in 2005. Kilchoman simply isn't old enough to be producing anything but adolescent whiskies. But with all the tender qualities that come with being young, I find it hard to imagine Kilchoman ever producing anything other than the clean, zesty, mineral whiskies that it currently does so well.

No one would have predicted 10 years ago that an eight-year-old malt could fetch £50 ($85), and even though some distilleries (The Macallan and Ardbeg, to name a couple) had previously explored young releases, it's Kilchoman that has really leveraged the demand... you could say that it created the demand. This is good news in more than one way, as it may be the only option going forward. John MacLellan, the distillery manager, hints that the current demand for young whisky means that little is being held back to develop older stocks.

John previously worked at Bunnahabhain Distillery. He is eagle-eyed as he walks me around the farm in wellington boots, pointing out cask numbers and telling me who or what the contents will be allocated for. He's checking valves and scanning notes as he casually recounts the trouble he has had with an airlock in the water supply 200 yards up the road, on that blustery, wet Islay morning. Only a sheepdog and a pipe are needed to complete the picture. The entire operation does feel agricultural and some of the publican barley used to make Kilchoman is grown on the farm itself (Anthony Wills, the director, refers to the business as a farmyard distillery) before being sent to its own floor maltings, which can process two tons per week. Kilchoman's floor malting is the only one I have seen that has a family of birds whizzing around the rafters; it gives the barley a kind of soundtrack, but hopefully not any flavour. The barley is peated to around 25 ppm and used in the 100% Islay malt, a unique product since every part of the production takes place at the Kilchoman farm, from growing the barley to malting, ageing and bottling. It has an ABV of 50%.

Machir Bay is Kilchoman's core expression, built from the same malt specifications as Ardbeg and bought in from Port Ellen Maltings. It's matured in a combination of bourbon and Sherry casks. There's no age statement but a little maths tells us that it certainly contains no whisky over eight years old in it.

Half-a-mile down the road is Machir Bay itself, which is where Kilchoman's core expression gets its name. Apparently Machir Bay is a popular retreat for locals in the summer months. On my visit, my travelling companions and I had just returned from that windswept bay where, at the risk of contracting hypothermia, we had witnessed the sun come up over the Islay coast.

KILCHOMAN MACHIR BAY

The colour of damp straw immediately gives the game away; this is a young whisky. The aroma of sweet chestnuts leads on to moss and peat, then ripe plums. Tastewise, unsurprisingly, we're getting medicinal iodine notes accompanied by black pepper and perhaps a hint of juniper. The addition of water reminds me of rainfall on sturdy oak casks, but further enhances the iodine note, which is really prevalent in this malt.

Left The oldest cask of Kilchoman in existence is a mere nine years young at the time of writing.

100% ISLAY

To begin with, this whisky is much cleaner than Machir Bay on the nose, with dominant citrus notes. Give it a minute and it becomes completely clear that it's indeed a relation to Machir Bay, but the peat is far more subdued, beautifully combining with cask character to provide a preserved-lemon note and brine. On the palate, the 50% ABV is not obvious, given that the smoke has been dumbed down. The addition of water makes this malt sweet, with a hint of some pastel-coloured lemon candy coming through nicely at the end.

2007 VINTAGE

The palest of the Kilchoman expressions, probably due to the (re)use of old bourbon casks (and the short ageing). It has a clean, mineral-like quality at first that gives way to moss, warm wellington boot and well-worn wax jacket. These descriptors roll

Above Kilchoman is fast becoming one of the most sought-after whiskies out there.

over into the taste, too, which seems somewhat drier than Machir Bay, with that distinct mineral note also making an appearance, even when diluted.

SINGLE CASK

Distilled in September 2008 and removed from the first-fill bourbon casks in September 2013

Ethanol is the first thing that grabs you with this; lots of it, too. But the esters begin to kick in on the third or fourth sniff, brandishing banana and liquorice, with a touch of butterscotch. Back again, and the smoke makes its presence known, but this is a very light dram. Good action in the centre of the palate, with a surprising wood influence (given the aroma) and plenty of pepper on the mid-palate. It definitely benefits from a good splash of water.

LAGAVULIN

The 'other' Diageo-owned distillery on Islay produces much less whisky than its big, friendly brother Caol Ila. However, the quality of the liquid is prized so much that a far larger proportion finds its way into official bottlings as opposed to blends.

Records of 'The Mill in the valley' go as far back as the mid-1700s and the distillery proper was first established in 1816, only a year after the neighbouring sites of Ardbeg and Laphroaig first officially filled their washbacks. There was another distillery that existed on the same site as Lagavulin, betwixt 1908 and 1962. It was humbly known as Malt Mill. The distillery came about as a result of a trade dispute between the Mackies of Lagavulin distillery and the Johnston family of Laphroaig. For over 50 years Lagavulin had acted as an agency for the Laphroaig brand, selling its product alongside its own, but in 1907 the Johnston family decided to go it alone. Furious, Peter Mackie attempted to sabotage their operation by building a small dam that blocked the water supply. After this attempt

failed, he took measures to seize control of the Laphroaig distillery. When that failed too he instead poached workers from Laphroaig and set up the Malt Mill distillery within his own Lagavulin site with the aim of emulating the Laphroaig taste. Ultimately Malt Mill also failed, but not until long after Peter Mackie's death. Today Malt Mill holds the title of being the rarest whisky in the world, with only one known bottle in existence. The bottle in question is actually a new-make whisky, which is totally unaged and therefore not classifiable as whisky itself. It was thought to have been bottled from the last run of distillate to come off the stills before they were dismantled.

The stills at Lagavulin are worth a mention as they purportedly have the steepest lyne arm in the industry and are particularly squat in appearance. The fact that they are short means that very little

Below Beautiful both outside and in, Lagavulin can prove to be a challenging whisky for many, though.

reflux takes place and the resulting spirit is dense and characterful. The steep lyne arm is thought to maintain the same by effectively catching dropping volatiles in the condenser before they have a chance to reflux down into the still.

Lagavulin takes a much lower cut of spirit from the run than Caol Ila. This further explains the big differences between the two products, despite them using the same raw material – malted barley, peated to around 37ppm. The spirit collection at Lagavulin runs from 71% ABV down to 59% ABV, which ensures that it captures all the heavy phenolic compounds and results in a rich, almost oily spirit containing many of the alcohols associated with the end of the spirit run.

I spent an interesting afternoon in the warehouse at Lagavulin with Iain McArthur, a compact and characterful man, who, based on that and many other things, is about as close as you're likely to get to a human embodiment of Lagavulin. His family are from the village of Lagavulin, and his mother was brought up in a tin shack not a stone's throw from the distillery itself. Iain has spent over 40 years working on site, having also spent time at Port Ellen in the past. He dances around a row of casks, sucking up samples through his whisky thief (master distiller's tool for extracting whisky from a barrel) like it's a giant straw and talking about cask character and the unpredictability of flavour during ageing. 'Colour is no indication of quality,' he tells us, a statement I wholeheartedly agree with.

The array of colours he produces from the various casks at his disposal is indeed a kaleidoscope of hues and intensities and the afternoon quickly descends into a deep and happy discussion among friends, surrounded by thousands of gallons of patient Lagavulin whisky.

NEW MAKE (63.6% ABV)

Among the best new-make I've had. Coal scuttle, cattle shed and sea mist are immediately apparent, but underneath there's nougat and a hint of candy floss/cotton candy. Briny and sharp on the palate, like fisherman's tears, leading into sweet liquorice/licorice (when water is added) and plenty of peat.

LAGAVULIN 9-YEAR-OLD (58% ABV)

Lagavulin 9-year-old Sherry cask retains some of the more pungent 'livestock' aromas of the new make, but here it's tempered by the finesse of warm yellow fruits, grape juice and a lingering of peat. The taste is surprisingly mellow for its strength, with tobacco, soap and lingering sweet sootiness.

LAGAVULIN 11-YEAR-OLD

Pale in colour, with sulphur and rubber, this whisky is like a drag race on salt flats. Water reveals a honey note, with underlying smoke (obviously). It has plenty of chilli/chile spice on the palate, along with a nutty vanilla note that doesn't quite manage to keep the hot smoke in check. It has a lighter, more fragrant finish but a long linger of smoke on the tongue. Water makes things a bit more gooey, but the spice returns with unexpected resilience.

1998 SHERRY REFILL CASK

Possibly the best Lagavulin I have tasted. The nose is hazelnut praline, bonfire and Dr. Pepper (basically the ideal Scout camp!). Almost inconceivably soft in the mouth, it develops from melted white chocolate and peat smoke into spicy dried fruits, pimento and iodine, all the time preserving a rich and dense texture. Delicious.

LAGAVULIN 16 (43% ABV)

The core expression of the distillery and certainly one of the most unique among the samples is the one from my year of birth. The 1982 refill bourbon cask has a most peculiar sulphurous aroma that I would associate with cabbage or a fermentation that's gone on a little too long. After a short time, it gives way to notes of marzipan, sponge cake and dried apricot: a delight. On the palate it is absurdly sweet and gentle, with initial soft fruits leading into lightly peppered mackerel, cantaloupe and wood resin. The finish is prickly and wicked.

1966

The oldest cask in the Lagavulin warehouse was distilled in 1966. The story goes that a woman on the island purchased the entire cask outright some years back, but when she died her family were hit with substantial death duties and were forced to sell the cask. The distillery, which had been keeping it safe, bought the cask back and has been dipping in and sampling its progression ever since.

* SPEYSIDE *

Speyside holds around half of all Scotland's malt distilleries, a statistic that makes it by far the most concentrated whisky-making area in the country. It's hard to move more than a metre within its fictive yet somehow appreciable borders without catching a glimpse of a pagoda roof, a truck loaded full of malted barley, or the distinctive aroma of fermenting wort. The wedge-shaped region encompasses the town of Elgin in the north, Rothes in the middle, Keith in the east and Dufftown heading south. Scotland's fastest river and the district's namesake, the Spey, traces a rough line betwixt these towns and finally comes to rest in the Moray Firth. The fantastic growth and success of Speyside is often attributed to the clear fresh water of the Spey and that might have once been the case, but no distilleries use Spey water anymore. A better argument for the growth of Speyside would be the perfect barley-growing land that it presents. Rich and fertile, enjoying long hours of sunlight in the summer months and a mild climate in the winter. But there's more than just the romance of geography and climate to the secret of Speyside.

Over a dozen farmyard distilleries in the area took advantage of the 1823 Excise Act. These included such names as Aberlour, Cardhu, The Macallan, Mortlach and Longmorn. But most notable amongst them was The Glenlivet. The Glenlivet should be awarded points as much as

Below After a long day's fishing on the Spey, there's no better way to warm your bones than sipping on one of the many whiskies that the region has to offer.

Speyside

SCOTLAND

Above The Cragganmore Distillery;
an excellent example of a distillery
with a working farm attached to it.

anyone when it comes to establishing who set things up things in the first instance. George Smith was the enigmatic founder of The Glenlivet, but when he took out a licence for his distillery in 1824, his former 'co-workers' and smuggler friends threatened to burn his operation down. Smith ignored them and instead carried about his person a pair of loaded pistols at all times and even employed a close protection racket to fend off potential assailants.

He might have been disliked among his former comrades, but George was smart enough to realize that the smugglers had enjoyed their time but that a new era was upon them. The 1830s and 1840s saw whisky of The Glenlivet ascended to such high esteem that other producers in the surrounding area would adopt the name on their own products, a practice that continued right up until the 1960s. I have even seen casks of Glenfarclas from the 1950s bear a 'Glenlivet' denomination.

Another string to the Speyside bow was that of the Strathspey rail line, which opened in 1863. Industry was growing rapidly during that period, blended whisky was on the rise, and the Spirits Act of 1860 allowed for products to be mass-mixed in centralized locations. The new rail line was a godsend to an industry that was poised on the verge

of a boom, and presented an excellent logistical solution for whisky-makers. The region leveraged its chance and production rampantly increased.

Between 1885 and 1900 there were 23 distilleries built in the area around the river Spey, but when the bubble burst at the beginning of the 20th century, many operators were mothballed. A pulse still remained, however, and during the second boom period of the mid-20th century they were revived to live another day... and another 10 or so built at the same time. Despite some hiccups in the 1980s, all but one remain in production today, with Pityavaich being the odd one out.

It would be easy for me to tell you that Speyside whiskies conform to a specific style. I could tell you that they are mostly fruity, fragrant and with well-integrated wood influence. Sometimes sherried, sometimes with a hint of smoke. But I'll stop myself there. Speyside conforms to no one style; it is a cross-section of malt whisky as a whole – the sheer number of distilleries alone stops any chance of consistency in its tracks. But something keeps us coming back – a lucid character, restrained heat, residual sweetness? Lurking within the DNA of this 'sacred zone' is a tangible nuance that unites them all, and whatever it is, it appears that we like it.

MORTLACH

Mortlach is a bit of an enigma among the distilleries in the Dufftown cluster of Speyside, both in terms of its production methods, unique flavour and its closed-door attitude to persons seeking to learn more. The distillery is owned by Diageo, and has long been an important element to its blend portfolio, with 90–95% of production destined for a Johnnie Walker, and prized for the hearty backbone it provides. But with all that intrigue and suspicion, Mortlach is making a name for itself as a stand-alone malt. Whether it's through demand for the malt itself, or a need for more Mortlach for blending, Diageo has recognized it and is building a complete replica of the distillery on the same site, due to begin distillation runs in September 2015.

Mortlach was founded in 1823 by James Findlater. The name comes from Dufftown's historic title of Mortlach, which was only changed to Dufftown six years before the distillery was registered as a legitimate operation. It's entirely possible, given the history of smuggling and illicit activity in the area, that Mortlach was in some form of existence prior to the town's name change. Given Dufftown's near-saturation of distilling operations today, it's hard to believe that Mortlach was the only distillery resident for a clear 64 years until a veteran Mortlach employee, William Grant, left to set up Glenfiddich in 1887.

Mortlach produces one of the most interesting malts in all of Scotland and much of its character is put down to its unique distillation process. The stillhouse holds six different stills of different sizes, one of which – wash still no. 3 – has a strange cone shape that you don't often see. Spirit still no. 3 has a water jet fitted where the lyne arm meets the condenser: evidence of an experiment that was neither removed nor deemed a great enough success to be applied to any of the other stills. A big refurbishment and expansion in 1897 increased the number of stills here and it's also at this time that the mystical distillation process was thought to have been put into effect. No one knows for sure, however. For the most part, the methods have simply been inherited down over the years and accepted by one head distiller after another as 'the way'.

The so-called 2.81x distillation process goes like this: wash still no. 3 and spirit still no. 3 work in tandem just like any other distillery. Wash still no. 1 and no. 2 give the first 70% of their run to spirit still no. 2, which then conducts a normal run and collection. The remaining 30% from wash still no. 1 and no. 2 is sent to spirit still no. 1, named – and subsequently famed – 'Wee Witchie' by a former distillery manager. Also added to Wee Witchie are the foreshots and feints from spirit still no. 3. Wee Witchie then distills those liquids twice to increase the intensity, and on the second and third runs the distillate is cut, but only on the third is it blended in with the spirits from the other two stills to form Mortlach new make. Combine that with 100% use of cold worm tubs that help to reduce copper contact, and the result is an unpeated, meaty, sulphurous distillate that makes the whole stillhouse smell of soy sauce and your muscles flex that little

Left A dark cask of Mortlach, which more than likely contains a dark beast of a whisky, too.

bit larger than normal. It is complicated, but is it necessary? Yes! Even though it may seem like a pointless process, it's one of the best demonstrations of the art of distillation. It's an example of how manipulating a liquid with complex configurations of distilling apparatus can create a unique product.

Like no other that is, until Diageo completes the construction of Mortlach II. That's the plan, at least. Mortlach is as close to witchcraft as you're likely to see in the world of whisky, which is why it will be interesting to see whether Diageo's replica distillery actually produces the same spirit as Mortlach.

RARE & OLD (43.4% ABV)

Cracked nectarine stone, pomegranate molasses, crushed velvet and hot jets of fleshy fruit on the nose. Raw and muscular on the palate: Bovril and plum wine and peppered steak, but still quite light and lean. The finish is unsweetened summer fruit sorbet, with just a lick of... well, a lick.

SPECIAL STRENGTH (49% ABV)

Flesh fruits and citrus on the nose first: nectarine pavolva, lemon cream and a hint of something really sweet, like pure wood sugar; chocolate fudge and salted liquorice/licorice complete the aroma. It's thick and hot on the palate: scarlet sauce, apricot jam and a slight salinity. The finish is spiced ceviche and black pudding.

18-YEAR-OLD (43.4% ABV)

Sherry-soaked forest fruits and veal *jus* – like a bodybuilder dressed in women's clothes; followed by moist tobacco and raspberry-topped chocolate pudding. Heated and free-flowing in the mouth: iron, quince paste and seasoned pigeon breast. The finish is profound: balanced and beast-like.

25-YEAR-OLD (43.4% ABV)

Sunday roast. with nut roast, ristretto, and concentrated stewed red fruit with star anise. But things ease up on return visits, revealing crème pâtissière and icing/confectioners' sugar-dusted macarons. Concentrated and complex on the palate, with pickled walnut, redcurrant jam, raspberry kriek beer and sweet glazed fillet mignon.

GLENFIDDICH

Glenfiddich is the best-known malt whisky in the world and in 2011 it reached the landmark sales figure of 1 million nine-litre/quart cases in a year. It had a headstart over other malts of course – in 1963 Glenfiddich became the first distillery to release and market a single malt whisky in the UK and in effect kick-started the malt whisky revolution. At the time the Grants had, like everyone else, been focusing on blended whisky. But a trade dispute with DCL over supply of grain whisky suddenly made blending rather difficult for the family. The solution was to bottle some of its malt whisky stocks, so a green triangular bottle was fabricated and filled with 8-year old Glenfiddich, which went on sale exclusively in the duty-free shop at Shannon Airport, Ireland. The rest is history.

But, as happens so often with hugely successful brands, familiarity breeds contempt, and Glenfiddich has become a back-bar staple of such proportions that it can easily be overlooked in pursuit of something (anything) a little more bespoke. Like it or not, though, Glenfiddich is here to stay, and if you're still unconvinced I would recommend a visit to the distillery in Dufftown – more than enough to convince even the most stubborn nonconformist.

William Grant had been working at the Mortlach Distillery for around 20 years before he had saved enough money to buy a field near the river Fiddich. A year later, on Christmas Day 1897, the first spirits ran off the stills. Five years after that he set up the neighbouring Balvenie Distillery. William Grant & Sons is still family-owned today and despite only currently operating three malt distilleries, its spirit accounts for over 10% of all the malt whisky in Scotland.

The cavernous rooms containing the 24 Douglas fir washbacks are connected by low archway entrances, giving the effect of a hall of mirrors, except that it isn't a mirror you're looking into – it's just more washbacks! Everything about Glenfiddich should be big, industrial and soulless. But the opposite is true; it's a self-sufficient operation that feels like it expanded organically, according to demand rather than by replacing its old equipment

with bigger stuff. The warehousing space is enormous and accounts for a large chunk of the 36-acre (15-hectare) plot, which also contains a coppersmith, cooperage and bottling plant through which every drop of Glenfiddich in the world passes – the biggest it may be, but only a few distilleries can claim they bottle everything themselves.

A tour around the two stillhouses at Glenfiddich is like a tour around a copper workers' museum. To the best of my knowledge, Glenfiddich is the only distillery in Scotland that sports at least one of all three types of pot-still shape: the onion, 'boiling ball' and lantern. The stills are surprisingly small, but what they lack in size they make up for in numbers – 15 of the 28 stills are fired using steam coils and the rest are directly fired from gas. Not only that, they're all different colours: everything from deep bronze through to Moomin pink!

Looking at the core expressions only, it's fair to say that Glenfiddich err on the safe side of things, being as approachably malty and citrussy as they are tame. But these have been supplemented with some fantastic older expressions and great special releases, and in recent years Glenfiddich has responded to the demand for peated whisky.

12-YEAR-OLD (40% ABV)

Classic fruit and malt nose, like a picnic in a grain silo. It's nutty too, warm and wholesome. The palate is delicate, female and not at all disruptive. Finish trails off with soft fruit and a whiff of smoked honey.

18-YEAR-OLD (40% ABV)

Perhaps more citrus and freshness than other Glenfiddich expressions: kaffir-lime leaf and ginger are backed up by the usual malt, toffee and wood aromas. On the palate there's more vibrancy, with grapefruit peel, stem ginger and a faint salinity.

21-YEAR-OLD RUM-FINISH (40% ABV)

Chocolate malt, chocolate orange, Guinness, and the general smell of a festive oak bar top. Syrupy and full on the palate, with toasted pecan, plenty of vanilla and a sweet milky mocha as the length draws out.

Right Just a small selection of the many and varied stills that call Glenfiddich home.

Below A chalkboard ledger reminds us that despite Glenfiddich being the biggest producer of malt whisky in Scotland, things are still relatively down-to-earth here. I'd be lying if I said that the old truck (bottom right) is still used, though!

Cardhu

Cardhu has an interesting claim to fame; it is thought to be the only currently active distillery in Scotland that was founded by a woman – a fact that is seemingly reflected in the product produced at Cardhu. Here, the new make leans toward the Lowland style. It's clean, grassy, perfumed and green, 100% peat-reek free and generally a very feminine dram. Indeed, it was the delicate nature of the spirit made here that attracted the Walker family to the distillery. Ever since then, Cardhu has been a key component of the Johnnie Walker range, with as much as 75% of Cardhu's production finding its way into one of Walker's iconic square bottles. There's even a Johnnie Walker museum housed at the distillery.

Officially, Cardhu was founded on Cardow farm in 1824, but as with any malt distillery licensed around the time of the 1823 Excise Act, the operation at Cardow was almost certainly an illegitimate one for some time before then. John Cumming owned the farm at the time, but the story goes that John's wife, Helen, was the brains of the distilling operation. In the years before the distillery was officially licensed, Helen was well known for warning nearby smugglers and wrongdoers when the exciseman was close by. Helen would invite the gauger in for tea and freshly baked bread (a common tact she used to cover up the smell of her own illicit operations) then inconspicuously slip outside and raise a red flag of warning.

Helen died at the age of 97 – *nae bad* – but not before she entrusted the running of Cardow to her daughter-in-law, Elizabeth Cumming. There were no flies on Elizabeth, either. In 1885 she relocated the distillery to a new piece of bigger land and sold off the old equipment for

Below Cardhu: green, clean and effeminate, just like its very pretty setting in the village of Archiestown, Moray.

£120 ($204) to a man named William Grant, who was setting up his own operation in nearby Dufftown. You might have heard of Grant's distillery – it's called Glenfiddich. Eight years later, in 1893, Scotland was experiencing its first whisky boom, and Liz masterminded the sale of the distillery to the Walker family for £20,500 ($34,780), but only on the proviso that the Cumming family continued to run the operation at Cardow and that Liz's 29-year-old son, John Fleetwood Cumming, be appointed to the Johnnie Walker board of directors. Sadly, Elizabeth died suddenly the following year and never lived to see the astonishing success that the Walker brand went on to have. It wasn't until 1981 that the name officially changed to Cardhu.

But surely there's more than just a history of female distillers to account for the fragrant nature of the spirit. Cardhu puts much of it down to the mash tun, the arms of which don't drop as low as other examples. This means the wort is churned up far less than normal, making for a very clear and sweet wort. There's a long conversation with copper in the stills, too, which will further amplify floral and fruity characteristics in the new make.

Above Don't be fooled: it's not a nearly-200-year-old cask of Cardhu, but a barrel end to commemorate the founding of the distillery.

12-YEAR-OLD

Cool and very light. Mint chocolate chip ice cream, green pea and coriander-seed citrus dominate the first sniff. Vanilla and cocoa butter are there, too. Initially green, generally herbal and especially minty in the mouth; coconut husk and some light spice follow. The finish is breezy and refreshing.

SPECIAL CASK RESERVE

Quite mineral-like at first, giving way to pine nut and basil pesto, slick rice pudding and perhaps a spattering of hot grease. More greenery on the palate: mint is back, this time dried, and there's soft vanilla butter and balsa wood. Bitter endive and cocoa powder finish it up.

18-YEAR-OLD

Minted butter and soft toffee on the first sniff. The mint persists, but there's also peanut, chocolate fudge and just a hint of lemon zest. The taste is much fuller than the 12-year-old, involving cool butterscotch, spicy toothpaste and some nicely integrated wood bitterness.

Glenfarclas

On the first trip I took to Glenfarclas, my travelling companions and I felt as though we had unwittingly driven into Narnia, when snow descended upon us as we traced the long straight driveway that approaches the distillery. The snow only subsided once we left. It's microclimates like this that remind us of the remoteness of some of the glens and peaks of the area, and it's also their seclusion that has made them excellent spots for illicit operations in the past. Glenfarclas is no exception; distilling activity has been taking place on the foothills of Ben Rinnes since at least the 1790s. George Grant, the sixth generation of the family-owned distillery, has a painting from the time to prove it!

George's great-great-great-grandad, John Grant, and his son, George Grant, bought the distillery in 1865 for £511 and 19 shillings. Since then there has been a steady succession of Johns and Georges in the family, who have carefully built upon the Glenfarclas legacy, right down to the current owner, John Grant, and his son... George.

It was only on my second trip that I was awarded a proper tour of the distillery and warehouses. And it's in the warehouses that we find what sets Glenfarclas apart from the competition. Of the 55,000 casks the distillery currently holds, nearly all are of the ex-Sherry variety, made from European oak dating back as far as 60 years. So expansive are Glenfarclas's older stocks that its excellent visitors' centre even offers a 'Five Decades' tour and tasting, allowing those with £85 ($145) to spare a taste of the past half-century. I'm told that, today, Glenfarclas is only buying Sherry casks, and soon hopes to have eradicated the evil scourge that is the bourbon cask (that's a joke, by the way) from the warehouse inventory. You won't spot anything bourbon-sized in any of the 30 dunnage warehouses, mind you. They covered their tracks by converting them into 250-litre (264-quart) hogsheads with a few extra staves. Even during my tour, as if planned, a delivery of 120 Sherry casks arrived by truck. For many distilleries, 120 casks would fulfil a year's quota, and while Glenfarclas does have a policy of reusing its ex-Sherry casks up to four times, the current production volume of 3.5 million litres (3.7 million quarts) of pure alcohol a year requires that they receive regular deliveries. A highly unusual wood policy such as this puts a very firm stamp on a spirit, so expect to find tobacco, fruit cake and vibrant florals throughout the Glenfarclas range. Of course, not all of the spirit made at Glenfarclas is destined for a long life of luxury in a fancy European container – an undisclosed amount of new-make spirit is sold on to blenders (the identity of which is also undisclosed).

Get inside the guts of the distillery and size matters. The three pairs of wash and spirit stills are the biggest in Speyside and direct-fired from gas. It's the direct firing and its associated browning of the still contents that can take responsibility for the robust and sweet new-make spirit. Steam coils were trialled in 1982, but promptly removed a couple of weeks later. The stills flank a typical polished brass spirit safe and a quite atypical 1970s *Star Trek*-style control console that is still in continuous use today. The mash tun takes a whopping 16.5 tons of malt per cook, a statistic that I believe makes it the biggest in a Scottish malt distillery.

All that remains to be said is that Glenfarclas was the first distillery to launch a cask strength whisky, way back in 1968. Most distilleries hadn't got around to bottling a malt whisky at this time, so the marketing meeting that established this bold move showed significant foresight – one of many benefits afforded to those with 150 years of family ownership, no doubt.

GLENFARCLAS 10

This whisky has scents of cut sandalwood, cream cheese and moist pipe tobacco. There's just a whiff of dried cherries. The palate is very soft and full, hinting of fruity biscuits/cookies, with a nutty almost rye-like dryness on the finish. Delightfully youthful.

GLENFARCLAS 15

Vibrant. There is a cream-soda vanilla aroma about it that drifts over to a sticky dessert trolley and finally a soft warm leather. There's powerful ester development at play here. The palate is drier than the 10, but with superb Sherry finesse coming over that serves to lift the whisky up rather than dominate it.

GLENFARCLAS 21

Wood is beginning to come through more powerfully now. There are dry spices like nutmeg and clove developing, as well as a polished, resinous note. Fruit is in the direction of nectarine and peach. A jasmine flower garnish. Thick and gooey on the palate, which drags out the suspense nicely. A tremendous long, concentrated fruit finish. This is a fantastic dram.

GLENFARCLAS 25

Intense cherry liqueur and sweet-running cherry juice coupled with yellow marzipan and well, the definitive smell of an ageing warehouse. Raw honey and thick cream with just a touch of dessert apple, too. Fragrant and almost underwhelming in its softness in the mouth. Very little heat; just subtle remnants of pollen and cut grass leading to a dry, musty finish.

GLENFARCLAS 30

Warm, sunny porches and a massive explosion of floral aromatics – geranium, honeysuckle and patchouli. The intensity of floral esters would be overpowering if it wasn't so wonderful! Underneath there's a hint of gingerbread, allspice and nutmeg. A good integration of heat and spice on the palate; the flowers get squashed but the spice washes over and fills the senses. With water, the floral is better preserved. One of the most floral whiskies out there.

GLENFARCLAS 40

Brown hazelnut wood with big, well-aged fruit cake. Bags of sultanas/golden raisins and brandy-soaked sponge massively contrast this whisky to the 30-year-old. On the tongue is where this whisky really comes into its own, however: big body and a stern set of features. Chewy fudge and hazelnut cream. A great whisky to match with chocolate.

Above Glenfarclas 15-year-old is widely regarded as one of the best sub-£50 ($85) whiskies available today.

GLENFARCLAS 1953

Old Sherry. This 59-year-old whisky has a distinct aroma of Sherry *flor*, nuts oxidized wine and plenty of complex wood resins. A slight macaroni-cheese aroma, too. The texture is massive and the build-up in flavour is – quite frankly – staggering. Like laser beams coming from all angles, there are deep, dark wood notes overlaid with nuttiness, baked fruits, a slight acidity that only serves to promote the perfect sweetness and pungent floral and raspberry overtones to boot. Wow!

THE BENRIACH

Back in November 2013 I was keen to make a special trip to The BenRiach for one very good reason – of the seven distilleries that conduct their own floor maltings, The BenRiach was the only one to have malt actually on the floor during my weeklong tour. Couple that with the fact that it had only re-introduced the process about six months prior to my visit and it's easy to see why this was gearing up to be a fascinating visit.

The BenRiach was founded in the 1898 boom period by John Duff, owner of the neighbouring Longmorn Distillery. Duff intended to produce an identical spirit to its sister distillery, which was already running at absolute capacity. But the whisky boom went bust only a few years later and The BenRiach closed without even a fighting chance at establishing itself. The malting floors remained functional, however, providing extra malt for Longmorn for the better part of the entire 20th century. It's for this reason that, even today, BenRiach is often affectionally referred to as Longmorn II.

It re-opened as a distillery in the 1960s and changed hands a few times over the following 30 years, but only really playing the role of blender's lapdog. In 1994, the first official BenRiach bottling was released: finally a taste of the limelight! But once again success was short-lived. In 1999 the floor maltings were decommissioned completely, 101 years after they had started, and the distillery was mothballed by new owner Pernod Ricard in 2002.

All seemed lost. That was until Billy Walker, the former director of Burn Stewart Distillers, came along in 2004 and bought the distillery for £5.4 million ($9.1 million). Production at The BenRiach nervously groaned back into action and has since grown to over 2 million litres (2.1 million quarts) of alcohol per year. The majority of this goes into the Chivas blend, where once more The BenRiach encounters its older brother, Longmorn. But malt expressions are popping out of this distillery left, right and centre, and with the re-opening of the malting floors there's a clear appetite for growth and innovation.

Unusually for a distillery tour, on this occasion I was met by an engineer called Les who worked at the distillery. He had, at one time, delivered trucks of barley to the distillery, but joined the team after being offered a part-time job and never looked back. Puffing his chest a little and bouncing on his toes as he explained to us the physical demands of turning the malt by hand, he said honestly, 'Aye, I ached like hell for the first week, but after a while you get to feel quite strong.' He's not kidding, either. I can testify to both the demands of the job as well as the sizeable stature of the man himself. The floor was only around one-fifth covered with malt at the time, but even pulling the hand rake from one end to the other was quite a strain on my muscles. To do over 20 lengths a few times a day, every day? Maltmen really are athletes.

Thankfully, there's an overhead pulley system used to move the germinated barley up for kilning, which has the appearance of a Heath Robinson

Right Over 115 years on, and now under new ownership, The Benriach Distillery is on the up…

creation – old but still entirely functional. And that statement neatly sums up The BenRiach, too. This distillery has been through the wars over the years, opportunities have been cruelly snatched away and even in good times, The BenRiach only ever played supporting roles. It's clear that this is not the intention of the current owners, however; I expect to see good things from The BenRiach in the future.

12-YEAR-OLD

Yellow. Golden delicious apple, fresh apricot and manchego cheese initially, faint cinnamon and vanilla cream folded in shortly after. Apple chips and just a light café latte character on the palate, that slips into chai spice and a finish of toasted oak.

16-YEAR-OLD

Mellow and elusive. Banana split, sesame and soft caramel initially on the nose, then warm fruit pie and lavender. Light and free-spirited, with more wild flower and woodland character. Peppered barley on the finish.

Below Just south of Elgin, The Benriach is located next door to the Longmorn Distillery.

15-YEAR-OLD (DARK RUM CASK FINISH)

Treacle/molasses and brown sugar on the nose initially, with dried sage and black onion seed. Concentrated and hot on the palate; liquorice/licorice, soft brown sugar and clove dominate, leaving a streak of hot white pepper in the linger. A force to be reckoned with.

SOLSTICE 17-YEAR-OLD (PEATED PORT FINISH)

Warm rubber boots, smoked paprika and tomato pureé/paste. There are more burnt red things, like beef ribs, pepper and brandy. More meat and umami figure on the palate, along with Bloody Mary and gazpacho, leading into rosehip, strawberry-scented wax and smokehouse sauce.

30-YEAR-OLD HOGSHEAD

Heavy cheese rind with a lemon twist. Nuttiness comes in the form of walnut oil, then yolk-rich vanilla custard and brown butter. Clean, mineral and citrussy on the plate, with a buoyant texture and lemon-drizzle cake moving through to savoury spiced wood and a whisper of field mushroom. Then gone.

ROSEISLE

Roseisle. The name paints a picture of a sleepy farmyard distillery, where ducks waddle across a barley-dusted pathway and an old gate lazily creaks to the gentle trickling sound of precious new-make spirit running off a small pot still. But names are sometimes deceiving. 'New North Supplemental Malt Spirit Facility' (for example) conjures a slightly murkier image, so you can hardly blame them for naming this shiny new distillery after the nearby Roseisle forest. Let's not sugar-coat it anymore then... this, dear reader, is the Death Star of malt whisky distilleries. Built at a cost of £40 million ($67 million) and opened in 2009, Roseisle is the most technologically advanced malt distillery in Scotland today.

The purpose of this 12.5-million litre-a-year (13.2-million quart) starship is to provide a large chunk of the malt whisky requirements of Diageo's stable of blended whisky, not least of all the ever-thirsty Johnnie Walker family. By taking some of the pressure away from Diageo's portfolio of malt distilleries (most of which are running at maximum capacity) it will allow for those whiskies to be matured and bottled as single malts. In a sense, Diageo has built one big distillery instead of upgrading lots of smaller ones. 'But how can one distillery do the job of many different ones?' I hear you ask. Blends are, after all, a blend of different styles of malt whisky. Well, it's in this field that Roseisle comes into its own, having been purpose-designed and engineered to produce multiple styles of whisky all under the same roof. This is achieved through clever twists in the production process that enable the distillery to produce 'fruity', 'grassy' and 'waxy' new makes, all using the

Below Little wonder that this distillery is affectionately referred to as The Death Star...

same production kit. The hope for the future is to produce a further three styles: 'nutty', 'smoky' and 'floral'.

From the outside, Roseisle looks every bit the spaceship. Mounted on huge stilts, the massive glass fascia demands that you pay respect to the 14 pot stills that line the length of the building. Half of the stills have two shell-in-tube condensers, one made of copper and one steel. This is the most obvious of Roseisle's manipulative abilities, allowing the team to produce differing degrees of sulphurous spirit. Other flavour manipulation tactics include the fill level of the stills, how fast the still is run, fermentation time and even wort cloudiness. William Grant & Sons has chosen a similar path with its new Aisla Bay distillery, which began production in 2007, and also wields unique forces in the crusade for moulded spirit flavour.

This approach to distilling is a fiendish move, and when Roseisle first opened it was met with a significant level of scepticism from malt whisky enthusiasts, who became fearful that it marked the beginning of a new era of faceless malt factories, churning out generic malt spirit categorized by a barcode or serial number. Malt whisky for the digital age. The fear turned to anger, which in turn led to hate, and the distillery became unofficially (and unfairly) known as 'Glen Mordor' – a none-too-subtle reference to the perpetually miserable wilderness of *The Lord of The Rings* trilogy. The same people also complain when distilleries undergo significant upgrades, or pretty much whenever anything at all changes in the fairytale whisky world that they believe exists only to serve their limited demand for special release bottles from mothballed distilleries.

My opinion? Whisky is a growing spirit category right now, and that is good. Expansion is inevitable and I for one would personally prefer that Roseisle malt go into blends than be taken from the likes of Clynelish, Mortlach and Cragganmore – liquids that deserve to have a bottle to themselves.

The secondary goal of Roseisle was to do all of the clever plate-spinning with a zero-carbon footprint. The seven wash stills are warmed by plate heat exchangers that capture heat from other distillery processes. Hot water from the condensers

Above The new distillery, which opened in October 2010 is Scotland's first new major distillery in a generation.

is pumped out of Roseisle at 60°C (140°F) and sent two miles up the road to Burghead Maltings, where it is used to heat the kilns. It's then sent back around to Roseisle and once again used for cooling the condensers. I'm told that only the Dufftown Distillery has a lower carbon footprint in Scotland, thanks to its biomass plant, which burns waste products for heat energy and uses an anaerobic digester to produce biogas for energy.

When I visited, the team was warming up to its first successful 'waxy' spirit distillation, emulating the style of Diageo's Clynelish distillery (see pages 142–143). To do this they needed to build up residual matter in the feints receiver, a task that was proving to be quite a challenge. Even despite half a dozen computer screens, some of the greatest engineering minds in the industry and a stillhouse from *Star Wars*, 'waxy' remained elusive.

What's happening at Roseisle today is re-writing the malt whisky rulebook. The frontiers are being stretched and traditional practices are being scrutinized. Like painting with colours, the distillers team at Roseisle is creating impressionist pieces, but it remains to be seen how diverse the gallery will be, and how detailed the compositions can get. Perhaps they'll get there; perhaps the most desirable malt whisky traits will forever remain beyond the understanding of science and engineering.

LONGMORN

I have heard Longmorn referred to as a hidden gem among malt distilleries, which would imply that Longmorn is small. But with a capacity of 4.4 million litres (4.6 million quarts) of spirit a year, it sits in the top 20% of malt distilleries based on production capability. But if it is a gem, it's certainly hidden. The long distillery walls are a pebble-dashed affair and among the least inviting of any I have seen. Bottles of Longmorn are reasonably well hidden, too. The vast majority of it ends up in one of Pernod Ricard's blended whiskies, not least of all the Chivas range, and only a small proportion is bottled as a single malt. The stuff that does make it into a bottle (on its own) deserves the respect it receives, however. Longmorn walks a tightrope between being powerful and subtle, complex and well defined. It was at Longmorn in 1919 that Masataka Taketsuru first learned his craft as a young intern. Fifteen years later and back in Japan he opened a near-replica of the old Longmorn in Yoichi.

So a distillery can be big yet still be a hidden gem, but whisky writer Dave Broom compares Longmorn to an underground musician that 'builds a reputation among an obsessive fan base who then somehow resent the fact that their hero might just be becoming better known'. My advice is to not mention the 'L' word when mixing in exclusive whisky circles, for fear that you might upset someone who still holds precious memories of a time when an elite group of connoisseurs met in dark, misty alleyways and, trembling with excitement, exchanged tasting notes with one another in whispered tones.

But aside from the whisky at Longmorn becoming more mainstream, the dedicated 'fan-boys' of Longmorn may have some additional cause for complaint. You see, Longmorn from the 1990s is held in very high regard – it was available as a 15-year-old bottling back then. Go back even further, to the independent bottlings of the 1980s and you'll find that they, too, are of exceptional quality – some would say better than

the Longmorn 16 bottle available at present. Perhaps this can be attributed to the wash stills, which were converted from direct coal firing to steam coils in 1994. An old steam engine still sits in the stillhouse, which was used to run the rummager in the wash stills. Around 20 years prior to that, the spirit stills were converted from coal to steam. So if you want my advice, try to buy Longmorn that was distilled before 1994. You'll be hard-pressed to find a bottle distilled before 1972 (at a sensible price anyway), but if you do, buy it!

If Longmorn really is *all that*, why then is most of it sent off to become a small cog in a big blend? Well, it's for the fact that it's great. Blenders prize it for its ability to, in very small quantities, grab a blend by the short and curlies and impart meaning and complexity into it. Blended whisky is still by far the biggest category of whisky sold globally, and awesome malts like Longmorn are like a flourish of spices in an otherwise bland curry of mixed whisky.

LONGMORN 16

Toffee apples are my first instinct on the nose, with a good hit of pear cider, porridge oats and honey coming through, too. There's a complex, resinous fruit characteristic here. Green and clean on the palate, drifting into dry bark, nettle, grapefruit zest and superb tactile balance. Water reveals a slight soapiness.

LONGMORN 1992 (20-YEAR-OLD) ADELPHI BOTTLING

Grassy and slightly vegetal initially, giving way to tarte tatin, crab apple, desiccated/shredded coconut and vanilla custard. The taste is bright and prone to wander. A blast of damson shifts to soft oak spice, mixed fruit and nuts and an elegant long finish. Once diluted there's a tenacious aroma of sage.

Benromach

Speyside's smallest distillery has well-tended lawns, warm white walls and splashes of red here and there, making it the very epitome of 'chocolate box' quaintness. Take the lid off this box and you'll discover that on the inside it's all very prim and proper, too. Benromach is in fact so squeaky clean I really wish I could have dug up a little dirt on it. But the best I could come up with is the gaelic translation of Ben Romach, which means 'shaggy mountain'.

Of course, the whisky made here hides a few skeletons, given that the general attitude towards whisky production at Benromach is 'traditional Speyside'. In the first instance this starts with barley, a proportion of which is peated, and all of which is sourced from Scottish farms. Barley is mashed in a tiny 1.5-ton steel mash tun, then the resulting wort is fermented with both distiller's and brewer's yeast for up to 120 hours. The logic behind this is that the distiller's yeast will do all the heavy lifting and produce a strong, healthy wash, while the brewer's yeast will concentrate on the details, adding character and complexity.

Short and small stills limit copper conversation and the resulting new make is sweet, gutsy, light on peat smoke and full of fruit. In other words, not typically Speyside – or at least, not like the Speyside we know today.

Only 240,000 litres (253,500 quarts) of alcohol is made here a year, all of which is matured on site in one of the 8,000-cask capacity dunnage warehouses. Almost all of it goes into a Benromach single malt bottle, with less than 2% destined for blends.

Back in 1999, Benromach began purchasing organic barley, which went on to make spirit that goes into their 'Organic' labelled bottles, and remains the only malt whisky to date that is certified by the Soil Association as organic – even the new American oak used to make their barrels is certified organic. Add in some other special releases, like the unctuous 'Origins' (made with Golden Promise Barley) and 'Peat Smoke' with a comparable phenol count to your average Islay whisky, and you can begin to recognize the experimental efforts of this little distillery as it quietly toils away in the upstairs room of Speyside.

ORGANIC

Barrel char and vanilla bean are up first here, with super-sweet coconut and white chocolate. But the second sniff brings more dark peat into the fray with an aroma of sooty, extinguished candle wick. Keep going back and you'll eventually find grapefruit soda and brown toast. The taste is relatively light and fragrant; roast pistachio, sweet meringue and a smoky grapefruit finish with a slightly mechanical linger.

Right The Benromach Distillery is the very picture of quaint, small-scale distilling on Speyside.

✱ HIGHLANDS ✱

The Scottish Highlands represent the most sparsely populated area in western Europe today. The most obvious reason for this is the region's geography; moor, mountain, hill, crag and loch feature heavily, in both the epic landscape and in the names of the whiskies that are made there. The second reason is cultural and sociological history, the impact of which has whittled down the populace through the Jacobite Rising of 1745, the forced Highland Clearances that followed, and the Industrial Revolution that drew the few-remaining highlanders ever closer to urban areas or overseas. Today, the Scottish Highlands account for less than 5% of the overall population of Scotland, despite the fact that they make up over half of the country's total land mass.

With all that land, from the southern tip of Loch Lomond right up to John O' Groats, and over 30 active distilleries that mostly cling to the coast or the border, it's no great wonder that it's difficult to pinpoint the 21st-century Highland style. The hope would be that the three main clusters of distilleries – the southern collection of 'Perthshire malts' in the east between Speyside and the North Sea coast, and the Northern Highlands near Inverness and the Moray Firth – might offer some regional traits that can better help us dissect the anatomy of Highland whiskies. But individualism is the way of things throughout, and that is about as close as you'll get to categorizing Highland whisky.

The 1787 duty on spirits imposed different tax laws on the Highlands and Lowlands of Scotland. In the north, distillers were taxed based on production volume (in much the same way as today) and in the south, the lowlanders were taxed based on the size of their stills. It's unlikely that the government was aware of the repercussions of this move, but it drove a fork in the road for Lowland and Highland whisky. For the lowlanders, quantity was the name of the game, since tax was a fixed cost, but in the Highlands, stills were run more slowly. The result was a fruitier, better-quality whisky. The only snag was that Highland whiskies were forbidden to be sold below the Highland Line.

The 1787 duty also paved the way for thousands of illegal distillery operations, keen to avoid taxation, and like scattering seeds on fertile land, some prospered and became successful

legitimate operations that remain with us today, while others have been lost to time. Politics and geography were unwittingly conceptualizing the broad style of Highland whisky as we now know it.

But only a fool would ignore the part that terroir has played in the shaping of Highland drams. Rugged coastlines seem to impart a certain maritime character to whiskies made nearby, whether it be a faint salinity, a vegetal seaweed note, or just the unmistakable sense of sea spray and wet wood. Peat terroir continues to place a unique fingerprint on the whiskies that choose to use it, imparting anything from rib sauce through to tar and feathers. Speaking of tar...

If anything, the Highlands are the glue that binds together the fragmented whisky regions of Scotland. There are whiskies made by committed traditionalists and by contemporary trailblazers. Some are fragrant and perfumed, emulating the tighter mould of the more recently popular Speyside malts – like Glencadam and Glenturret. There are rich and bold malts, too, sometimes with a heavy Sherry influence, such as The Dalmore and The GlenDronach. Then there's the 'shock and awe' spicy whiskies that seem to leap out of the glass at you, like Oban and Balblair, as well as docile, textured whiskies that disarm with a 'slow and steady' approach, typified by Clynelish and Teaninich.

Highlands

SCOTLAND

Left The sprawling Highlands. Diverse in the sense of its terroir and the flavour of its whisky.

Below Some of Europe's most stunning scenery can be found in the Scottish Highlands.

BALBLAIR

Balblair is not perhaps a distillery that immediately jumps off the page at you. As part of the coastal Highland cluster that also contains the likes of Glenmorangie, Clynelish and The Dalmore, poor Balblair is an undeserved victim of overshadowing by big, noisy neighbours. It would not be wise to ignore what's happening here, though. Besides being one of the oldest active distilleries in Scotland – it was originally founded in 1790 – Balblair also has a unique and carefully streamlined range of products not to mention a progressive and refreshing way of packaging them (more on that shortly). Couple that with idyllic settings, a new visitors centre and – if I may – some very friendly staff members, and you have a hidden gem here on the banks of Dornoch Firth.

The founder of the distillery was John Ross. The Rosses are to Edderton what the Beams are to Bardstown (see pages 196–197) and even today, five out of the nine people who work at Balblair have the surname Ross and two of them are even called John (none are known to be direct descendants of the founder, and rather interestingly, none are known to be directly related to each other, either.) Archive records of Balblair date back as far as 1800, making them some of the oldest malt whisky records of any distillery currently in operation. John Ross himself wrote an entry on 25th January of that year, which read 'Sale to David Kirkcaldy at Ardmore, one gallon of whisky at £1 and

8 shillings'. The distillery was operated by John Ross's sons and grandsons until 1894, when it was subsequently sold and relocated about half a mile up the hill in order to, as Victorian whisky writer Alfred Barnard stated, 'get the benefit of gravitation working in the distillery... so no pumps are necessary'.

The town of Edderton was affectionately dubbed the 'Parish of Peat' back then, and Balblair would certainly have burned its fair share – at the time it was outputting nearly thrice that of the nearby Glenmorangie Distillery (it's the other way around today). No Balblair whiskies are peated these days, mind you, although in 2013 they did release a 1990 vintage that had spent some time in a 'peaked cask' from Islay.

Below Balblair feels every bit the family operation. In fact, over half of the distillery workers share the same surname.

And that leads us neatly on to Balblair's labelling policy, which sees 'years' take precedence over 'time' – if you get my meaning. In the words of Balblair itself: 'Our whisky tells us when it's ready; not the other way around'. As sickly as that statement may sound, it does kind of make sense. Imagine that your distillery continuously bottles a '12-year-old' whisky but you get a bad set of casks one year. It could cause a spot of bother, right? Balblair takes the stance of only bottling casks that are ready, then simply putting the year in which the liquid was distilled on the bottle. A little maths tells us that its core range is roughly 10, 16 and 20 years old, but the sticking point is that they are not confined to (or defined by) those parameters in the following year's releases. Shrewd and sensible, if you ask me.

Today, the distillery is labyrinthine in nature, with walkways emerging and disappearing here and there in an impossible Penrose staircase-esque fashion – at times it feels a little like a treehouse for robots. A single man can operate the entire distillery from the computer screen that was installed in 2011, outputting around 1.8 million litres (1.9 million quarts) of alcohol a year. About three-quarters of that goes to blends, with almost all of the rest going into bourbon casks for maturation as malt. There are some ex-Sherry casks knocking around, too.

If you want to see a little more of Balblair without actually visiting, be sure to watch the 2012 movie *The Angel's Share*, which sees the co-conspirators and heroes of the movie siphon whisky from a sadly mythical 'Malt Mill' cask through the window of one of the Balblair warehouses.

Above A masterclass in whisky packaging, Balblair radiates understated complexity.

BALBLAIR 03

Clean and breezy. There's a cool mint character on the nose, which is enough to give you goosebumps. This continues into a mineral slate/flint-like quality that is matched by some soft coconut flesh and a spritz of lemon oil. In the taste it remains frigid and stony, with some sweetness and curried spice on the finish.

BALBLAIR 97

A sweet and fresh affair, with lemon bonbons, dried mango and cool spices. Oh, and fizzy pineapple. Delve a little further and glossy wood notes begin to emerge, providing more dry fruit and winey notes. On the palate there are soft, dried apricots backed up by well-integrated wood spices and a vice-like grip on the tongue.

BALBLAIR 90

A full array of raisins, PX wine, tobacco leaf and spice draw, supported by tangerine... wait, lamb tagine. On the palate we have a more Moroccan influence: soft apricots, almond and dark wood, leading into a lingering aftertaste of floral incense and vanilla cream.

BALBLAIR 2000 CASK STRENGTH

Honeycomb, praline and brown buttered popcorn on the nose. Chewy and gooey on the palate, with a consistency similar to maple syrup. A long, candied cashew finish, checked by a constant alcohol presence.

CLYNELISH

The coastal village of Brora in Sutherland is the setting for Clynelish Distillery, a town also famous for its salmon and herring fishing, old wool industry and being the first town in northern Scotland to have electricity, a luxury that gave rise to its local nickname of 'Electric City'. Brora sits within the parish of Clyne, which took its name from the fact that the parish kirk was sited on the slope of a hill, or *cleinadh* in Gaelic. In 1818, the Marquis of Stafford, who later became Duke of Sutherland, established the Clynelish Distillery along with a brickworks, a coal mine, roads and a new harbour. All this industry for farming folk might make the duke sound like an alright fellow, but in truth, it was part of a larger and more sinister relocation and ethnic-cleansing operation that was taking place, later known as the Highland Clearances.

By the end of the 19th century, Clynelish whisky was the most expensive on the market – trade orders were refused altogether and all output sold directly to private customers. Back then it was producing a peated malt whisky, but through the 20th century the peatiness fizzled out and became more like the Clynelish whisky we recognize today. In the 1960s, a new, much bigger distillery was planned on the same site as Clynelish, and it began producing whisky in 1968. The old Clynelish Distillery was closed in May of 1968 and its name handed over to the new distillery, which is still known as Clynelish today.

By all accounts the story should have ended there, but a sudden demand for smoky whisky in the same year, mostly due to a drought on Islay, meant that the old Clynelish Distillery could still be useful. Production of a heavily peaked whisky resumed there in 1969, under the new name 'Brora'. The two distilleries operated side-by-side for a few years and Brora lowered its phenolic content in 1973 – a sluggish reaction to consumer demand. Then, 10 years later in 1983, Brora closed for good.

The 'new' Clynelish Distillery lives on, and it is here that we find one of my favourite whiskies in the world and a great friend of the blenders. Clynelish will undergo significant expansion over the coming years as Diageo, the current owner, attempts to increase production of this honeyed, lustrous and infamously 'waxy' whisky, which offers a unique experience to malt drinkers and unparalleled adhesive qualities in a blend.

Left & below The epic mash tun at Clynelish is made from cast iron and the top is plated with copper. The spooky green haze inside hints at the docile waxiness that typifies the dram.

Right Clynelish Distillery exists on the site of the Brora distillery, which was formerly known as Clynelish. It's complicated, basically.

Snooping around the guts of the distillery, I sought to discover how Clynelish develops its rare character. The distillery operators believe that textbook Clynelish is en route when a strong pineapple aroma emanates from the washback. The aptly named Jim Beveridge, Diageo's master blender, boldly states that Clynelish is the only malt whisky in Scotland that possesses this particular character trait during its fermentation. Perhaps this is down to its unique use of two yeast types. Both are of the distiller's variety, but one is thought to produce more residue (gunk) than the other, and through careful balancing of both types and an 80-hour fermentation, the Clynelish character is expertly sculpted.

Moving through to the still room you find that, rather bizarrely, the spirit stills here are larger than the wash stills by a full 1,000 litres (1,057 quarts). No one knows exactly why this is, but it effectively means that two wash-still runs are required for every spirit run. The spirit stills are run quite hard (around four hours for a single run) and this results in a build-up of a black waxy substance in the feints receiver. It's this tar-like gloop that is thought to award Clynelish with its docile mouthfeel: a long flavour release that teases a smile out of even the gruffest of warehouse men. Ever the opportunist, I tasted the black wax and the experience was like licking a new tyre.

At present, the distillery has a capacity of almost 5 million litres (2.28 million quarts) of pure alcohol, yet only sells around 100,000 bottles of Clynelish malt. Clynelish is the backbone of Johnnie Walker Gold Reserve, famed for its honeyed aromatics and waxy mouthfeel. It's alleged that Alexander Walker II had Clynelish in mind when he first penned the idea for Johnnie Walker Gold around 100 years ago.

CLYNELISH 14

A faint smell of copper on the nose, which probably shouldn't be as surprising as it is. Clarified butter, oiled leather, waxed cotton and honey. A true mélange of flavour integration that makes it hard to pick much out, but certainly shouldn't detract from the mouthfeel and complexity. A long, swooping finish with just a touch of astringency for grip.

CLYNELISH DISTILLER'S EDITION

Honey and raisins on the nose, like the perfect topping to Greek yogurt. There's wax-a-plenty, too, with pungent oak notes creeping ever closer. The palate is a near masterpiece of soft dried fruits, honeyed nuts and a long, gluey mouthfeel.

CLYNELISH CASK STRENGTH, NO AGE STATEMENT

Honeycomb and milk chocolate, with some mineral honeyed notes on the palate, too... but when water is added there are pineapple cubes, and the generic smell of fabric conditioner and freshly laundered cotton. Very sweet on the palate, with clean sheets and slick honey leading the way.

CLYNELISH 24-YEAR-OLD

Raw honeycomb, beeswax polish, fruit cake, saffron and overwhelmingly, the colour orange. Voluptuous, sticky and slow in the mouth. Warm honey, sea air, orange curd and lashings of salted butter.

EDRADOUR

The Edradour Distillery in Pitlochry has the feel of a model village about it. Clean, white farmhouse-style buildings, white picket fences, and a perfect little stream winding through the middle of it all. Edradour is every bit the cliché farmyard distillery, and a tribute to the others that saturated the Highlands in the 18th and early 19th centuries. The grass is so green that it must have undergone the lawn equivalent of a fake tan, and even on a damp-coloured Scottish morning, this tiny distillery puffs out its chest and looks gloriously proud. In fact, so perfect is its appearance that you'd be forgiven for wondering if the building fascias are actually cardboard scenery, supported by a flimsy wooden framework from behind – surely this cannot be a working distillery? But step through the lipstick-coloured doors and you will find an inner character and charm to this operation that far outweighs its picture-postcard facade.

A whisky-making operation called 'Glenforres' was founded on this site in around 1825 and the first mention of Edradour came about 10 years later in 1935. A mere two years after that, a statistical report from 1839 shows that Edradour produced 90,000 gallons of whisky that year, which is about twice the quantity produced there today. This makes Edradour currently the smallest distillery in Scotland, with the exception of the very new Strathearn Distillery (see page 149), which is yet to bottle a whisky. But to attach a simple label like 'Scotland's smallest' to Edradour would be doing a major injustice to the well-preserved beauty of the buildings and the skill of the people who work there.

The distillery makes two different whiskies: the unpeated Edradour and the heavily peated Ballechin. The tiny 1.15-ton cast-iron mash tun that sits opposite the stills is of the open-top raked genus, and a gaudy green and red affair, looking suspiciously like it was built out of a boiler engine salvaged from an old steam locomotive. In fact it was installed in 1904, making it 110 years old at the time of writing and one of the oldest working examples of any malt distillery. The Morton wort cooler is a one-of-a-kind piece of kit, too, an exact replica of an older cooler that was recently replaced after 100 years of active service. The stills are also very small and use old-fashioned worm tubs, cooled by water from the distillery's tiny lake (pond), giving the two types of spirit distilled here a sweet and oily character.

But it's Edradour's 6,000 casks that Des McCagherty, distillery manager, is committing the most time and energy to. Having passed through many owners over the years, Signatory, the current proprietor, became the current regent in 2002. Upon acquisition, the team was immediately faced with a wood-themed nightmare of epic proportions. Much of the stock was held in tired old bourbon casks, like a convent full of injured soldiers, so the team set about nurturing the spirit back to good health. This involved new stocks of first-fill Sherry and bourbon casks; a standard of living which Edradour has since become highly accustomed to. As for the whisky already in cask, much of it was picked up and dusted off by way of a wine finish. Edradour now has 12 'Straight from the Cask' expressions, each bottled at cask strength and finished from 6–24 months in a wine cask – from Barolo to Burgundy and Chardonnay to Châteauneuf-du-Pape – all of your old favourites are featured. Then throw in a growing range of 10-year-old whiskies matured solely in ex-wine casks, a Cask Strength range, and a few Ballechin 'Heavily Peated' expressions, and the list of whiskies coming out of 'Scotland's Smallest distillery' exceeds 30.

'No one in Scotland invests more money in wood per litre of spirit than we do,' Des tells me. And after the barrel-ordering spree that they've been on over the past decade, I can believe it.

CALEDONIA 12

Plenty of sweetness on the nose, with pine wood, sugared cashews, bay and béarnaise. There's also a faint linseed oil note, quickly replaced by poached pear and other autumnal aromas. Sweet initially on the palate, too, which is carried by some oily texture. Some grassy fennel tones on the finish.

EDRADOUR 18 – (OLOROSO FINISH)

There's an immediate aroma of fruited tobacco, ginger and soft brown sugar on the aroma of this mahogany-coloured whisky. This is pursued by Soreen malt loaf and a touch of beef stock. Huge dark fruit liqueur on the palate, accompanied by warm spices, ginger ale and orange sherbet.

Below Even on a miserable Scottish morning, Edradour is beautiful. It's hardly surprising that it is one of the most frequently visited distilleries in Scotland.

BALLECHIN – SAUTERNES CASK FINISH

Prawn/shrimp cocktail crisps/potato chips, and sweet rib glaze on the nose. This is followed up by post-campfire clothing, charred green pepper and sweet antiseptic lotion. The palate is juicy, with a quick lashing of alcohol announcing the beginning of the oily finish, which gradually deteriorates to a warm, smoky fuzz.

8 YEAR BOURBON CASK / 2.5 YEAR BAROLO CASK

Shiny. All sorts of nuttiness, pecan, hazelnut praline and almond. Pungent and ripe as the aroma continues, with black polished boots, tawny Port leading into chocolate-coated cherries. Barolo is more prominent on the palate, bringing dark fruit compote, more black leather and a lovely lingering heat.

ROYAL BRACKLA

There are only two distilleries in Scotland prefixed with 'Royal' – the other is Lochnagar in Aberdeenshire. I've never been to Royal Lochnagar (although I have driven past many times) but I'm told that it's a real beauty. Royal Brackla, on the other hand, while beautiful in setting, is not an especially attractive distillery. But it was the first of the two to be awarded a royal warrant, by William IV back in 1835. Since then it has undergone significant expansion and renovation, to the point where only the detached office building stands as part of the original operation. Of course there's no shame in being a bit ugly; we're here to talk about whisky after all, not the aesthetics of the staffroom.

In all fairness, I am probably being a little harsh on poor Brackla; from the inside looking out, this distillery becomes a far more bonny prospect. The huge retractable windows of the stillhouse look out over two small reservoirs and a handful of old farm buildings. The reservoirs were purpose-built to provide process cooling water for the distillery's shell-and-tube condensers. The assistant distillery manager, John Mackenzie, informed me that the water was once good for fishing and that on one occasion he has witnessed an otter scampering past the front of the stillhouse with a whole trout in its mouth. Some of the cottages that sit adjacent to the reservoirs are still inhabited and make up part of the wider estate of Cawdor, an area made famous by Shakespeare's play *Macbeth,* which has its setting in the nearby Cawdor Castle. I'm told that Brackla means 'small, speckled hill', but the lay of the land here is actually very flat and mellow. So much so in fact that when the distillery was closed during World War II, the adjacent field was converted into a runway and for a short time the distillery became RAF Brackla. Traces of the runway still remain visible today.

Whisky-making at Royal Brackla is a relatively straightforward process. Two hundred and twelve tons of malt arrive at the distillery every week and the total is split between seventeen 12.5-ton mashes. There are eight 59,000-litre (62,000-quart)

washbacks, which are of the vented variety. The wash-still run takes about four hours, and the spirits-still 10 hours, which is longer than most and makes for a very fruity and fragrant new-make spirit. Brackla does not officially conduct tours and the stillman shared his regret with me that the onion-shaped stills were not better lacquered for our cameras. Pots like these are the backbone of the malt whisky industry, though, and their tarnished exteriors and tired joints are testament to the many millions of litres that pass through them.

No filling is conducted at Brackla and the small amount of warehouse space is actually leased out to Diageo, so new-make spirit is shipped down to Glasgow for the next stage in its journey. Ninety-eight per cent of Royal Brackla will find its way into a Dewar's bottle, as it has played a prominent role in the make-up of the blend for quite some time now.

You might wonder why I chose to feature Royal Brackla in this book at all. From the description I have provided it would appear to be a monumentally unexceptional distillery. But there are dozens of distilleries like Brackla in Scotland, whose malts are rarely seen bottled, yet they have significant roles in the hands of a blender. Ardmore, Auchroisk, Blair Athol, Braeval, Glenallachie, Craigellachie... all are similarly sized distilleries with capacity potential exceeding that of A-list operations such as Bowmore and Highland Park. Distilleries like Brackla are the Ford Transit van of the malt whisky industry: prosaic and straightforward, but you'd damn well miss them if they were gone.

NEW MAKE

Rounded. The initial hit of pungent blackcurrant leads to hot hay barn, cereal and musk. Cheap chocolate and prune come through on the second time around. Almond, gorse and more blackcurrant on the lips.

OLD PULTENEY

Pulteneytown, now part of Wick on the far north-east coast of Scotland, was purpose-built in 1810 by the British Fisheries Society to leverage the huge opportunity presented by nearby herring stocks and a homeless workforce. Named after the chief protagonist in the town's creation, Sir William Pulteney, the Old Pulteney Distillery was set up in 1826 by James Henderson, who had previously run a nearby whisky-making operation for circa 30 years. The inaccessibility of the town meant that both barley and finished whisky were shipped in and out by sea, and most of the employees were also fishermen. Self-sufficiency was the key to survival, and that seasoned determination was reflected in the distillery's ability to endure the whisky downturn, along with two wars and economic depression. Having thousands of thirsty fishermen helped too, of course, but that created its own problems in 1922, when a state of prohibition was enacted, heavily lobbied for by the Wick Salvation Army Group, whose chieftain was the aptly named 'Captain Dry'. Rather unsurprisingly, the distillery closed, and until 1939 herring were the only pickled creatures that you'd find in Wick.

Get into the guts of this distillery and if prizes were being given out for peculiar-looking distillation apparatus, Old Pulteney would almost certainly win a double gold. The wash still has a grossly oversized 'boil ball' and a flat top, giving the effect of a giant copper snowman wearing an elongated fez. There's a purifier on the spirit still, and like a whirlpool, it whips the vapours around in a copper and chemical maelstrom, before plunging them into cold worm tubs for condensation. Alfred Barnard described the stills in 1886 as 'of the oldest pattern known, similar to the old smuggler's kettle.'

Weird stills means weird new make, and in this instance we're talking oily, briny, sulphury and full of all fruity maritime aromas. This lends itself nicely to the confined space of an oak cask and it means that old Old Pulteney is really rather delicious stuff, redolent of sea foam, salt-caked fruit and old waxed leather.

NAVIGATOR

A big blast of blackberry jam on an initial sniff that gives way to biscuit, honey and brown sugar, turning the jam into a crumble. Water reveals orangeade and a touch of rose. On the palate it's a bracing salted-citrus accent that wins over, lingering to some wood vanilla and just a hint of bitterness.

17-YEAR-OLD

A more complete package. The heady sweetness of Crunchy Nut corn flakes lurks about this glass. There's plenty of malty honey to supplement it, too. The distinct pear aroma couples nicely with this, but there's honeydew melon, as well as crystallized citrus-fruit slices and a clean, soapy note once water is added. On the palate there's granola, vanilla fudge and a long honey/cereal finish.

21-YEAR-OLD

Smoked lemon and tonic water quickly emerge from this surprisingly clean and crisp-smelling dram, but water reveals a tinned pineapple fruit salad. On the palate it is thick and oily, like trawler engine grease splattered with saltwater. The finish is the business end of this dram, however, ranging from sweet oak lactones right through to tropical fruits and lime oil. Smoke gets the last laugh.

Below Old Pulteney Navigator is autumn in a glass.

BEN NEVIS

As its name suggests, Ben Nevis sits at the foot of the most famous 'Ben' in Britain. I found myself driving past this distillery late one cold and windy November night, and thought it only proper to stop by on the off-chance of a snoop around and having a chat. To the surprise of myself and my travelling companions, the distillery, which is contained within a large aeroplane hanger-esque building, was in full operation – with stills glowing hot, the smell of mashing and fermentation in the air and the sound of pumps humming. Rather bizarrely though, there was not a soul about the place. It was as if the warning siren had been sounded, and the entire facility abandoned in fear of death or worse. The glow of copper that emanated from the open doors was almost more than we could take, but after a quick glance around we got on our way and left the spirits to their important work.

Besides invisible stillmen, this is a distillery that's seen its share of weirdness over the years. In 1878, a Siamese-twin distillery was opened next door, simply called 'Nevis'. The two sites operated together for 30 years then eventually merged into one. In 1955, a Coffey still was installed and for the next three decades the distillery was unique in being the only one in Scotland producing both malt and grain whisky side by side. Most of these spirits were mixed together prior to maturation in a similar fashion to some Canadian brands and after some years sold as blended whisky. The early 1980s saw the Coffey still removed and a big refurbishment and expansion take place. Then, like so many others, the distillery closed in the mid-1980s.

But in 1989 the most unexpected of saviours sailed in from the east: the Japanese giant Nikka. Quality has improved, as you might expect, but the mantra at Ben Nevis is really all about sticking to traditional practices. It is still the only distillery in Scotland that uses only brewer's yeast for fermentation. Brewers are usually less concerned with high alcohol strength and more concerned with flavour, so even though this type of single-celled organism isn't great for the bank balance, it does score well in the flavour department, something that is evident in the robust new-make spirit distilled here. You might question why more distilleries don't explore other yeast strains, but the dependancy and dependability of distiller's yeast by the rest of Scotland is a dull truth. From their perspective, though, I suspect it is better to stick to what you know than flit between varieties and helplessly watch your product alter. Fortunately for Ben Nevis, brewer's yeast has always been the way.

10-YEAR-OLD

Aroma gives the impression of youth that belies the whisky's age. Flint, black pepper and olive couple with vanilla ice cream and a touch of heather. The taste is sweet and dynamic, starting softly and crescendo-ing to buttermilk and warm jam tart, with a sticky, almost cloying, afterthought. What the aroma seems to lack in age, the tongue makes up for.

25-YEAR-OLD

Maltesers, sultanas/golden raisins and soft leather. Oily and full on the palate, with a fantastically silky texture. Cherry chocolate, white chocolate and bitter dark chocolate. The finish is long and compact.

BEN NEVIS – THAT BOUTIQUE-Y WHISKY COMPANY – NO AGE STATEMENT

Dried cranberry, rubber boots, and that smell you get when it rains on a hot day. There's wood here, too, and the conspicuous note of tinned pineapple. A good blast of sweetness on the palate is accompanied by bags of fruit and a rich and spicy walnut-whip finish.

Go back 300 years and most of the distilling activities in the Scottish Highlands would have been farmyard operations capable of only minimal production volumes. Scotland's newest distillery (at the time of writing) aims to recreate this tradition, by being both the smallest and the most authentic distillery among those we have seen so far. Strathearn farm in Perthshire is the location of this distillery, just about an hour north of Edinburgh. The brainchild of Tony Reeman and David Lang, they have combined their knowledge of brewing, distilling and engineering to set up the operation. Strathearn has a current annual output of only 12,000 litres (12,680 quarts), or to put it in simpler terms, it is one-thousandth the size of the biggest malt distillery in Scotland, Glenfiddich. To put it yet another way, Glenfiddich will produce in eight hours the same quantity of spirit that Strathearn produces in a whole year.

So small are its barley requirements that it must go through the agricultural equivalent of cabbage flogging, by having 20kg/44 lbs. bags of the stuff delivered by hand. 'We plan on setting up our own maltings,' David Lang tells me, 'The farm grows both Optic and Concerto barley, which we hope to germinate and dry ourselves, fulfilling all our malt requirements.' Not that they'll need much.

The distillery uses a brewer's yeast to create a fruity, delicate wash, which is then distilled in two alembic pot stills. Strathearn is the only distillery in Scotland using this traditionally shaped still and the resulting new make smells like digestive biscuits/graham crackers and orange zest. There's no automation here at all; even the steam pressure is controlled by a valve. David tells me that they will be able to make two types of spirit in the future by simply disconnecting the lyne arm by hand and reconnecting it the other way around, encouraging more (or less) reflux, depending on their requirements.

Maturation also errs on the traditional side of things, with the team choosing to use 50-litre (53

quart) octave casks in place of something four times the size. This move will of course also accelerate certain elements of the ageing process, meaning that we can expect to see three- and four-year-old releases in the not too distant future. Tests are being conducted in three and five litre/quart casks, too, as a means of approximating the flavour profile of a fully matured whisky. I've included tasting notes on one below.

If you're eager to get your hands on some of Strathearn's first releases, they offer the option to buy an entire octave cask for as little as £800 (+ duty). Obviously you won't get to drink it for a few more years yet. They may be in higher demand than the distillery can cope with, however. Besides the malting floor, there are no plans for expansion going forward. 'Distilleries these days are running the arse out of it,' says David. 'We're taking a more relaxed approach.'

STRATHEARN 10-WEEK-OLD 3-LITRE PORT CASK (CASK STRENGTH)

Salmon pink, with aromas of plum pudding, sloe gin and pitch. In the mouth you're in for more dark stone fruits, with a powerful feinty note, and finishing on soft spice and alcohol heat. Clearly not ready yet, but good to see the direction it's taking.

Right The low-profile octave casks at Strathearn will help speed up some elements of the maturation process, but it'll still be a little while before we see a finished product.

GLENCADAM

I have consciously refrained from offering too much of my own preference when it comes to distilleries in this book, but I must make an exception here and tell you that I believe Glencadam to be one of the most underrated whiskies in Scotland today.

It seems almost inconceivable then that this distillery was mothballed in 2000 by its then owners, Allied. Montrose, the home of Glencadam, once had three distilleries and now it feels fortunate to have one. The Hillside Distillery was closed in the 1980s and demolished in 1996, and Lochside was closed in 1992 (also by Allied who it would appear had taken it upon themselves to act as distillery liquidators at this time) and subsequently burned down in 2004. The reason for all this? Overproduction. Too much holding stock and not nearly enough demand for whiskies perceived as too generic from blenders, made distilleries like Glencadam unfeasible. It did well to hang in there until 2000, mind you. This was the time of peat, where smoky Islay malts were on the rise and delicate whiskies like Glencadam were trampled underfoot.

The good news is that Glencadam was bought by Angus Dundee in 2003 and production is now set at 24 hours a day, seven days a week. The secret to the concentrated but light character of this spirit is the downward-sloping lyne arm on the wash and spirit stills, which encourage plenty of reflux. 2005 saw Glencadam's first ever single malt release, a 15-year-old, which was subsequently re-released in 2009 and is now augmented by a 10-year-old and a 21-year-old, as well as port- and oloroso-finished expressions.

As a stand-alone malt, Glencadam is a hidden gem. Blending it, in this author's opinion, is like putting sashimi-grade tuna in fish pie. Vulnerability, poise, a slight salinity and crisp florals make this a whisky that deserves to stand on its own. What do I know though? A blending and bottling plant was installed at the distillery in 2007 and a good chunk of Glencadam's 1.5-million litre (1.6-million quart) capacity is still filling the blender's bottle.

12-YEAR-OLD PORT FINISH

Rhubarb and custard, toffee apple and mulled wine-stewed pear. Chewy and full-bodied texture and the perfect juxtaposition between fruit and candy. Sweet and nutty on the palate; pine nut, cough candy, vanilla, soft sage. The finish is gentle raspberry shisha.

14-YEAR-OLD OLOROSO FINISH

Air-fix glue on sticky fingers welcomes you, giving way to cantaloupe melon and hot shingle. A subtle maritime quality continues into fino, salt cod and samphire. The palate is a fruit bowl of flavours, leading into nutty sherry notes and a pleasant brine finish. The linger is fleshy fruits on the beach.

15-YEAR-OLD

Raw honey, buffed teak and fresh cherry juice on the nose. Elegant and finessed in the taste, with all sorts of polished wooden fruit, and plenty of residual sugar, balanced by just a hint of salty acidity and a touch of pepper. A brilliant dram.

21-YEAR-OLD

Initially orange soda and sugared plums on the nose, which relaxes into sticky wood lustre. Complex wood spice and resinous notes on the palate, with just a touch of clean bitterness on the finish that structures the whole thing. A long understated finish of salted caramel and melted citrus butter.

Left Glencadam is a hidden gem and definitely one to watch for the future.

With its proud stag's head and blood red colour, only the mighty Macallan can claim a greater degree of prestige among malt whisky investors over The Dalmore. Just like Macallan, The Dalmore is a powerful whisky, capable of holding its own through extended periods of time in European oak casks. This means old Dalmore can be especially complex stuff, like stuffing a cigar box filled with fruit cake and liqueur chocolates into your mouth all at once.

Whyte & Mackay, which has owned the brand since 1960, has taken full advantage of these superpowers by more recently augmenting the core range of The Dalmore expressions with a vast array of special release bottles that promise high statements and deliver a high price. Indeed, The Dalmore seems to have well and truly found its place within the realms of high-rollers of this world, who tend to place at least as much emphasis on the status that a bottle affords them as they do the flavour of the liquid inside. Never had this been more true than with The Dalmore's 2012 Constellation Range of travel-retail-only whiskies. Twenty-one bottles of 20-to-60-year-old whiskies can be yours for an astronomical £158,000. Collect them all and you get a free badge*. Perhaps the major catalyst for all this ludicrously expensive whisky was an event that took place back in 2005, when a 62-year-old bottle of The Dalmore broke all previous records and sold at auction for £32,000 ($53,309). It was one of only 12 that had ever been produced and contained whisky distilled in the 1860s and 1870s.

It was around that time in 1874 that the first water-jacketed spirits still was installed at The Dalmore, which is one of the unique features of the distillery today. There's a second one there now; both of them promote a tremendous amount of reflux within the still and grant the distiller heightened flavour selection abilities. The wash stills are also geared towards copper contact, with flat tops and lyne arms protruding from one side. This is reflected in the new-make spirit, which is broad in character, being both heavy and robust as well as light and effeminate. It's this distillery character that affords the spirit resilience to long periods in oak and differentiates The Dalmore from other brands.

Who could fail to appreciate the allure of an industry where plain and harmless engineering decisions made in the Victorian age resonate through the centuries, ultimately defining the nature of a product that is sought-after all over the world today?

THE DALMORE 12

There's a depth of aroma that defies the age of this whisky: red fruit and bright nuttiness of lightly roasted coffee, tempered chocolate and a spoonful of orange marmalade. On the palate, it's robust, round and full of Christmas spices.

THE DALMORE 15

Warm honey, cedar wood and jam-filled sponge cake on the nose. Initially, it pats your tongue with dry wood, but then leads into a nutty Sherry *flor*, orange blossom and sweet spices, before reverting to a long, wood finish.

THE DALMORE 18

The aroma begins with sticky toffee pudding, supple leather and horse hair. There's big, pungent chocolate orange here, too, which carries into the taste and is bolstered by a soft Sherry note, along with a good spattering of wood spice. The finish is a spice and sugar battle – and a long drawn-out death.

*You don't get a badge.

Right The Dalmore is the only distillery I have visited that has its own petrol/gas station!

* CAMPBELTOWN *

It's said that Irishman, Fergus Mór established the first Scottish Parliament in 503 AD in the area formerly known as Dalruadhain. They renamed it Kilkerran, a shortening of Kinlochkilkerran (head of the loch by the kirk of Ciarán) and later, James V transferred the territory from the MacDonalds to the Campbells of Argyll, who gave it their family name. The area where Campbeltown sits has long been an important fishing port and shipbuilding site, as well as a safe haven for ships at sea due to its natural sheltered harbour afforded by the deflection of winds by the stormy Mull.

I've been told that Campbeltown is the most remote mainland town in the British Isles, located near the bottom of the drip-like peninsula of Kintyre that hangs off the south-west coast of Scotland. As the crow flies, it's only 97km (60 miles) from Glasgow, but by road, the drive around Loch Fyne takes around three hours. Even on misty days, the northern coast of Ireland is visible in the distance, and on the oft occasion that visibility is truly terrible your mobile phone may alert you to Ireland's close proximity by connecting to one of the Irish network providers, since it has better coverage than the British ones in this corner of the Isles. Campbeltown itself appears out of nowhere and you could be forgiven for doubting the road signs that tell you there's only a short way left to go as your journey to the end of the earth continues. But Campbeltown is still there, with its three distilleries, now a quiet and peaceful relic of the town that was once dubbed 'the whisky capital of the world'.

The first reference to distilling in Campbeltown goes back to 1591: not surprising, given its close proximity to Islay. When whisky historian Alfred Barnard conducted a two-week visit in 1885 there was a ferry service from Glasgow that ran daily. Barnard avoided it in fear of 'women and children tumbling about in all direction'. I'm led to believe that it's the men tumbling about that you're best to avoid these days. It's said that the now innocuous-looking Glebe Street was at one time the wealthiest street in the UK outside of London and the town was a very popular tourist destination for those with enough money. Back then there were 850 tons of barley arriving every week, which is more than Glenfiddich get through even today. At least 34 legal distilleries opened in the town between 1815 (Campbeltown Distillery) and 1879 (Ardlussa Distillery); all but two were closed by 1934, and one of those – Glen Scotia – was up for sale. There were so many factors going against Campbeltown during this period: war, economic depression and Prohibition in America all shoulder some of the blame. And there was the rise of Islay and particularly Speyside as producing regions, and the replacement of Campbeltown malts in blends. Some would say that Campbeltown's comparative inaccessibility (be it by road or boat) was a hammer-blow too, but I would reckon Islay should have struggled more in that sense, and it didn't.

Perhaps Campbeltown whisky simply belongs to another time; like it wasn't cut out for the new demands of a quickly modernizing industry. There's a reflection of Victorian industry in the character of the dram, with oil, soot and grease being good indicators that it's something from Campbeltown that you're drinking. Old reports seem to agree that it has always been mechanical and briny in its nature. In 1930 Anaeas McDonald called them the 'Double Basses of the whisky orchestra... potent and pungent.'

Left Multi-coloured barrel ends are often used to indicate whiskies that are intended for independent bottlers.

Left The Mitchells of Campbeltown have a 200-year unbroken history of whisky distillation.

SCOTLAND

Campbeltown

Below Campbeltown harbour: as bonnie as ever, but not the tourist destination it once was, alas.

⫸ SPRINGBANK ⫷

There's no other distillery in Scotland that approaches the production of malt whisky in the same manner as Springbank and it's not surprising, really; Springbank has been in the same family for around 200 years. Founded in 1828 by illicit distiller Archibald Mitchell, the distillery has been passed down through the generations to the current owner, Hedley Wright, Archibald's great great grandson, the heirless king of the Springbank throne.

The list of claims here is a big one: the longest continuous family-owned distillery; the only distillery to floor malt 100% of its barley requirements; the only distillery to use the same water source for every stage of production; the only still that combines both direct firing from oil and a steam coil; one of the only distilleries never to chill-filter its whisky; and the only distillery to conduct every step of its entire operation, from malting to bottling, all in one location.

With that in mind, one of the best reasons to visit Springbank is to see the working floor maltings. Sadly, on my visit, the maltings were not in operation, since the distillery was closed for a nine-month cleaning and maintenance programme. Malting floors are lonely old places without any barley to fill them and Springbank's reminded me

of an abandoned car park in miniature. All there is to be seen are round marks on the floor like giant coffee cup stains, left behind by casks that were stored there in the 1970s. Combined, the two floors hold 22 tons of barley, which will be raked and grubbed for a continuous six days. It sounds like a lot of barley, but when you consider that Glenfiddich gets through 100 tons of barley a day, the modesty of the operation becomes very apparent. There are no air conditioning units or even a fan in sight; all of the malting is conducted by hand and airflow controlled by simply opening and closing the window.

After germination is complete, the barley is sent to the kiln, which has both a peat furnace and an oil-powered hot-air blower (basically a giant hairdryer) that can be used individually or in tandem to generate a desirable peatiness to the finished malt. Once a year, the distillery holds a £350 ($590) a ticket dinner for 20 people inside the kiln on its perforated floor. I've never heard of anything like this being done elsewhere, but looking at the ticket price I can imagine a few other distilleries considering it in the future.

There's one other first that Springbank can claim by my reckoning – the weakest wash strength of any distillery in Scotland. At only 4.5% ABV it is around half that of the industry average. But the long 100-hour fermentation and low starting gravity affords the distillery high levels of bacterial development and a very fruity beer.

Springbank Distillery produces three different labels of whisky: Hazelburn, Springbank and Longrow. With the former being unpeated and the latter heavily peated malt, Springbank itself sits in the middle. Both Hazelburn and Longrow are named after old Campbeltown distilleries; Longrow is also the main road that runs through Campbeltown's centre. During kilning, the Hazelburn malt has 30 hours of continuous hot air, Springbank malt has six hours of peat smoke

Left The dunnage warehouse at Springbank holds stocks of their Hazelburn, Longrow and Springbank expressions.

Right The 'CV' in Springbank CV stands for curriculum vitae, and just like a CV, this non-age-statement bottling aims to explore the past experiences of the whisky by combining casks of various different ages.

followed by 30 hours of hot air, while Longrow malt has 40 hours of peat smoke (using two different types of peat) followed by a blast of hot air to finish it off. The three labels are also distilled in that order (the order of peatiness) to prevent Hazelburn from contracting peat reek from the other two. There are three stills in Springbank; Hazelburn uses all of them, Longrow two of them, and Springbank is somewhere in the middle whereby a proportion of the low wines from the first distillation are distilled with feints from the second.

Every inch of Springbank's cluster of buildings hints at it not being a hard-nosed, commercially driven operation, yet the decisions that have been made over the years are well calculated and it's that attitude that has led to its continued survival. If the whisky industry went bust tomorrow, I'd wager that Springbank would be the last distillery standing.

HAZELBURN 12

This whisky has a sesame oil and general nuttiness on the nose (but I'll avoid saying hazelnut) and these qualities integrate nicely with the Sherry influence, with wood from the same providing dried plum, date and raisins. The texture is soft and oily, with some citrus qualities and dried fruits coming through in the finish.

SPRINGBANK 10

Green and nutty, with raspberry leaf, pine cone and burnt grass. Green lemon oil, too, with a smattering of wet sand and seagull feather. Thick and juicy on the tongue, with spikes of green peppercorns, sea salt and waxed lemon. Unique.

SPRINGBANK CV

Cracked brown toffee and almonds, and a big bag of sugared doughnuts. There's a touch of something herbal present, too, perhaps savoury. Coastal on the palate, a glint of something shingly and some yeasty masculinity. Dessert fruits and that doughnut note continue through to a lingering spice in the finish. One for the pastry-lovers.

LONGROW PEATED

The smoke has an oily pungency to it, and reminds me of when you find oil on a beach. Perhaps a touch of something vegetal in there, green pepper or even mild chilli/chile. Rich and well balanced on the palate, with the smoke building slowly, then drifting away just as slowly. It leaves the taste of steam engine and a touch of iodine. A very nice dram.

GLENGYLE

The story of Glengyle begins, like any good story, with a family feud. In the 1860s, William and John Mitchell ran their father's Springbank Distillery, but an argument, apparently relating to sheep (bear in mind that most distilleries were connected to farming operations back then), caused the brothers to separate. William set up the Glengyle Distillery right next door to Springbank and it was one of a number of operations that enjoyed the good times of the Campbeltown boom period, then was forced to close in the downturn of the 1920s. Since then, the property has changed hands numerous times and operated under a number of guises, including a petrol station, a rifle range for the 'Campbeltown Miniature Rifle Club' (every town should have one) and an agricultural supply shop. A couple of attempts were made to re-open the distillery in both the 1940s and 1950s but nothing ever came of it. Glengyle remained the best-preserved distillery of the veritable cemetery of former Campbeltown operations, however, and in 2000 it was purchased by Hedley Wright, the owner of Springbank, and the great-great-grand-nephew of Glengyle's original owner, William Mitchell. Stills were bought in from the closed Ben Wyvis Distillery in Aberdeenshire, and a spirits safe from Craigellachie, among other things. Finally, after 82 years of inactivity, Glengyle hissed back into action in 2004.

When I visited, I managed to catch the brief six-week production run that was taking place to fill the year's quota. The stills, mash tun and washbacks are all contained within the same open space and the distillery certainly had a feel of a holiday home that only becomes 'lived in' for a short period of the year. A battered old desk and plastic classroom chair had been placed within warming distance of the spirits still and a few simple notes recording the day's run scatter its surface. Nearby, a glass-fronted wine chiller was completely filled with 20kg (44 lbs.) bags of yeast

Left The Kilkerran label celebrates Campbeltown's Longrow church, which is visible from a barred window at the far end of the distillery.

that would be used in the days to come. New make was generously offered, served in a coffee mug. And very nice it was, too.

The name Glengyle may not be familiar and you're unlikely to see it on a bottle any time soon, since for legal reasons the distillery cannot use it. You see, 'Glengyle' is actually already in use by a blended malt whisky, owned by Campbeltown's third distillery, Glen Scotia. I tried to track a bottle down, but failed. Anyway, that's why Glengyle is bottled as Kilkerran, the old Gaelic name for Campbeltown.

Since 2009, Glengyle has released a yearly insight into the spirit's progression, entitled Kilkerran 'Work in Progress'. These releases seem to indicate a waxy lemon character that runs through the spirit. In 2013, there were two 'Work in Progress' expressions made available, one matured in ex-Sherry casks, the other ex-bourbon. A 12-year-old will be the first official release in 2016, which seems an odd move since there can be no way for anyone to know if a 10-year-old Glengyle might be better than a 12, or indeed a 12 not quite ready yet. Either way, a big party is planned to commemorate it. I asked for an invitation, but I'm still waiting to hear back...

WORK IN PROGRESS #5 – BOURBON WOOD

A pick 'n' mix bag of lemon sherbet, Black Jacks/aniseed candy and plenty of bright floral esters. On the palate there's some nutty brown butter, liquorice allsorts, damp cardboard and wood caramels developing in the end. A work in progress I would agree, but not far off at all.

WORK IN PROGRESS #5 – SHERRY WOOD

This is more fruity than the bourbon cask, with the lemon still present, but now candied, along with orange, sultana/golden raisins and dehydrated apple. There's warm spice on the palate, turning to buttery fruit cake mixture – dark, full and fatty.

* Islands *

Depending on the time of the day and the corresponding tides, there are almost 800 islands off the coast of Scotland. For many people, the wild nature of these scattered pieces of land epitomizes the beauty and sometimes brutality of the Scottish landscape as a whole. These are places of salt-caked skin, smudged landscapes and wind-shattered rock, where precarious yet enduring settlements do dogged battle with nature in its most devastatingly graceful form. But in some ways, the commonality between islands ends there. Each one possesses an identity of its own, and many are quite far removed from that of the mainland, both physically and culturally. Seven islands (including Islay) have operational distilleries, and all choose to approach whisky-making in their own unique way. Ignoring the benefits of the magnificent surroundings that island life provides, these are often places of survival in solitude, where a great deal of effort is required over a long period of time for anything to get done. Let's not forget, though, that the best grapes often come from disadvantaged vines. Similarly, maybe the challenges of island life galvanize the soul, leading to a 'can do' attitude that's reflected in the whisky. The distilleries on Orkney, Skye, Lewis, Jura, Arran and Mull have not only weathered the storm, but emerged through it as some of the most diverse, gritty and thrilling whisky producers out there today.

Even though the winds are generally quite ferocious – the reason why there are so few trees on many islands – the winters are usually quite mild. Like a collection of individual countries,

Below The old, weathered island landscape plays host to some old and weathered distilleries, too.

Islands

SCOTLAND

the islands each have their own ecological backdrop, where wind, light and temperature all have a final say on the character of the whisky. So it's no wonder that each distillery reflects its surroundings — you can expect to find old sea rope, sticky tar, salted heather, the catch of the day and much else besides in each one.

Like Islay, illicit distilling was commonplace through the islands during the 18th and 19th centuries. After the 1823 Excise Act, there were 22 registered distilleries, of which only two — Highland Park (in Orkney) and Jura — remain active today, although neither carried the same name back then. Besides the legal distilling operations, there were probably around 10 times the number of illegal stills, run by those who sought to take advantage of the remoteness of the setting. Joining the two I have already mentioned, we now have Arran on the southern Isle of Arran — a place with a long history of distilling and now sporting a distillery that is almost in its 20th year. There's also Tobermory on the Isle of Mull, and Talisker on Skye. Scapa Distillery, which was once owned by Highland Park, is the other Orkney offering and the newcomer (and catchily named) Abhainn Dearg

Above The Highland Park Distillery is not particularly easy to get to, or to get away from, so it seems. On my most recent trip, the flight was cancelled and my companions and I spent an evening on Scapa Bay drinking Highland Park 25 by the light of a beach fire. So not all bad, then...

sits on the Isle of Lewis, sporting the weirdest stills (looking rather like a one-legged insect) of any I have ever seen.

HIGHLAND PARK

The Highland Park Distillery is located on the outskirts of Kirkwall, the main town on the Orkney Islands, just off the north coast of Scotland. Orkney comprises around 70 islands in total (some only appear when the tide is low!), of which around 22 are inhabited. The islands sit at 59° latitude, which is almost the same as Bergen in Norway, making Highland Park the most northerly malt distillery in all of Scotland – for now anyway.

What this means is that the temperature does not fluctuate so much according to the season; what it affects, however, is the amount of light. Summers peak at about 16°C (61°F), typically accompanied by 18 hours of sunlight. Winter rarely drops below 0°C (32°F), bringing with it a mere six hours of daylight. Wind, on the other hand, is a constant feature. The islands actually feel like they are near the top of the world; the sun and shadows behave differently in Orkney, the clouds appear low, distant and somehow squashed.

The isolation is palpable, and it's said that only 1% of Scots ever visit, which is why it might seem surprising that the islands were so highly prized by first the Romans and then the Vikings. Orkney is highly valued by the Royal Navy, which used Scapa Flow, one of the world's largest natural harbours, as the chief tactical British naval base during both world wars. The distillery ceased production during both world wars. In fact, during World War II, the washbacks served as gigantic bathtubs for sailors!

The rather Nordic-sounding Magnus Euson first founded a distillery on the Highland Park site in the late 18th century, and the operation was founded properly in 1798 by David Robertson. Before the 1826 Excise Act. it would have operated illegally, which is the reason for the tactical placement it holds; with views out to Kirkwall harbour and the incoming roads from the south, there'd be no unexpected visits from excise officers here!

Obviously the distillery is a totally legitimate operation today, owned and operated by The Edrington Group, which plays parent to the The Macallan brand as well as The Famous Grouse blend, which Highland Park contributes towards.

From a production perspective, Highland Park's most interesting feature is its malting floors. It is the largest of the seven distilleries that malt their own barley and supplies 20% of its total requirements and 100% of the subtle peat influence that lingers in the final product. The remaining 80% (unpeated) malt is bought in from Simpsons Maltings on the mainland. I'm told by Highland Park's distillery manager, Graham Manson, that when all is said and done, the barley malted at the distillery effectively costs twice as much as it would if it were it bought in from the mainland. But Highland Park considers the Orkney peated malt to be a part of its whisky's DNA, so the accountants are fighting a losing battle in this instance.

The peat smoke on Orkney is different to that of the mainland, partly due to the lack of trees on the island, which gave up braving Orkney's salty winds a long time ago. Highland Park's peat is a soil-like brown, rich with heather roots and not a lot else. Peat cutting takes place on Hobbister Moor in late spring, where over 350 tons is cut, mostly by hand, in the space of two weeks. The peat's influence is that of a light sootiness, rather than the iodine phenolics of a comparable Islay malt.

Bookending the production process neatly, the second most interesting feature of Highland Park is its wood. Every cask, whether made from American or European oak, is constructed in Spain and loaned out to be filled with Sherry for two years. No bourbon casks have been filled since 2004. Even for Highland Park's core 12-year-old expression, the distillery must be thinking about supply and demand a full 20 years in advance. Daryl Haldane, global brand ambassador, tells me that 'The acid in the Sherry removes the flavours from the wood that we don't want in Highland Park.'

The multitude of expressions that Highland Park produces trace out a battle between Old and New World casks, fought by fresh first-fill warriors and tried (and tested) refill veterans. Each expression is like a debriefing of the aftermath, where one side usually tips the other. For me, it's the strict code of malt and wood that Highland Park adhered to, coupled with the open attitude to explore complex avenues of wood influence over time that defines Highland Park whisky. It's this that makes it some of the most highly respected stuff out there.

HIGHLAND PARK NEW MAKE

The new make has a touch of the quince jelly about it. There's apple, too, with a wisp of smoke and a citrus, grapefruit-zest aroma.

HIGHLAND PARK 10-YEAR-OLD

Nutty, with a syrupy sponge-cake note. Very light and clean on the palate, almost ethereal. Flash of cold tropical fruits and Juicy Fruit chewing gum. An altogether chilly, almost menthol-like dram that is reminiscent of the cold winter winds that haunt the Orkney Islands.

HIGHLAND PARK 12-YEAR-OLD

The first expression ever released and comprising around 25% first-fill American oak Sherry casks. A sweet smell, if that's at all possible, living up to the Highland Park doctrine of sweet honey and soft smoke. Very light heather honey, dried apricots and restrained smoke. Soft on the palate, with a slight cooling effect.

HIGHLAND PARK 18-YEAR-OLD

The malt that put Highland Park on the map, made from 60% first-fill European oak Sherry casks. Bombay mix, dried fruit. Wood spice on the palate. Not a complex dram, but a very well-rounded and complete package.

HIGHLAND PARK 21-YEAR-OLD (47.5% ABV)

Comprising 30% first-fill American Oak Sherry casks. Nutty sherry *flor*, zingy tropical fruits including dried mango and papaya, dried dates and plums, too. Bircher muesli and vanilla custard plus the general linger of an ageing warehouse. Great grip on the palate when mixed with water. Fruit-and-nut-bar finish. A fantastic dram.

HIGHLAND PARK 25-YEAR-OLD (48.1% ABV)

Comprising 20–25% first-fill European oak Sherry casks. Slightly softer on the nose. Benzaldehyde,

Above A strict wood policy is one of Highland Park's defining features.

dried cherry & marzipan and sultana. Warm cotton sheets, toast and butter. Mouth-puckering flavour. Bitter almond linger and a trail of smoke that appears more readily than the 21-year-old expression.

HIGHLAND PARK 30-YEAR-OLD (45.7% ABV)

Intensely floral – think orchid flowers and honeysuckle. Florals are tenacious, too, but give way to some beeswax polished oak and warehouse mist. Powerful on the palate, with a resounding resinousness that leads into a whole bag of candy and a long lick of wood.

HIGHLAND PARK 40-YEAR-OLD (48.3% ABV)

Floral. Elderflower, ground ginger, fenugreek and perfumed honeysuckle suck you in initially. Behind that there's just the lightest whiff of smoke that, over time, has evolved into something medicinal and intoxicating. The palate is chewy – if oak were edible it would feel like this. Darjeeling tea, blinding florals and plenty of dark, brooding wood spice, that drifts into a mixture of sweet dried fruits. Kill me now.

Jura

Jura was the first bottle of whisky that I ever received as a gift. It was a Christmas present from my aunt, who later owned up to the fact that she herself had received it as a Christmas gift the previous year and promptly placed it in the 'unwanted presents' box. I must confess that I wasn't overjoyed and took an immediate dislike to the bottle and branding, but forced the liquid down none the less. I wasn't that delighted with the prospect of visiting Jura, either, but I will admit to having grown to enjoy some of the whisky made here over the years. Just like the whisky bottle, the island's proportions are very lumpy and generally not at all inviting. It's the very definition of remote. In fact, George Orwell, Jura's most famous resident (likely its *only* famous resident) lived there for some time and described the island as 'extremely un-get-at-able'. Even today you must travel via Islay to get there, which in itself is a bit of a hassle. Of course, unless you're visiting the distillery, there's very little reason to 'get-at' Jura at all, as despite being only a little smaller than Islay, it has only one road, one pub,

one shop, and fewer than 200 permanent residents.

The enormous 'paps' (the three towering mountains on the western side of the island) of Jura are the first things you see, which represent an immediate contrast to Islay's flat and feathered terrain. What might not be so obvious, however, are the bogs. Peat bogs. Lots of peat bogs. Which makes it all the more strange that in the past, no peated whisky was made on Jura. Actually, that's not technically true. If you travel back to 1810 where we find the origins of the distillery, we'd no doubt have found that the whisky produced there would have been smoky, as was the general style. The main town of Craighouse – and one-time name of the Jura Distillery – was chosen to be the setting for the premises. For a good 30 years before then, whisky production had been a smugglers' operation, set in the seclusion of a small cave, the walls of which had been tapped to channel a small stream through its

Below Jura's main town. Ok, it's not really, but Craighouse isn't a great deal larger.

middle. After becoming a legitimate distillery, it ran for about a century before finally grinding to a halt in 1910. When distillation historian Alfred Barnard visited in 1885 he found the equipment to be 'of the most modern description', but it would appear that things ran into disrepair over the years (not for the last time) and all the equipment was removed upon its closure. In the 1960s, Jura was brought back from the dead, however. Two local land owners, Robin Fletcher and Tony Riley-Smith, refurbished the distillery to an exceptional standard for the time, and began producing light and fruity malt whisky, which was in great demand by the blenders during that period.

This light and unpretentious approach continued with current owner Whyte & Mackay up until quite recently. The flavour of young Jura is that of mushy yellow fruit, warm cereal and pleasant green things. Not at all offensive, but not especially thrilling either. Now though, we're beginning to see more interesting releases as the distillery finally gets the chance to stretch its legs. Some of them peated, some feature more Sherry influences, on top of the fact that there are some very good older expressions, too. Even though the distillery is once again in fairly poor repair, the future of Jura's whisky is looking more promising. All that remains is to change the style of the bottle and Whyte & Mackay might just have a serious competitor to the Islay.

Above Distillery visitors are offered a free dram for life, every month at the Jura Pub – all part of the Diurach promotional programme.

10-YEAR-OLD (40% ABV)

Golden delicious apple and porridge/oatmeal, with a touch of ripe plum on the nose. Pear drops and lavender on the palate. Drying alcohol sensation on the finish. Not at all deep or complex, but it's not trying to be.

SUPERSTITION (43% ABV)

Light and mineral to begin with, revealing a touch of smoke from the heavily peated portion of malt. Peat continues to come through, but it's softened by fruit and nuts. A graze of tannin on the palate (rhubarb, my father-in-law describes it as), which gives some structure to a dram that needs it.

16-YEAR-OLD

A pungent, honeyed note accompanied by a touch of Wensleydale cheese leads into a familiar citrus tone. On the palate, the cereal is prevalent, sweet as granola and nutty to boot. The sweetness continues into the finish, with just a touch of spice to remind you it's whisky, not a sweet cereal.

PROPHECY (46% ABV)

BBQ ribs, banana and coconut. Intense sweet smoke (but not peat) on the palate, drying into malt and vanilla. Finish is a lingering BBQ pork.

21-YEAR-OLD

The cheese is back again, but this time it's a dry mature Cheddar, giving way to grist, marzipan and rotting apple. Wood comes through when tasting, with sweet cedar and welcome spice to balance it. There's a sturdy mouthfeel in the finish with a touch of sultana/golden raisin and pimento, mellowing into dry, resinous wood spice.

TALISKER

Breathe in a glass of Talisker and it's hard not to be reminded of the coast, with its aromas of seaweed, fishing nets, wet wood and pitch. Squatting off the western coast of the Isle of Skye, the largest of the Inner Hebrides, the tiny remote village of Carbost is Talisker's home, with the head of Loch Harport on one side and the protective teeth-like basalt deposits of the Cuillin Hills rising up inland. The setting is as dramatic as it is fitting for a whisky that is every bit a movie trailer of its own history and setting. As crazy as it may sound, the essence of fire and brine seems to be somehow encapsulated in Talisker.

Even in the early 18th century, when the clans of MacLeod and MacDonald still ruled the land, the whisky from Skye was highly sought-after: Bailie John Steuart, who also gave us the earliest written example of the word 'whisky', was also known to send 'Isle of Skye Champagne' as gifts to foreign wine merchants as far back as 1735. Back then, the population of Skye would have topped 20,000, but 100 years later, it was less than half that.

The island was a headline victim of the Highland clearances that erased whole communities to make way for sheep farms. 'Big' Hugh MacAskill took control of the Talisker Estate in 1825 and set up the Talisker Distillery five years later. The operation required a workforce, which presented an opportunity for families who would otherwise be expedited to the cities and towns. In this manner, the Talisker Distillery was born.

In its first 50 years, the distillery was an epic failure and the cause for at least one bankruptcy and a jail term. Despite all the economic washouts, though, someone (or perhaps the island) was obviously doing something right, leading to Robert Louis Stevenson's famous assertion that Talisker was 'The King 'O drinks, as I conceive it' in 1880. Ten years after that the distillery was rebuilt and went on to enjoy some success. It eventually fell under the umbrella of DCL in 1916, so henceforth became a key component of Johnnie Walker. A fire in the stillhouse destroyed pretty much everything in 1960,

Below Pretty in green and black – colours that neatly summarize the nature of Talisker whisky, too.

but the site was rebuilt and remains a jealously guarded possession of its present owner, Diageo.

And it's in the stillhouse that we find the most intriguing anatomy of the Talisker Distillery. The two wash stills have a kind of drooping U-bend in the lyne arm, as if the plumber earned his money per inch of pipe laid. The bend actually has a purifier pipe at its base that channels less volatile compounds back into the base of the still. Allegedly the spirit here was triple-distilled up until 1925, so the purifier and U-bend, along with the unusual practice of distillation through two wash stills (and the resulting low wines split among three spirit stills), likely goes a long way towards emulating that practice. Copper contact is key in all that, but it's offset by the use of cold worm tubs as condensers, which scavenge back character that would otherwise be lost in a shell-and-tube model. All weird as hell, but it works – the new make is fruity and perfumed, but also briny and oily, with just a touch of sulphur.

Bizarre and ingenious distillation mechanisms put to one side, there is a character on Skye that finds its way into a bottle Talisker. Even in old expressions, there's a primordial battle between mineral and volcanic elements on one side and the wind and the ocean on the other. The good news is that soon we will get to find out whether Skye truly possesses elemental superpowers, because a new distillery is planned. Named Torabhaig, it hopes to conduct its first spirit runs in late 2015 and release its first whisky in 2018.

10-YEAR-OLD

Chocolate coins, heather, blackened cod, warm horsehair and a childhood beach hut. Light and surprisingly delicate to begin with on the tongue, it's perfumed and sprightly like Alka-Seltzer, leading into sweet soot and salty seaweed.

'STORM'

Aptly named, as the aroma is that of fresh peach bellini, banana skin, tar and gull feathers leading into black olive and vanilla paste, with dried seaweed on driftwood. Full and punchy in taste, there's hot chilli and the lingering taste of burnt clothing.

Right Storm is one of many new non-age-statement whiskies that is leading the charge for in-house blending of young and old malt whisky stocks.

18-YEAR-OLD

Beach bonfire, mirror-polished mahogany, and that particularly brittle variety of dark/bittersweet chocolate lead into shortbread and nougat. Full and complex on the palate, beginning with a fruit-compote explosion, honey and a glossy mouthfeel, then the alcohol spices things up revealing nuts, tobacco, pepper, and an electric streak of smoked lemon and lashings of sea breeze. Bitter smoke eases away the long finish.

25-YEAR-OLD

Smoked black pepper and cracked caramel arrive at first. Then there's dried banana with occasional puffs of smoke. Some aromatic spice – ginger and turmeric – lifts off, too, as well as nori. Initial soft and sweet fruit on the palate – creamy, pungent and slightly spicy like sourdough. Then comes a build in heat, with some nougat and a freak splash of seawater taking us into the finish.

* LOWLANDS *

As unromantic as it may sound, the Lowland whisky that we know today has been engineered more by politics and economics than the pursuits of craftsmen and innovators. At the rear end of the 18th century, Lowland distillers were taxed on the size of their stills, not the volume of alcohol they produced, peaking at a rate of £54 ($90) per gallon. This meant that a 200-gallon still would cost you £10,800 ($18,000) a year in taxes – equivalent to over £1 million ($1.68 million) today. The good news was that you would never pay any more tax than that, no matter how much spirit you made. As one would expect, this encouraged the distillers to run their stills as fast as possible, effectively reducing the rate of tax per litre/quart of pure alcohol.

Now, when I say fast, I mean fast. The Lord Commissioners of the Treasury alleged that the Scottish distillers had 'by the ingenuity of their contrivances, found means to discharge their stills upwards of 40 times a week'. The truth was actually far worse, as distilleries developed very shallow, broad, saucer-shaped stills that would speed up the process. The Canonmills Distillery in Edinburgh, owned by John Stein (father of Robert Stein of continuous-still fame - see page 78) is just one example from the time: they were charging their 253-gallon still with wash once every 15 minutes! Naturally, this kind of practice was not conducive to a tasty dram. The Lowlands became synonymous with the affliction 'rot gut', making spirits that were 'only fitted for the most vulgar and fire-loving

Below A patient line of washbacks at the Auchentoshan distillery near Glasgow.

palate'. The gin rectifiers of London were less concerned with this, though, as they flavoured the Lowland spirit with oil of turpentine, oil of vitriol, sulphuric ether and salt to satisfy the London craze. Given that this kind of adulteration was designed to improve the palatability of the product, one can only imagine the filthiness of the raw spirit. Stacked high and sold cheap, the market was wide open for the Lowland distillers, who produced over one-quarter of all the spirit consumed in England at the time.

The introduction of the continuous still in the 1830s (see page 78) was exactly what the Lowlanders had been waiting for – even larger production potential and a far more agreeable spirit. If there was ever any doubt that the Highlands and Lowlands were destined to walk different paths, the industrial revolution sealed the deal. The Lowlands became the base for the powerhouse blends that emerged through the later part of the 1800s, seasoning their 'silent spirit' – named for its comparable neutrality – with the more characterful but less consistent products of the Highlands.

When Alfred Barnard toured Scotland in 1886 there were 31 active distilleries in the Lowland region and all but five were making some kind of pot-distilled whisky. Many of them diversified, like Dundashill in Glasgow, which produced double and triple distilled whisky (as well as continuous-distilled whisky) and sold them separately for blenders. Dundashill wasn't alone in producing triple-distilled pot-whisky; it was one of six distilleries, whether influenced by Irish techniques or simply attempting to emulate the effects of the more price-restrictive continuous still. It's here that the Lowlands' lighter style of malt cemented itself.

Today there are five distilleries currently making whisky in the Lowland region: Aisla Bay, Auchentoshan, Bladnoch, Daftmill and Glenkinchie. Bladnoch very recently fell into the hands of the administrators, and its future is currently uncertain.

Expect to find orchard fruit, grassiness, citrus and clean, sweet traits in younger Lowland malts. As time presses on, the style is diversified by wood influence, but on the whole, this is arguably one region of Scotland that does conform to a specific formula.

SCOTLAND

Lowlands

AUCHENTOSHAN

This distillery that won't be winning any awards for its setting any time soon. Just off the Great Western Road in Clydebank, but notably not actually on the bank of the Clyde itself, it's the thrum of overpasses and the smell of cafeterias doing a roaring trade in square sausages (it's a local speciality) that fill the senses in this suburb of Glasgow. Fortunately, the local spirit is 'nay half-bad'.

Auchentoshan is the only Scottish distillery to distil 100% of its whisky three full times. This, along with a highly selective middle cut of spirit at 80–82% ABV, makes for a very light, fruity and delicate new make. At such a high strength, one would imagine that the spirit is all but devoid of character and more akin to a grain distillate, but that's not the case. The high cut gives the new make a tropical-fruit character that reacts in weird and wonderful ways when introduced to an oak cask.

Nobody is entirely sure when the triple distillation started at Auchentoshan. The distillery was officially founded in 1823, although references to activity on the same site go back further. Certainly towards the end of the 19th century, there were only two 'Old Pot Stills' installed, as recorded by Alfred Barnard in *The Whisky Distilleries of Scotland* (1887). Investing in a few tons of copper before trialing triple distillation would have been a risky move. For that reason, it's likely that triple distillation was going on before the third kettle was introduced and some say, regardless of the number of stills, that Auchentoshan was influenced by Irish methods and likely always triple distilled. Suntory, the current owner, believes that the process was firmly in place by the beginning of the 1900s and the distillery changed hands in 1900 and again in 1903, so perhaps the third still was introduced around that time. Either way, as a keen documenter of the facts, there's something exciting about asking a question that no one knows the answer to!

If anyone knows, it's distillery manager Alistair McDonald, who seems to have a sixth sense about the goings-on at the distillery. He occasionally pauses during our chat, as the pitch of a barely audible background humming rises ever so slightly.

Then, as we walk through the distillery, he sniffs the air and brushes his hand over valves, like the distillery equivalent of a horse whisperer. There's little in the way of automation at Auchentoshan. Most of the valves have pen marks scribbled on.

NEW MAKE
Guava, lychee and pineapple complete the tropical trio of fruits on the nose, which are also reflected on the palate and joined by a buttermilk, nutty flavour and a hot, creamy finish. Essentially, a very delicious new make.

THREE WOOD (43% ABV)
Chewy dried mango, palm sugar, spruce and hazelnut are prevalent on the nose. Water opens up more wood – barrel staves this time. Texture is full and vibrant, with a hit of spice and wood resin, followed by a silky milk chocolate finish. Nice lingering flavours without being too deep or meaningful.

18-YEAR-OLD (43% ABV)
Log cabin and hot chocolate. The wood is beginning to dominate the light spirit here. Creamy to begin with on the palate, with a powdered milk taste protruding through, that is then overpowered by nicely integrated wood spice, vanilla, soft toffee and cacao.

2001 CASK SAMPLE (58% ABV)
Bags of esters on the nose, then nail polish, sweet/candy shop and bubblegum. Water reveals a burst of lemonade and lime leaf. The palate is clean and mellow (with the addition of water) with lemon sherbet, melted marshmallow and a light spattering of wood spice.

1996 CASK SAMPLE (54.5% ABV)
Dark chocolate, caramel and nougat initially on the nose, but a splash of water reveals citrus notes, lemongrass and orange oil. Good grip in the mouth due to some friendly tannins. Not an especially interesting dram to taste, but there's some whacky stuff going on in the smell.

GLENKINCHIE

Glenkinchie was the first malt whisky distillery that I ever visited, and it is a great choice for any first-timer. It's in a beautiful setting for starters, only 30 minutes from Edinburgh, surrounded by the gently undulating fertile farmland of the prosperous East Lothian countryside. The distillery even features a bowling green and gardens that were laid down in 1920. This is barley country, and has been for 2,000 years. Some of the best cereals in the UK are still grown near Glenkinchie – something that Robert Burns didn't fail to notice, describing the land of East Lothian as 'the most glorious corn country I have ever seen'.

Some of the buildings at Glenkinchie date back to the whisky boom of the 1890s, even though operations go back as far as 1825, when the land belonged to the de Quincey family – hence 'Kinchie'. Besides the agriculture that no doubt made Glenkinchie a model of self-sufficiency, there are reasons inside the distillery that warrant a special trip for a first-timer, too. The old malting floors were decommissioned in 1968 and have been tastefully converted into a visitors' museum – the only one of its kind that I know of – complete with not-at-all-miniature model of a working distillery filled with a small army of tiny workers.

For the antique-lovers out there, you'll no doubt love the intact Porteus grist elevator that used to transfer ground malt from the mill into the mash tun. This particular beauty was a feature back when Alfred Barnard visited the distillery in the 1880s.

There's something here for the statisticians, too, as Glenkinchie has the largest wash still in all of Scotland. Weighing in at 30,963 litres (32,700 quarts), it's more like some of the monsters you'll find mentioned in the Ireland pages of this book. The still was actually replaced in 2008, shortly after my initial visit, and I'm told that the whole roof needed to be removed and the new still lowered in by crane. Despite the typical double-distillation process that takes place here, the gigantic proportions of the lantern-shaped stills do mean greater copper contact, more reflux and a lighter, more Lowland-y spirit. However, this is tempered by a very steep descending lyne arm that sweeps volatiles down into a massive cast-iron worm tub containing (wait for it, worm-tub fetishists) an unusual rectangular coil, as opposed to the standard tube configuration.

Only 250,000 bottles of Glenkinchie single malt are sold in a year and, given the 14 nine-ton mashes that occur every week, along with the big stills, this means that the production quota for malt bottling for the year is completed in less than three weeks. Mind you, that malt won't see the light of day for at least another 12 years. The rest will be used in Diageo's many blends, where this Lowland malt tips the scale in a lighter, more fragrant direction.

GLENKINCHIE 12 (43% ABV)

Fragrant and delicate, with a dry malty note and some honey and sweet cut grass. Stewed stone fruit on the palate, but the lightness carries through to with an almost winey character. Wood makes its presence known as the finish creeps in and dries off.

Below Glenkinchie's close proximity to Edinburgh has afforded it the title 'The Edinburgh Malt'.

IRELAND

When Alfred Barnard visited Ireland on his 1885 tour of the 'The Whisky Distilleries of the United Kingdom' (which then, of course, included the whole of Ireland), he found 28, many of which had already been around for a century and a few that had a terrifically large production capacity. Thanks to the consistency that the big distilleries in particular offered, up until the end of the century, Irish whiskey was the obvious choice of tipple for England and the British colonies. Jump forward 100 years and there was only one company making whiskey in the whole of Ireland and no one outside of Ireland drinking it. What the hell happened?

In truth, it was Ireland's complacency and unwillingness to adapt and evolve that became the thorn in its side. While the world tentatively dipped its toes into blended Scotch at the turn of the 20th century, the Irish persevered with pot-distilled whisky and blindly became a victim of their past successes and tradition. It was Ireland's non-committal attitude towards the continuous still that was the crux of the problem. I say this with a sense of irony, since now it's the continuous still that forms the pillar of the currently fast-growing Irish whiskey scene.

By the time they'd cottoned on, the Irish whiskey market was soon subjected to one of the most cut-throat business moves I have ever heard of. In an attempt to cement the dominance of Scotch whisky (but also to destroy the entire memory of the Irish whiskey market), the powerful Scottish Distillers Company Ltd. (DCL) began buying Irish grain distilleries and closing them down. Something needed to be done quickly to protect the industry before all-out meltdown ensued.

The profoundly unromantic solution for Ireland was amalgamation, and so Irish Distillers Ltd. (IDL) was born – a merger of various distilleries that resulted in only the Old Bushmills Distillery in County Antrim, and Midleton Distillery in Cork, remaining in operation. IDL's ensuing dominance over the Irish whiskey market allowed the necessary stock control and pricing that was something akin to inducing a medical coma to keep the body alive. Since then, a new distillery – Cooley – opened in Ireland in 1987, the first new Irish distillery in over 100 years. Eleven years later, and IDL was bought by mega-giant Pernod Ricard, which, in turn, sold the Old Bushmills Distillery to even-more-mega-giant Diageo in 2005: a flicker of the eyelids after a long period on life support for the Irish whiskey market.

It has been the blending of both column and pot whiskies to produce a light and easy style that has propelled the category over the past three decades. This momentum is typified by the most reliable of Irish liquor brands, Jameson, which achieved global sales of around 50 million bottles in 2013, placing it firmly in the top-10 whisky brands of the world. Like a green-and-gold-clad knight doing battle with the white spirits of this world, Jameson has grown by over 20% every year, for the past 10 years – quite incredible.

With positive stories like that filtering around the camp, it's hardly surprising to hear that others have been inspired to fight the good fight. There are 15 new distilleries planned in Ireland over the coming years, three of which are in Dublin. Dave

Left In-house blending is the name-of-the-game in Ireland, achieved through the diversity of mature whisky stocks.

Quinn, master of whisky science at Midleton, tells me they've been giving the new guys a leg-up. 'We're given some of them advice on the technical side of things and see more good-quality Irish whiskey as a positive force for the category', he says. New producers will, of course, open up new blending opportunities – an area where options have been thin on the ground in the past.

New European legislation is on the way, too, which will see the rules regarding the labelling of 'Pot Still', 'Grain' and 'Malt' scrutinized and defined in a similar fashion to that of the 2009 Scotch Whisky Regulations. It's not like it will squeeze any current producers into doing anything differently, but this kind of thing is always a good sign that there's growing interest in a category.

If anything, the final feather in the cap for Irish whiskey today is its massive potential for diversity. From an industry salvaged from the brink of collapse, Irish distilleries now find themselves in the powerful position of being able to tread whatever path they choose. Light and musical flavours have dominated, but I expect to see diversity as the

IRELAND

Teeling

Midleton

overriding theme of the coming years, where some of the oldest distilleries in the world do battle, while the newest and perhaps even the half-forgotten whiskies of saints and scholars once again become a reality.

Below An immense old copper pot-still stands as a garden feature at the front of the Midleton Distillery in Cork.

MIDLETON

When travelling around whisky distilleries, you encounter many people who have spent their entire working lives, and sometimes even some of their childhoods engaged in whisky-making activities. But perhaps none can better claim that whisky runs through their veins and lubricates their bones than the men of Midleton Distillery near Cork. Barry Crocket, the master distiller who retired in 2013 after 31 years in the position, was literally born at the distillery. His father was the master distiller, too, and young Barry's first blinking glimpse of the world was of the bedroom in the Distillers House, where he still works today. Ger Buckley, the master cooper, is the fifth generation of his family to raise and repair casks for whisky-making. Entering his fully functioning workshop at Midleton is like slipping between rips in the fabric of the universe and the musty man-cave of timeless craftsmanship – complete with tools that were handmade by Ger's grandfather.

It's not all tips of the hat and quaint stories of Irish ancestry here, however. The New Midleton Distillery, which opened in 1975, produces seven different brands of whiskies and dozens of expressions, using a range of corn, barley and malted barley recipes, and various combinations of triple pot and column distillation. In fact, it's more like five distilleries under one roof (actually, several roofs) – a result of the amalgamation of John Jameson & Son and John Power & Son, both from Dublin, with Cork Distillery Company back in 1966 to form The Irish Distillers Group – a shrewd move, as the individual distlleries might otherwise have been swallowed up by the impending downturn.

Over 200 people work on the site today, which is nearing the end of a 24-month £160 million ($270 million) renovation that aims to double capacity. They're not stopping there, though, as master distiller Brian Nation tells me: 'We've three more pot stills on order from Forsyth's... they're due for delivery in three years'. The long lead-time is a telling reminder of the demand that the Rothes-based copper fabricator is currently seeing

for distillation equipment. Perhaps Midleton should recycle some of its old copper to speed things up; the adjacent old distillery, which now forms part of the visitors' centre, still holds three inactive pots stills, one of which is the biggest in the world at 143,000 litres (151,000 quarts).

They have seven pots and three columns at present, which already affords a production capacity of 68 million litres (72 million quarts) of pure alcohol per year. The brand-new 'Garden Still House', as it is referred to, is like a giant terrarium of the future, installed on some atmospherically controlled post-earth space-platform. With huge floor-to-ceiling glass walls, it does a great job of celebrating the scale of the three 80,000-litre (84,535-quart) pots, though.

The gigantic column stills work as a set of three. The first is a vacuum still, operating at an air pressure comparable to the summit of Mount Everest, which is heated entirely by energy recycled from the second (atmospheric) and third through a vapour recovery process.

Even cooking cereals here is a state-of-the-art process – the corn for grain whiskey is milled to a superfine consistency, mixed with water and pumped around a flume at 150°C (302°F), before being vacuum-cooled and mixed with malted barley for conversion. There are 24 fermenters, which could easily be mistaken for missile silos, with a total capacity of almost 5 million litres (5.28 million quarts). They're located outside the main distillery housing to keep them cool, but still require additional cooling lines to avoid overheating during the production of the whopping 14.5% ABV grain wash. Midleton also synthesizes all of its bottles using laser beams and genetically modified shamrocks. OK, that last bit isn't true.

Things return to normality when it comes to the wood policy and warehouse management. Most of the 44 warehouses are palletized, containing roughly 1.1 million casks in total. There are a wide variety of barrels used here, from the usual bourbon and oloroso Sherry ones, through

Right & below The brand-new still house at Midleton is truly jaw-dropping.

to Madeira, Malaga wine and even a few Bordeaux casks holding liquids that we might see bottled in the near future, so I'm told. Different casks further diversify the products made at the distillery; like mixing colours on a palette, it gives the blenders a broader range of hues to paint the picture with.

The current range of excellent malt bottlings (Redbreast, Green Spot, Yellow Spot) can be partly attributed to the foresight in developing a diverse wood policy during the difficult period of the 1980s. Green and Yellow Spot, which are both relative new releases, are named after the practice of blobbing coloured paint on casks deemed fit for dumping. Green is daubed on the barrels of 9–10 years in maturity, yellow on a barrel of 12 years old, and blue on a 15.

GREEN SPOT (40% ABV)

Peachy hand cream and a touch of spearmint gum on the nose. Very soft, supple, and sweet. A good hit of tobacco, with vanilla and a finish of soft and ripe guava, with just a hint of tannin. A highly approachable whiskey, with a good amount of subtle complexity.

YELLOW SPOT (40% ABV)

A good hit of bourbon 'air fix' glue on the nose, followed up by honeycomb, vanilla and sandalwood. I could definitely believe this was a

bourbon if tested, but the corn greasiness is replaced with some soft-sherried fruit, dried apricot, crisp tannin, and a long, glossy, wood finish. One of the best Irish whiskies out there.

REDBREAST 12 (40% ABV)

Relatively simplistic on the nose, with a Sherry/caramel battle going on that fizzles out and leaves only generic vanilla descriptors. If ever the word 'smooth' should be used to describe a whiskey, it's probably this one. Soft and clean, to the point of leaving me wishing for perhaps a little more guts... that is, until the spice kicks in accompanied by candied orange and bitter almonds.

MIDLETON VERY RARE 2013 (40% ABV)

Melba of two varieties: toast and peach. Pine cone, black peppercorn and crème pâtissière, which is propped up by a good hit of resinous wood and treacle/molasses. Suspiciously soft, and dare I say it, disappointing on the palate, with lemon balm and nutty vanilla notes.

JAMESON 18 (43% ABV)

Peach yogurt, and musty, dried football-boot mud. Winey and lax on the palate, but delicate with it. Some orange blossom comes through in the soft and short lingering finish.

Through the entire Victorian era, Dublin was a powerhouse of whiskey production. The areas around Thomas Street and the Grand Canal basin were filled with breweries, malting houses and four of the biggest distilleries of the time... of any time: John Jameson & Son; John Power & Son; George Roe & Co.; and William Jameson & Co., which between them had a combined output of over 5 million gallons of pot-still whiskey per year – over twice that of the whole of Campbeltown (the 'whisky capital of the world') during the same era. The spectacle, with the dust, smoke and army of horse-drawn carts carrying people, casks and cereals, must have been remarkable to behold.

The downturn forced the merger of these distilleries into IDL, keeping the brands alive but dampening their identity and individuality in the process. Even today, there are no distilleries in Dublin, although at least three are in the planning stages at the time of writing. In the meantime, The Teeling Whiskey Co. has opened up shop as Dublin's only independent Irish whiskey bottler. Its own distillery may be a few years off right now, but this event will truly herald the Dublin whiskey revival.

And this revival extends to the Teeling family themselves, whose connection with whiskey goes back at least as far as 1782, when Walter Teeling set up a distillery in Marrowbone Lane in Dublin's 'Liberties' district. Skip forward a couple of centuries and Walter Teeling's descendant, John Teeling, becomes the founder of the Cooley Distillery in Co. Louth. The site had formerly been a government-run facility converting potatoes into industrial ethanol, and just before being bought by Teeling it also produced the spirit that went into Bailey's Irish Cream Liqueur. Teeling himself allegedly didn't drink much whiskey, but recognized the need for an independent Irish distillery. It wasn't an easy ride – the distillery was threatened with closure, or worse still, purchase by DCL, but Teeling kept things afloat and increased the portfolio of products to include Connemara, Greenore, Kilbeggan, Lockes and Tyrconnell brands, among others. In 2011, the distillery was sold to Beam Inc. for €71 million.

And so begins a new legacy of Teeling whiskey in Dublin, operated by a new generation of Teeling brothers, John and Stephen. Granted, they're not distilling the stuff themselves yet, but a good amount of the aged stock used to fill these bottles is likely to be from Cooley, so you could argue it was made under Teeling supervision. Early releases seem to be exploring the extremities of the Irish style, which it appears will be the operating manual for things going forward, too. This is important stuff for the category and It's very likely that the products that fill the Teeling portfolio now will later become benchmarks for the fledging Irish distilleries of the coming years.

SINGLE GRAIN (46% ABV)

Supple leather, snapped pencil, oak shavings and pipe residue on the nose. On the palate there's a persistent spice that travels like a white spark towards the back of the tongue - most alarming! And with it comes dryness, oak lactones, vanillin and a finish of brown sugar and rice pudding. In taste alone I could believe it was a very good rum.

SMALL BATCH (46% ABV)

Very perfumed, with orange blossom, walnut, pimento and more than a touch of musk... which together mean one thing: carrot cake. Oil-slick mouthfeel with bouncy fruit that leads into a good hit of wood spice and a clean, mineral finish.

SILVER RESERVE 21 (46% ABV)

A medicinal whiskey, starting with the cool spice of nasal decongestant. There's also a haunting wet dog and mild iodine aroma, reminiscent of a veterinary surgery. On the palate, the iodine is also a constant presence, but more typical whiskey characteristics also join the fray, including soft yellow fruits, damp wood and a slightly astringent finish.

Right Snazzily packaged and delicious to boot, Teeling is ushering in a new era for Irish whiskey.

USA

* TENNESSEE *

I know of no other country or state with a more confusing and contradictory relationship with alcohol than Tennessee. Despite being home to by far the biggest single whiskey producer in North America – Jack Daniel's – in many parts of Tennessee it is still not legally possible to buy a bottle. Temperance and Tennessee go hand-in-hand. With its origins largely in religious teachings, temperance began in the early 1800s and grew deep roots in Tennessee. Temperance leaders attempted to discourage the consumption of alcohol among labourers in order to improve their working habits. Even today there's a tangible stigma in the air when it comes to alcohol, perpetuated largely by an ingrained commitment to the Bible – the sheer number of churches testify to this.

Prohibition law was enforced there as far back as 1838 – the first state to do so – forcing the closure of what they called 'tippling houses' and making the sale of spirits punishable by a fine. The Civil War of 1861 set the Temperance movement back a decade or so, but in 1897, the general retail of spirits in towns of fewer than 2,000 inhabitants was prohibited, meaning that nearly all of rural Tennessee was effectively dry. Incidentally, the production of alcohol in Tennessee was healthy enough, with over 100 registered distilleries at the turn of the century. However, legislation introduced on 20th January 1909, made it illegal to sell any alcohol within a four-mile radius of a school. Then, just under a year later, the Manufacturers Bill came into effect – essentially an all-out ban on the production of intoxicating beverages in Tennessee. In the weeks leading up to the ban, distillers ran at full capacity, selling low-quality hooch and putting anything left over in cask. The numerous people involved in the industry were left jobless. Some distilleries relocated to Kentucky, but their efforts were dashed by nationwide Prohibition a few years later. Only two producers ever returned to Tennessee.

Tennessee whiskey was first officially defined in 1941, and it differentiates itself from bourbon in that must be filtered through sweet maple charcoal prior to maturation. You'd be forgiven for thinking that this would add a sweet-barbecue character to the product, especially since Tennessee whiskies do tend to exhibit that kind of flavour, but the process actually removes certain flavour compounds and adds no sweetness. The important point to remember is that by removing some of the heavier congeners (the substances produced during fermentation other than alcohol) from the white dog, the barrel has a crisper and cleaner sheet of paper to scribble on. Mellowing like this is thought

Left Tennessee Straight white dog runs off the copper pot still at Prichard's distillery in Kelso.

to have been popularized by distillers in Lincoln County around the mid-1800s (hence the name Lincoln County Process), with some sources referencing Alfred Eaton of Lynchburg as the first to trial it, back in 1820. However, there are plenty of examples of charcoal being used as a filtration medium for spirits in Europe before this date.

For the most part, Tennessee whiskies are high in corn content, typically above 80% in their mash bills. This makes for a rather more dessert-like glass of liquor when compared to the dry and fruity high-rye, or wheated bourbons from Kentucky.

Until 2009, it was only legal to distil spirits in three of its 96 counties: Lincoln, Moore and Coffee. State law now extends to a further 41 counties, so expect to see many more distilleries cropping up.

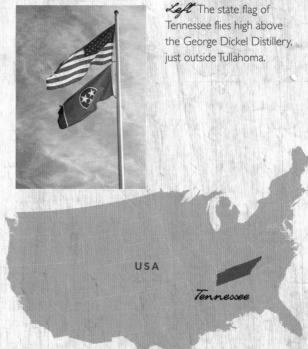

Left The state flag of Tennessee flies high above the George Dickel Distillery, just outside Tullahoma.

USA

Tennessee

Below A life-size statue of Jack Daniel watches over a modern-day operation of staggeringly epic proportions.

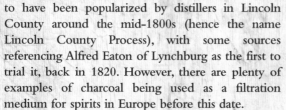

GEORGE
Dickel
TENNESSEE WHISKY
· CASCADE HOLLOW ·

PLEASE ENJOY GEORGE DICKEL TENNESSEE WHISKY RESPONSIBLY

TURN HERE

GEORGE DICKEL

Tullahoma is a mere 20km (12 miles) from Lynchburg, but the former is much bigger on account of its history as a significant railroad town in the late 1800s; this goes some way to explaining its Las-Vegas-style strip (but with fast-food outlets rather than casinos). It also happens to be one of the reasons why John F. Brown and F. E. Cunningham were compelled to establish the Cascade Hollow Distillery there in 1877. The other good reason is the nearby Cascade Springs, which provided all the water required for the operation.

Over the 10 years that followed its opening, the distillery changed hands a few times until the Geo. A. Dickel company bought it in 1888–89. George Dickel was a German immigrant, born in 1811, who practised as a cobbler until he opened a liquor wholesale store in Nashville in the 1860s. His brother-in-law, Victor Schwab, joined the firm some time later and the company became well known for blending and 'rectifying' (flavouring) whiskey, including that sold by the Cascade Distillery. Things went well until 1903, when a new bout of Prohibition fever set in, followed by George's death a year later. From 1910 onwards, the Cascade distillery sought asylum in Kentucky and, for a time, was made in limited quantities at the Stitzel Distillery – that is, until Prohibition was enacted there, too. There is some evidence to suggest that the Cascade brand was made and sold as medicinal whiskey during this period. In 1937, after Prohibition had ended, the Schenley Group purchased Geo. A. Dickel & Co. and shoe-horned production into the George T. Stagg distillery – now called Buffalo Trace.

After Tennessee whiskey's official classification in 1941, the 1950s saw the Jack Daniel's empire begin to swell. Schenley put in an offer for the Jack brand, but this was refused (Brown-Forman later bought JD instead), so Schenley made the decision to re-build the Cascade Hollow Distillery, to increase competitiveness and product range. In 1958, it began bottling a very young corn whisky called 'Pride of Tennessee' while its stocks matured; young Tennessee whiskeys were still bottled under the Cascade brand, but since 'Pride of Tennessee'

competed with Cascade Bourbon, also owned by Schenley, the new product was marketed as George Dickel's Tennessee Whiskey, in 1964. By this time, the recipe had almost certainly changed somewhat when compared to the pre-Prohibition Cascade, but Schenley did go to great efforts to flavour-match old bottles that it had acquired.

George Dickel, just like Jack Daniel's, uses the Lincoln County Process (see pages 176–177). Dickel approached the process in a slightly different way, though, by steeping the whisky in the charcoal pellets for 10–15 days, as opposed to dripping it through continuously. This gives a much longer contact time between the charcoal and spirit, which I liken to steeping coffee in hot water (as in a French press) as opposed to percolating water through coffee. The spirit is also chilled down to around 6°C (43°F) before filtration, which improves the clarity of the final product and helps to remove fatty acids in the same manner as chill-filtering Scotch.

The effect of this proprietary filtration technique is distinguishable when comparing the potent aroma of Dickel's white dog and the soft, buttery nuances of the newly released George Dickel No. 1, which undergoes mellowing, but no maturation in oak. In normal circumstances, a whiskey, by federal law, must be aged in the USA, but this is not the case if it is a corn whiskey – Dickel No. 1 meets that criteria.

At the time of writing the 11 racked Dickel warehouses can hold up to 140,000 barrels, but new palletized warehouses are currently being constructed and will increase capacity by a further 50,000. When I toured the warehouses, one particularly unique practice stood out: as is the norm, the racked warehouses are loaded one barrel at a time by rolling each cask down the shelf. Besides the weight of the cask, one of the biggest problems with rolling casks along the rack is ensuring that the bung resides on top of the barrel when it stops in its final resting place – to minimize the risk of leaks. If the barrel is rolled into position

Right George Dickel is one of only a handful of American whiskies that spells 'whisky' with no 'e'.

Left The person responsible for this particular marketing slogan clearly deserves a pay rise.

GEORGE DICKEL NO. 8 (40% ABV)

A big punch of vanilla, with apricot and tangerine gnashing away in the background. This is followed up by some solid oak lactones and a generous helping of maple syrup. The palate is given a heavy dose of vanilla, with clear and present early maturation characteristics of glossy candy. The finish is soft and subtle, with just a touch of rye spice carrying the flavour through.

GEORGE DICKEL NO. 12 (45% ABV)

The wood aromas here are more butch and burly. Hardwood resin, sticky vanilla toffee and a welcome spiced dark-fruit compote – a result of the wood getting in its stride and working in cahoots with the rye. More voluptuous on the palate than No. 8, this is a golden-corn oil slick of a whiskey, flexing its muscles and showing off deep black-pepper spices and a refreshingly dry finish.

GEORGE DICKEL BARREL SELECT 10–12-YEAR-OLD (43% ABV)

Soft stone fruits shine through with canned peaches and ripe plums. The backdrop is undoubtedly wood, though, but it certainly does not overwhelm. Vanilla sugar, coconut surfboard wax and chamois leather all paint a vivid oak picture. On the palate it is perhaps flatter than I would like, but when the prickly finish subsides, you come to realize that it wasn't the finish at all. All hail oak!

GEORGE DICKEL RYE (45% ABV)

Absurdly sweet aromatics bounce of this glass, like a bag of banana, strawberry and especially chocolate-orange flavoured sweets/candy. The palate offers little in the way of argument, either; the sweet shop continues... but this candy is evil. The sting in the tail is hardy rye spices, which wage bloody warfare with the sugar-coated candy.

with the bung on the bottom, this presents a problem, since all 350 kg (770 lbs.) must then be turned in the highly restricted space at the end of the rack. The burly barrel-men at George Dickel have devised an ingenious method to stop this happening, by marking each rack with a series of numbers that represent hands on a clock face. Before being rolled into position the bung is rotated to a 'minute' that corresponds to its position in the rack. For example, position three in the rack requires the barrel to be loaded at '25P' – positioning the bung at 25 minutes past the hour. With this knowledge, every cask can be loaded on to the elevator in the correct position, then rolled into its final resting place, safe in the knowledge that the bung will finish on the top. Genius.

GEORGE DICKEL WHITE DOG & NO. 1 WHITE WHISKY (45.5% ABV)

The white dog is mossy, with a touch of jalapeño pepper and talcum powder. On the palate, it's spiky and nutty, with just a hint of pear drops and aniseed. The No. 1 White Whisky smells of a cardboard popcorn carton, brown butter, lilacs and chanterelle mushrooms. On the palate, it's very light and rum-like, with just enough nuttiness to convince you otherwise.

JACK DANIEL'S

Jack Daniel's is the best-selling non-blended whiskey in the world. Its iconic square bottle, with black-and-white label, is a brand icon, which, in many ways, transcends the American whiskey category as a whole. Its iconic status is further enhanced by the fact that the same amount of Jack is consumed annually as all the other American whiskeys put together. In 2013, there were 135 shots of Jack Daniel's poured every second. A staggering 750 tons of corn arrive at the distillery every day – enough to fill over 15,000 barrels with white whiskey every week. Brown-Forman currently owns 84 warehouses to hold all this stock and has experimented with gigantic eight-tier steel warehouses, but they were so big they buckled under their own weight and are now held together by huge steel cables.

It seems strange, then, that this global product originates from the tiny town of Lynchburg in Moore County (where it is still produced today), which has a population of less than 400. And even more strange is that Moore County is legally classified as a 'dry county', so JD can't be sold at stores or restaurants in the county. It's this kind of head-scratching logic that surmises the confusing relationship that Americans, and in particular Tennesseans, have had with alcohol for over 200 years.

Mr. Jack, as he is affectionately referred to, was the youngest of 10 children, born to a farming family based in southern Tennessee. Jack was (not to put too fine a point on it) the runt of the litter, and measured only 5 ft. 2 inches (157cm) as a grown man. His problems didn't stop there, though. Jack's mother tragically died giving birth to him, and his stepmother showed him little love. Some legends suggest that Jack ran away from home at the age of six, but in reality, it wasn't until his father died in the Civil War that orphaned Jack moved in with his neighbour, in 1864. Two years later, under the watchful eye of his adopted father,

Right A familiar site in bars all over the world. Jack Daniel's is one of the best known brands, of any kind, in the world.

Dan Call, and a former slave called Nearis Green, Jack was tutored in the art of distillation. How long Jack had been distilling before that is anyone's guess, but the 'boy-distiller' was taught well about the value of corn and the importance of clean water in a distilling operation. On 27th November 1875, after almost a decade of distilling whiskey and moonshine, Jack registered his own company, Daniel & Call, and began distilling on Call's farm.

In 1884, the operation moved to its current resting place in what is now known as The Hollow. The Hollow caught Jack's attention due to its cave spring, the water of which is still used to make Jack Daniel's today. Over the years, the name of the distillery changed to 'Old Time' and eventually the product became known as Jack Daniel's Whiskey. Despite appearing for some time before, the 'Old No. 7' brand wasn't registered until 1908 and is the subject of many a tall tale and a good helping of intrigue. Tour guides of the distillery today prefer to play dumb and perpetuate mythical stories of Old No. 7's origins, but what follows is the truth behind the whole thing.

Every distillery in Tennessee was registered in a tax district, and within that district, given a unique number. Originally, Daniel & Call were registered in the fourth district, and they were given the

This page The small town of Lynchburg, Tennessee, is nothing short of a Jack Daniel's theme park. It's ironic then that the law prohibits anyone from actually buying a bottle of Jack Daniel's Old No. 7 in the county.

now-famous number 7. However, the fourth district was later merged with the fifth district, and they were given a new unique number, '16'. Their old number, by which they were recognized by wholesalers and customers alike, was lost. So they decided to put 'Old No. 7' on the bottle.

Despite reportedly being engaged six times in his life, Jack never married or had any children. In 1887, Jack's nephew, Lemuel Motlow, came to work for him, having been a part-time errand boy since 1880. Jack saw the opportunity, and began training 'Lem' to be his successor. This would pay off, as it was Lem that drove the Jack Daniel's brand in to the 20th century and establish the brand for what it is today.

As for Mr. Daniel himself, sadly his money got the better of him, but in a more literal sense than you might imagine. At the age of 55, Jack had the robust appearance of a man who enjoyed rich foods and whiskey. One day in 1904, he arrived at his Lynchburg office and, after struggling with the combination lock on his safe, he angrily kicked it. His foot was badly bruised, and perhaps broken, but it went untreated and over time eventually became gangrenous. Successive amputations over the coming years left him with no leg at all, and Jack eventually died from the infection on 9th October 1911. The guilty-looking safe can still be seen at the distillery in Lynchburg today.

When the Manufacturers Bill took effect in 1910, Lem Motlow moved the entire operation to St. Louis, Missouri. Sadly, a fire in 1913 ravaged the distillery, and Lem barely had it back in working order before nationwide Prohibition took effect in 1920. Production stopped altogether during this period and, even when Prohibition was repealed in 1933, much of the state of Tennessee, including Moore County, remained dry (and still does today). It wasn't until 11th November 1938, after a great deal of petitioning from Lem Motlow, that the law was relaxed to allow production in Lynchburg. The first new barrel of Jack Daniel's was rolled into the warehouse after 35 years of inactivity. By the time World War II had begun, the brand had barely had time to surface for air. Even in the years following the war, production slowed and even stopped due to the unavailability of the correct grade of corn – a stubborn insistence on

Lem Motlow's part that later granted Jack Daniel's a reputation for superior quality. Even as late as 1951, a reporter for *Fortune* magazine wrote an article with the opener 'If you've never heard of Jack Daniel's whiskey, so much the better. Its relative obscurity is part of its charm.'

After Motlow's death in 1947 (a full 67 years after his first day's work at the distillery), the company was run by Lem's four hands-on sons, who grew the business successfully until its sale to Brown-Forman (the current owner) in 1956. It was the clever 'backwoods' advertising campaign that propelled the product into stardom, by playing off the small-town, slow-paced lifestyle that the square black-and-white bottle stood for – similar ad campaigns can still be seen today. Before too long, the well-kept secret that was Jack Daniel's Tennessee Whiskey had become not so well-kept at all.

JACK DANIEL'S OLD NO. 7 (45% ABV)

Before you taste Jack, give it a good rub on your hands and have a sniff. That smell is as close as you can get to the aroma of a bourbon warehouse. The aroma is unquestionably banoffee pie and barbecue. There are glazed pecans, too, and a hint of butter and pancake batter. On the tongue, it is sweet and slick, like banana custard, with plenty of vanillin, a little hint of tobacco ash and a kind of vacant finish.

JACK DANIEL'S GENTLEMAN JACK (40% ABV)

Crisper, cleaner and generally more gentlemanly. The aroma is softer and less smoky, allowing the vanilla and banana to take a stronger grip. Softer and supple in taste, the finish has a lick of soft fruit and drifts off quite quickly.

JACK DANIEL'S SINGLE BARREL (45% ABV)

Maple-wood floor, banana and peanut-butter milkshake and superglue hit the nose. This leads on to more wood aromas, with treacle/molasses tart, anise, and plenty of vanilla. On the palate there are darker suggestions of some wood spice and a hint of pepper... and a neutral heat that's quickly covered up with honeycomb and clotted cream.

PRICHARD'S

The Prichard's Distillery is a relative newcomer to the whiskey-making game and Tennessee's first new distillery in 50 years. First licensed in 1997, Phil Prichard, the founder, gave up a life of farming and technical dentistry (he used to make dentures) and moved back to his home state of Tennessee with the dream of making American rum. Almost 20 years later, and the Prichard's ever-expanding portfolio now consists of over a dozen products, including rye, malt, Tennessee and bourbon whiskies. But Prichard's is an altogether more 'boutiquey' operation than its famous neighbour (its output in a week is roughly equivalent to what Jack Daniel's bottles in 10 minutes).

It was the mid-1990s and Phil Prichard was placing the finishing touches to his home-made still, pieced together from copper pipes and a large turkey baster. He eventually took the plunge and snapped up two old pot stills from a seller in Vermont. Phil Prichard chose the small settlement of Kelso as the home for his distillery, and an old grade school as the premises. It started in the back room to begin with but gradually, as the company has grown, the 30-strong team has begun to occupy the entire building and has recently opened a second site in Nashville to keep up with demand.

The haggard, worn exterior of the school in Kelso would have you believe that some unsavoury types were squatting inside. Inside though, there's a hive of activity going on. The stillhouse is the old cafeteria, the offices and bottling line are the old classrooms, and the gymnasium has been converted into a stock-holding area. Phil Prichard's office is the old teachers' lounge. Outside, two container units, vulnerable to heat and rain, have been dumped in the playground and filled with casks of maturing spirit.

Their 'Single Malt' is, as the name suggests, made from 100% malted barley and aged in new 15-gallon white-oak casks. It's a blatant attempt to accelerate the maturation process by using a tiny ripe cask, but the effect is a tasty dram. It would appear that the huge one-week fermentation period did a good job of drumming up some interesting esters and aldehydes.

There's a rye whiskey, too, as well as a Tennessee (more on that shortly) and two varieties of bourbon. Now, the bourbon is not actually distilled at Prichard's; they buy it in from one of the large Kentucky producers (Buffalo Trace is my guess) after four years' ageing, then put it back into a cask for another two years. The result is a deep, rich hue and the sensation of being bitch-slapped on the tongue with a stave. They have even trademarked its name, 'Double Barreled'. There's

Left This school cafeteria once dished out meals for kids. Today, there's a very different kind of 'cooking' going on.

also a Double Chocolate Bourbon (non-trademarked), which undergoes the second maturation with a helping hand from some cacao nibs, which are supplied by a local chocolatier. It's an interesting product that nicely balances the fine line between enhancing natural flavour and adulteration.

The Tennessee whiskey (70% corn, 15% rye, 15% malt) is unique among its peers because it isn't charcoal-mellowed. On 13th May 2013, new state legislation was introduced that required all Tennessee whiskey to be charcoal-mellowed. Prichard's had already been producing its own unmellowed whiskey for a few years by that point, so Phil Prichard sought an exemption from the bill and was successful. The revised bill now states that any distillery that was granted a license between 1st January 2000 and 1st January 2001 need not comply with the Lincoln County Process. Prichard's is the only Tennessee distillery that meets this requirement and, unless the law is changed further down the line, no other Tennessee whiskey will ever be able to, claim this. The irony of all this is that Prichard's is the only distillery currently operating in Lincoln County itself!

PRICHARD'S TENNESSEE WHISKEY (40% ABV)

There's a healthy hint of rye here that the other Tennesseean's don't have, giving it aromas of banana bread, sultanas/golden raisins and dried apricots. The taste also announces rye pepperiness and good action on the mid-palate. The dry grip continues, even exhibiting some tannin that both adds structure and flattens any subtlety that might have been there.

PRICHARD'S SINGLE MALT WHISKEY (40% ABV)

Immediately, you pick up aromas of green malt, golden syrup/light corn syrup, chestnut and damp meadowsweet. It's viscous, nutty and sweet on the palate. A highly approachable, clean and delicate single malt, but lacking some balls. More like an Irish pot-still whiskey than a Scotch malt.

Above A rather neat solution to the problem of where to store your barrels: a shipping container.

PRICHARD'S DOUBLE BARRELED BOURBON (45% ABV)

You pick up hard-ball caramel, sticky toffee pudding and the overwhelming sensation of being locked in a oak coffin; on the palate, it's like you're licking your way out! Massive resinous oak notes crush the fragile world around you. There's a long, dry finish with spikes of oak lactones that hiccup through you like the sobbing memory of an emotionally charged experience (it's nice, but unbalanced).

PRICHARD'S DOUBLE CHOCOLATE BOURBON (43% ABV)

There's overwhelming hazelnut praline on the nose, which slips into popcorn and chocolate foil (the wrapper). There's a touch of pistachio and cashew there, too, and in the mouth it's heavy and voluptuous. The initial flat chocolate notes subside to reveal nutty sweetness and a Szechuan-style fuzzy tingle. The finish is like scalding chocolate sauce and white pepper. The dry glass smells of dark oak resin.

PRICHARD'S RYE WHISKEY (43% ABV)

The initial hit of diesel fumes is followed by brilliant sour plum, nutmeg, cocoa and cherryade. The taste is pleasant, but lacking the exuberance that the nose alerted us to. There's nuttiness, spice and some vanilla, but distinction is sadly lacking.

* KENTUCKY *

It starts with perfect corn-growing conditions – the basis for all bourbon whiskey. Then, iron-free, limestone-filtered water, with a high pH and in need of sour-mashing – which in turn gives flavour. Hot summers and cold winters stretch and constrict new-oak casks in unnatural ways, accelerating maturation and injecting character into the spirit. New railroads and old rivers form the transportation network required to get the product to market. And finally, the first families of bourbon whiskey – Beam, Brown, Samuel, Van Winkle and Williams – provide the hard graft that forms the whiskey-making culture still resonating through the state today. This is Kentucky, where bourbon is made.

Bardstown and Lousiville make up the two spiritual homes of Kentucky bourbon. At the turn of the 20th century, Lousiville, Kentucky's largest city, had a population of 200,000 – more than Los Angeles and Atlanta put together. There were around a dozen whiskey distilleries there at the time and Louisville's infamous 'Whiskey Row' fluctuated between 60 and 90 vendors at the height of its powers. The whiskey boom had painted the town gold, and its residents were reaping the rewards. Just 20 miles south, in Nelson County, sits the much smaller settlement of Bardstown, where the most common surname in the phonebook is Beam. Once home to no fewer than 20 distilleries, Nelson County now has only two: Heaven Hill (also owned by Beam) and Tom Moore.

Below The old Labrot & Graham towers are still visible at the Woodford Reserve Distillery in central Kentucky.

Prohibition was, of course, the cause of all this. Only six distilleries in all of the US were granted licences to distil during Prohibition: Schenley, The American Medicinal Spirits Company, Brown-Forman, Frankfort Distilleries, W. L. Weller and A. Ph. Stitzel – all of them in Kentucky.

The marketplace for these producers had shrunk considerably, however, as whiskey was available only through a medical prescription. This meant that, in reality, only doctor's surgeries and hospitals were in a position to purchase it. The concept of prescription whiskey still echoes through to some of the bourbon products available today, present in the style of labelling and even the name of the product. Over 100 million alcohol prescriptions were issued during Prohibition and, while the prescription whiskey ticket afforded the six distilleries the opportunity to weather the storm, business was not at all good.

Following Prohibition, the Kentucky bourbon industry was miraculously brought back from the dead. Many distillers, who had turned their hands to other professions – like Jim Beam, who was for a short time a fruit farmer – came back to their former lives. Suffice it to say, the demand for good liquor was high. New regulation was introduced in the 1930s, which required that liquor could no longer be sold by the barrel, and that whiskey labelled as 'Straight' had to be aged in new- oak casks.

Today Kentucky bourbon is the fastest-growing whiskey category. In 2012, Maker's Mark grew by 10%, Evan Williams by 10%, Jim Beam by 8% and Wild Turkey by a massive 18% – making it the second-fastest-growing global spirits brand that year (Bombay Sapphire gin was first). This growth can be partly attributed to the demand for single-barrel and barrel-strength products, but much of it is simply a generally greater export demand from European nations, like the UK, Germany, France and Spain.

To truly understand what makes Kentucky uniquely special among American whiskey, you first have to understand the unique nature of each distillery. Pursuit of good liquor unites them, but the route to get there is what defines them.

Above Buffalo Trace is more like a well-maintained industrial town than a whiskey distillery.

Right Every corner and pathway is a picture-postcard of a scene at Woodford Reserve.

USA

Kentucky

Right Experimental casks of whiskey at Buffalo Trace only hint at the crazy schemes that are being dreamed up behind the distillery's doors.

BUFFALO TRACE

Driving up to the Buffalo Trace Distillery feels a bit like you're entering post-apocalyptic fortress, cobbled together over a century or so in efforts to make it secure and self-sufficient from invading packs of zombies. Parts of the original Old Fire Copper Distillery, which dates back to 1777, still remain, but newer buildings have been constructed, too, made from limestone, wood-fired clay bricks, timber, steel and marble. Names have changed over the years: OFC, then Stagg, Schenley, Ancient Age, Leestown and, finally, Buffalo Trace. The whole place is like a patchwork quilt of mismatched walls and roofs, workplace to a dedicated community of over 300 souls, and a distillery operation like no other in the world.

At one time, over 1,000 people worked here and they even had an onsite cooperage, fire department and hospital. The scale is still visible today and besides the fairly typical spirit-making equipment, Buffalo possesses one-of-a-kind machinery for processing distillery by-products. Every ounce of spent mash passes through evaporators, presses, mills and roasters, and gets processed into animal feed for dogs, shrimp, catfish and cattle. This means that trucks delivering the corn, wheat, barley and rye don't just go back empty to the farm they came from; the same truck collects animal feed that's ready to be sold back to farmers. Many ultra-modern distilleries do the same trick, but not with unique, antique machinery. There's a huge workshop on the grounds that fabricates replacement parts for much of this equipment, as, in many cases the original manufacturer went bust many decades ago. Freddie, our tour guide, who is the third generation in his family to work at Buffalo, tells us that the price they sell the feed for is almost the same price they pay for incoming cereals.

Freddie's grandfather worked at the distillery from 1912 until 1964 and his son (Freddie's father), James 'Jimmy' Johnson, handled every barrel of whiskey in the distillery from the commencement of operations after Prohibition until he retired over 40 years later. Jimmy was welcomed back to the distillery in 2008 to roll the 6,000,000th barrel since the end of Prohibition. This cask now stands proudly on its own at the distillery, in what is touted as the smallest bonded warehouse in Kentucky. Jimmy passed away in 2011 at the age of 94. In 2013, another legend was lost in the form of the long-time master distiller Elmer T. Lee, who worked there from 1949 until 1985.

'Honour tradition, embrace change' is the distillery motto, and it would be hard to argue that they don't live up to it. Harlen Wheatley, the master distiller, can monitor and control the old column still from anywhere in the world by using computer software and a mobile/cellphone application. The spent beer from the still is run through a heat exchanger, which provides 100% of the energy needed to heat the one-of-a-kind doubler. Most of the water requirements (1.5 million gallons a day, to be exact) come straight from the Kentucky River, which winds around the cluster of distillery buildings.

The distillery runs five different mash bills to facilitate its remarkable 40-plus product list, which includes Kentucky whiskey, wheated bourbon, rye bourbon, and straight rye. You'll recognize some popular brands – most notably W. L. Weller, Sazerac Rye, Blanton's, Eagle Rare and Pappy Van Winkle.

The master blender for all this is Drew Mayville, a man with an easy smile and a twinkle in his eye, like there's a joke and he's still deciding whether or not to let you in on it. 'The real fun', he says, 'is experimenting with warehouse conditions. The materials, the height of the rick, and the position of the warehouse in relation to the sun and environmental elements – all of these things affect the product.' To give you an idea of this in practice, when a warehouse was destroyed by a tornado and the surviving bourbon tasted delicious, they built a new warehouse ('X'), which is partially exposed to the elements to try and emulate the conditions. 'We're still learning' Drew tells me, pausing for a moment to widen his grin a little, 'and we haven't made our best whiskey yet'

BUFFALO TRACE WHITE DOG (62.5% ABV)

This white dog smells of apricots and polenta, with a touch of mustard seed coming through at the back. On the palate it's oily, but not greasy with a smattering of cut grass and warm smell of hay.

BUFFALO TRACE RICE MASH 9-YEAR-OLD (45% ABV)

Presents nothing too out-of-the-ordinary on the first sniff, with aromas of cocoa butter, vanilla and butterscotch all present and correct. A second dip, however, uncovers a floral note that's not normally present. On the palate there's a serious amount of sweetness and a cleanness that I would normally associate with sake. Besides that, typical Buffalo flavours prevail.

BUFFALO TRACE WHEATED BOURBON 10-YEAR-OLD (45% ABV)

Possesses much more brown flour, anise and peppery notes on the nose. At first it feels like an altogether more savoury affair, but the wheat sweetness soon kicks in. Very full on the palate, with intense heat (but I like it) and lip-smacking sweet/dry balance. A residual taste of brown sugar is accompanied by dates, crème caramel, nutmeg and vanilla.

EAGLE RARE 17 (45% ABV)

There's a (pleasantly) large amount of corn on the nose, along with exploding dark cherries and the aroma of the paint thinner shelf in my garage (I have a whole shelf for it). It's a brilliantly complex taste that builds up into a rich spice mixture with tannin adding structure to the whole thing. It's full-bodied, too, with a long, sleepy creme brûlée finish.

GEORGE T. STAGG 2013 RELEASE (64.1% ABV)

This one is nutty and corny, and less sickly sweet, but still gives off coconut sunblock and hot sand. Plenty of sugar on the palate, though – thick, syrupy and massively concentrated – crescendoing into jalapeño as fruit attempts to gain traction, but is vaporized in the maelstrom.

Above A Buffalo Trace beer font? No – that's white dog that runs out of there!

WILLIAM LARUE WELLER 2013 RELEASE (68.1% ABV)

Air-fix glue on the nose and that seems like all, but there's an effeminate, musky note in the background, like warm blonde hair. Fruit comes through eventually – blueberry ice cream. On the palate, the second sip (first is a dud and used only to overcome the alcohol) is creamy vanilla sponge cake leading into tempered spice. Back to the nose and there's white chocolate now. More pepper on the palate, easing away gently.

BUFFALO TRACE 19-YEAR-OLD EXPERIMENTAL (45% ABV)

Distilled in 1991 and bottled in 2010

Thick beeswax polish and remnants of pipe tobacco and glossy maple wood on the nose. The taste is not as sweet as expected; there's a dryness here from flint and old wood. The finish is disappointingly short-lived.

BROWN-FORMAN

George Garvin Brown, perhaps the most influential figure in bourbon's history, was born in Munfordville, Kentucky, in 1846. He moved to Louisville to attend high school, where his older half-brother had already established himself as a successful whiskey trader on 'Whiskey Row' in downtown Louisville. The pair joined forces in 1870 and formed J.T.S Brown & Brother Co. They released their now legendary Old Forrester (one 'r' was later dropped) bourbon in 1873 – named for the local celebrity physician William Forrester – to the trade exclusively in glass bottles, that is, you couldn't buy it any other way. The modern day Brown-Forman will tell you this was a move that guaranteed the quality of the product, and while that may be partly true, the real reason was to grow sales in the lucrative 'prescription whiskey' market. Most whiskey at the time was sold only in large containers, and by offering their product in small glass bottles, it became much easier for physicians to prescribe the whiskey to patients (for all manner of ailments) and to have some assurance of its quality. This marked the beginning of a new era of brand marketing for bourbon producers and brand-calling for consumers, along with counterfeiting activity by those looking to make a few bucks off the back of a successful bourbon brand.

George Forman joined in 1872 and took on a role in accounting. Two years later, J.T.S. Brown parted company and, in 1890, the company name became Brown-Forman. With Brown on sales and Forman on accounts, business grew quickly in the first 30 years. In 1894, Brown was elected the first president of the National Liquor Dealers Association and in that same year, he was elected president of the Wine & Spirits Association, an organization founded to fight the rising tide of Prohibitionist activity. In 1910, George Brown even published a book entitled *The Holy Bible Repudiates Prohibition*, which basically listed hundreds of bible references that mentioned 'wine' or 'strong drink', 'proving that scriptures commend and command the temperate use of alcoholic beverages'. In short,

George Brown was an everyday crusader for the steady consumption of quality bourbon whiskey. He died in 1917.

There's a lot of history between Old Forester and the town of Louisville. In 1937, intense rainfall caused the Ohio River to flood its banks, so a 550-metre (1,800-ft) floating pontoon bridge was constructed from empty Brown-Forman casks to move people from Jefferson Street to Baxter Avenue and dryer areas in Crescent Hill and the Highlands. Over 75,000 people crossed the makeshift bridge in four days.

In 1946, Brown-Forman acquired a rifle-stock manufacturing company on the outskirts of Southern Louisville and converted it into a cooperage. Today, Louisville's Bluegrass Cooperage is the only distillery-owned cooperage in America, producing approximately 45% of the world's supply of new whiskey barrels annually. The Bluegrass Cooperage raise around 2,500 casks a day and about 90% of them are filled with Jack Daniel's. The rest are used for Early Times, Old Forester and Woodford Reserve, which are made to a slightly different recipe than the other bourbons, with a heavier toast and lighter char. These barrels once used then go on to other whisky distilleries around the world, or to tequila and rum makers. Incidentally, the 'other' cooperage in the US is The General Stave Company, which supplies barrels to the remainder of the bourbon industry.

The modern-day Brown-Forman Distillery makes Old Forester bourbon and Early Times whiskey. The distillery today is not open to visitors, and has an unashamedly 'let's get down to business' feel about. It's clean, efficient, functional and not at all pretty. Old Forester uses a higher rye content mash bill than Early Times, and is aged entirely in new charred oak; Early Times uses some refill casks – hence the non-bourbon denomination.

One major point of interest in the distillery is the use a 'thumper' instead of a 'doubler' for distilling, wherein the alcohol vapours from the beer still are pumped through a small pot still containing water. (See more on this on page 79).

The warehouses on site hold a whopping 320,000 casks, and are split between Early Times, Old Forester and Woodford Reserve stock. The warehouse temperature is cycled using steam, which increases from 15°C (59°F) up to 26°C (79°F) and back again over the course of eight weeks. The benefit of this system is that it improves consistency and avoids stocks at the top of the warehouse getting hotter than those at the bottom. This also means that evaporative losses are more consistent throughout the warehouse and the alcohol content from cask to cask is consistent, too. Secondly, it speeds up certain elements of the maturation process by emulating seasonal effects. The mathematics doesn't quite make sense from my end, but Brown-Forman believes the effect can be compared to two complete seasonal rotations in the space of time that it takes to do one (for those not paying attention, that's a year).

EARLY TIMES (40% ABV)

Coconut, candy floss/cotton candy and bullets of popcorn. On the palate, there's more dark candy in the taste, but it's a layer over a backdrop of pipe tobacco and musty warehouse notes. The finish is sweet and surprisingly long.

OLD FORESTER (43% ABV)

Green apple (which was an aroma that powerfully emanated from the fermenters when I visited previously) is mirror-polished with toffee and allspice. There's crème Anglaise and vanilla popcorn, too, with some more bubblegum rye surfacing after a few sniffs. The taste is spiced and woody, leaving a slick caramel finish. The less-refined twin of Woodford Reserve.

Below Huge fermenters at the Brown-Forman Distillery emit the unmistakeable smell of green apple and lavender.

WOODFORD RESERVE

If someone dropped you inside the Woodford Reserve Distillery and asked you guess where in the world you were at that point, there's a good chance you'd say Scotland. The landscape of Woodford County is that little bit more undulating than the rest of Kentucky. Many of the Woodford Reserve buildings are made from limestone, in the style of a traditional Scottish farmhouse. The five striking red cypress wood fermenters are reminiscent of the Scottish washback. There are even three copper pot stills that would look just as comfortable in the still-house of Auchentoshan. The 202-hectare (500-acre) site seems peaceful and serene when compared to the 'factory' feel of some of the other Kentucky distilleries; Woodford even has a distillery cat, Elijah, that clambers around the warehouse ricks. All that's required to complete the picture is a lashing of rain and a couple of kilts.

There's a reason for all these nods to Scotland. Elijah and Sarah Pepper built a cabin here in 1812, which was quickly followed by a watermill and whiskey distillery. Their decision to locate there was no doubt a result of Glen's Creek River, and the mineral-rich spring – now known as the Pepper Spring – that emerges from the riverbank. In 1825, Elijah died, and Oscar Pepper, his son, took over. Oscar called in a helping hand from a Scottish distiller by the name of James Christopher Crow. Under the watch of Crow and Pepper the distillery grew, and it was 1838 that saw the construction of many of the limestone buildings that exist today. 'Crowpep' (as I like to call them) are often credited with revolutionizing the bourbon industry by drawing attention to the necessity of recording details and maintaining a hygienic and safe operation; we have them to thank for pieces of sanitary advice, such as 'Always keep sheep and livestock at least 200 yards (180 metres) from the fermentation vats.' As Chris Morris, the current master distiller puts it, 'They did not invent anything, but they perfected everything.'

All of the whiskey made at Woodford Reserve is made using Pepper Spring water, which the Woodford engineers have gone to great lengths to ensure does not surface before reaching the distillery; this trick neatly avoids what would normally be a legally required purification process. Instead, it is simply particle-filtered, then sent to the mash cooker. Chris Morris equates much of the floral aromatics of Woodford to the Pepper Spring water, but I'd say that the triple-distillation process and high rye mash bill (18% ABV) have a lot to answer for, too.

And speaking of mashing, Woodford grinds its cereals finer than any other distillery, into an almost flour-like consistency. Why? Well, that would be a requirement of its triple-pot-distillation process. Unlike malt whisky, bourbon and rye are almost always fermented and distilled without filtration – this means the liquid entering the still is like a thin porridge/oatmeal. Column stills handle the beer solids by ejecting them from their base once all the alcohol has been extracted. But during a pot-still cook, the solids are free to burn onto the sides of the still and cause all sorts of havoc. To overcome

Right The master distiller of Woodford Reserve, Chris Morris, takes a modern approach to retrieving cask samples.

Above Some things are still done the old-fashioned way.

this problem, (in truth they're only reducing the issue rather than solving it) Woodford performs a caustic wash every day (after every fourth run) on the beer still, to remove all the cooked-on crud. The beer still has a specially designed conical bottom that helps remove the spent beer solids as well – a unique innovation.

Both the beer and high wines still conduct two complete distillations before the 55% ABV liquid is sent to the third (spirits) still and concentrated up to 79% – just under the legal limit. The white dog is cut back down to 55% ABV for maturation. Chris Morris argues that the spirit requires less additional water after maturation because of its low fill-strength; ultimately the liquid in a bottle of Woodford Reserve has had 14% more contact with wood (his calculation, not mine) than had it been filled at 63% ABV. Either way, half the volume of the cask is lost during the seven-year average ageing period, when it emerges at around 67% ABV, gets blended with some column-distilled bourbon from the Old Forester Distillery – the details of this are a bit sketchy but I believe it's about 50/50 – and bottled as Woodford Reserve bourbon.

As for the 'masters collection' whiskies, I am told are all 100% pot distilled in Woodford County. The range has been met with mixed reactions. A word to the wise – if you can get hold of the two malt whiskies, both of which are unexceptional by themselves, try blending them and you'll be rewarded with what I believe is a superior product.

WOODFORD WHITE DOG

Heavy and round with sultanas/golden raisins, plums and cherry stone and something not dissimilar to a mince pie. There's a residual, fusel-oil note there, too, and a 'green' zing of youth. On the palate, it's hot and more than a little sulphury, which is no doubt the backbone of what is to come during maturation.

WOODFORD RESERVE CASK SAMPLE

Filled 07/11, Dumped 03/14

Initially on the nose there's buttered brown toast and pecan. This leads into some cereal aromas, finally picking up lychee, rose hip and other red fruits. On the palate, there is less in the way of complexity, with a streak of pepper and some vague glue-like notes. The finish is surprisingly long, slip-sliding away into a pit of wood toast and resin.

WOODFORD RESERVE DISTILLER'S SELECT (43.2% ABV)

Surprisingly citrus at first, with toffee coming through, like lemon bonbons. It smells syrupy, sweet and stewed. The taste is refined and defined, with more lemon and a herbal note that gets washed away by oak spice and some drowning burbles of rye fruit. The finish is citrus and wood.

WOODFORD CLASSIC MALT – EX-BOURBON CASK (45.2% ABV)

Bakewell tart, peanut shells and dust. A touch of toasted almonds. There's cereal on the palate, with a smear of dry cherry in the finish with even a hint of 'craisins'. Lacking a little on the finish and perhaps guilty of being a bit too young.

WOODFORD STRAIGHT MALT – NEW CASK (45.2% ABV)

Slap in the face of coconut ice cream, with a big vanilla hit to boot… this is all about the cask. Plenty of residual sugar. Traces of malt have been crushed here by the big, bumbling wooden container.

WOODFORD RYE – NEW CASK (46.2% ABV)

Treacle tart and warm sand greet the nose on this fruity-smelling whiskey. This follows into banana sugar, dry cacao, nutmeg and brittle, rotten wood, with a slightly herbaceous note. On the palate, it's full and juicy, with a hint of mint that is quickly trounced by fruity wood. The finish is fruity tobacco.

FOUR ROSES

Two years into Prohibition, the Paul Jones Company purchased the Frankfort Distilling Company and its Old Prentice Distillery (OPD). Although like all other distilleries it was rendered nonoperational, it was one of six distilleries granted permits to sell its existing stocks of bourbon for medicinal purposes. The OPD was actually located just across the road from a long-gone distillery that produced 'Old Joe' whiskey, which is thought to be bourbon's oldest brand. The Frankfort distillery is one of the only examples of a distillery that stayed afloat during Prohibition, accounting for roughly one in every five bottles of whiskey sold in the USA. When Prohibition ended in 1933, it had a good head start, and when Seagram bought the Four Roses brand in 1943, it was the top-selling bourbon in America. So it was slightly shocking when the company took the decision two years later to focus on export markets, like Japan and Europe, and bottle a blended Four Roses for US stores. Seagram was a Canadian company, so blends and blending came naturally to it, but by all accounts the liquid was pretty bad, a combination of aged and up to 66% unaged spirits from Seagram's Lawrenceburg, Indiana and Maryland distilleries. Consumer faith in the company plummeted in the US after Seagram attempted to dupe the public with identical packaging to the old bourbon, but with the word 'bourbon' quietly removed. This newly acquired 'bourbon' was ushered out of the marketplace to make way for Seagram's '7 Crown' and 'VO' Canadian whiskies – cannibalization, in effect.

Four Roses Straight Bourbon continued to be produced for export, however, but true to the Canadian way, it was blended from five distilleries (located in Athertonville, Fairfield, Louisville and Cynthiana), along with the Four Roses Distillery in Lawrenceburg. All five Seagram bourbon distilleries used the same yeast 'V' yeast culture at the time. Slowly the distilleries got mothballed, but each of their unique styles was re-imagined in Lawrenceburg by introducing new yeast strains into the mix. Jim Rutledge, Four Roses' master

distiller, doesn't draw any direct comparisons between the old whiskeys of the closed distilleries. 'It's the water they used that characterized the product,' he says. 'Instead, we use yeast to create a diverse stock of bourbon that can be blended to our unique flavour profile.' Jim uses five proprietary yeast strains, each coded by the letters 'K', 'O', 'Q', 'F' and the original 'V'. In addition to the yeast, Four Roses uses two separate mash bills: 'B', which contains 35% rye, and 'E'- which has 20% rye. This means that 10 unique white dogs are produced, each of them different before and after they're dropped into wood. Four Roses Yellow Label is a blend of all 10 yeast/mash combinations; Small Batch a blend of only the 'S' and 'K' yeasts with both mashes; and Single Barrel is always selected from the 'B' mash and 'V' yeast. Sounds a bit complicated? It is. But things become a little more straightforward when it comes to maturation. Four Roses has 20 warehouses in Cox's Creek – around 50 miles from the distillery – that cling low to the ground like military bunkers waging war with gravity. Casks are racked only one tier high, which explains the enormous footprint of the warehouse and the relative consistency of maturation between any two barrels. 'We only get a five-degree temperature fluctuation between the top and the bottom of the rack' says Jim 'which is nothing compared to the six-tier houses that other producers use.'

Jim Rutledge believes that he has already made the best bourbon any of us are likely to taste – the only problem is that it's all sold out already, and even he only has half a bottle left. The story starts back in 1995. Jim had only recently been appointed master distiller, and by way of gaining the approval of his colleagues, decided to give the staff a couple of weeks off over the festive season. The distillery operation was winding down, and for one reason or another, a sample of 'V' yeast was left in the propagator too long and began to mutate. A lab technician beckoned Jim over to the microscope and what he saw was the Arnold Schwarzenegger of yeast cultures, which had mutated into virile little hunks. They fermented the mash and produced a one-of-a-kind fruity beer; in turn, the resulting white dog was the best Jim had ever tasted. In his own words, 'Everything the mutated culture touched turned to gold.' Unfortunately, by that point the super-yeast in question had been disposed of and to this day remains extinct.

The white dog was put to cask, and as time went on, it developed slowly. Jim recognized early on that this was a bourbon that would require more time than most to reach its full maturity. But, eventually, it did, 18 years later – an unusually long time for a bourbon. The mutated 'V' culture whiskey was blended with two 13-year-old whiskies and bottled as the 2013 Limited Edition Small Batch 125th Anniversary. Also, Four Roses created a special selection bottling of the 18-year-old casks only (albeit in absurdly small volumes) – I have included tasting notes below.

As Jim recounted the story to me, he pensively gazed out of his office window at the custard-yellow 'mission'- style buildings that populate the distillery, then said 'If I'd have kept a sample of that yeast, right now I'd be making the best bourbon anyone has ever tasted, every day.'

FOUR ROSES 'YELLOW LABEL' (40% ABV)

A continental breakfast of a bourbon: marmalade, honey, fresh citrus and pain au chocolat... all served on a charred oak table. The taste is of hot and sweet oak, leaving a finish of sugar and spice.

FOUR ROSES SMALL BATCH (45% ABV)

There's a good heeling of wood on the nose here, but it quickly subsides, giving way to honeysuckle and jasmine. There's a subtle hint of orange oil, too, giving an almost sherried characteristic, with white chocolate sauce. On the palate, it's drier than I would have expected. Green peppercorns, peach and burnt milk shine through. The finish is short, drying and moreish.

Above The distinctive yellow label of Four Roses eloquently hints at what might be inside the bottle – honey, orange, spice and wood.

FOUR ROSES SINGLE BARREL (50% ABV)

The aroma here is softer, eclipsed somewhat by a good blast of alcohol. There's some saddle leather and warm oak on the nose, though, followed up by some spiced dark-fruit compote. It's heavy in the mouth, with a lot of spice, which trounces all over any fruit notion. Refreshingly non-vanilla-like, but hot, spicy and heavy with it.

FOUR ROSES SINGLE BARREL 2013 'V' YEAST 18-YEAR-OLD (57.3% ABV)

Silky-smooth butterscotch, candyfloss/cotton candy and trough-fulls of ripe, red fruits like cherry, plum and red grapes. Impossibly chewy and fat on the tongue, releasing a hot jet of wood resin, dates, prunes and dried apricot. The finish is long, warm and peppered with spice and fruit.

⋙ JIM BEAM ⋘

The undisputed first family of bourbon can trace its lineage back a full 216 years, which by my reckoning makes it the oldest whiskey dynasty in the world. The year was 1788 and America was independent, shiny and new, with immigrants flocking to its shores from Europe to stake their claim on its physical and metaphysical frontiers. One such person was a second-generation American of German descent called Jacob Boehm. Like many others at that time, Jacob was searching for a nice spot to hunker down in and build a life, and in that year, he and his family crossed the Shenandoah Valley of Virginia, along the Clinch River into Tennessee, then across the Appalachian mountains and along the Wilderness Road. The trip took months, but eventually they settled in Hardin Creek, situated in modern-day Washington County, Kentucky. Jacob quickly established a farm, rearing livestock and growing corn, which led to the common farmyard practice of distilling. He also changed his name, from Boehm to the less German-sounding 'Beam'.

Years went by and whisky production became lucrative for the Beam family. By 1810, they owned no less than 324 hectares/800 acres of prime Kentucky farmland. Jake's son, David Beam, took over the farm, followed by his son, David M. Beam, in 1853. David M. had more ambition than most and in the 1860s, he built a new distillery in Nelson County to take advantage of the railroad. He also incorporated a continuous still into the design. Also around that time, David M. brought his 16-year-old son into the family business; his name was James, but most people know him better as Jim. Jim took over running the distillery in 1892 and brought his own son, Jeremiah 'Jere' Beam, into the business. Jim's other child, Margaret, married a man by the name of Frederick 'Booker' Noe, and it's his grandson, Fred Noe, who stands as the seventh-generation Beam-distiller today.

Back in 1920, Prohibition shut the Beam operation down and Jim turned his hand to fruit farming. However, when Prohibition was repealed in 1933, he went back to Kentucky and purchased the old Murphy Barber Distillery at Clermont, and for

Above The Jim Beam bottling line – the part of the distillery that the current master distiller, Fred Noe, began working in.

the first time began producing bourbon under the Jim Beam brand name. The business wasn't sustainable, though, as there were simply too many family members requiring a cut of the profits, so factions began splintering off and new distilleries were established. Jim's cousin, Joseph L. Beam (grandson of David Beam), was involved in no fewer than nine pre- and post-Prohibition distilleries, including the likes of Early Times and Stitzel-Weller. Jim's brother, Park, who worked as master distiller at the Claremont operation, went on to run the Shawhan Distillery in Bardstown. Park's son, Earl, went on to set up Heaven Hill in 1934, which has continued to have a Beam running its stills ever since. The first distiller at Maker's Mark was a Beam, too, and there are today countless Beam descendants continuing the family tradition.

The present-day Beam distillery is a monster. It's so big, in fact, that a standard tour involves a walk around a fully functioning micro-distillery (although bigger than some others featured in this book) because the real distillery is simply too large for the average human brain to process. This distillery-in-miniature is overseen by Jim Beam's great-grandson

and namesake, Jim Beam Noe. Just over a gallon of whisky is made here every second – enough to fill almost half-a-million barrels a year. I've never been to a proper southern ranch, but I'd imagine that the big ones feel something like this. Rolling, sprawling landscape, with massive barns erected here and there, but in this instance they are filled with whisky. Despite the sheer scale of the operation, there is some self-sufficiency here and a good proportion of the product is bottled on site.

Just over 80% of total production ends up in a Jim Beam White Label (4-year-old) bottle, but there are quite a few other whiskies made in Claremont, such as Jim Beam Black (8-year-old) and Devil's Cut, which uses a unique process that liberates lost bourbon from empty barrels by soaking them in water. There are lesser-known products, too, like 'Old Crow', a 4-year-old resurrection of one of bourbon's oldest brand names; there is also 'Old Grandad', a spicy high-rye mash bill whiskey at 43% ABV, and Old Overholt Rye – one of the most readily available straight rye whiskies around. Finally, there are the small-batch bourbons of Knob Creek (named after Abraham Lincoln's childhood Kentucky home; Basil Hayden's, an 8-year-old high-rye; Bakers, an overproof 7-year-old; and the most revered of them all, Booker's - named after Jim Beam's grandson who played brand ambassador and distiller for 50 years.

KNOB CREEK CASK SAMPLE

Art room: lead pencil, poster paints and wet clay. Then comes the wood, rippling with intensity. Concentrated spice that holds the centre of the tongue, meaning this whisky is initially dry, but lingers into sugary coffee and nutshells.

BOOKER'S (63% ABV)

Hard to ignore the alcohol on this one. Once quieted, there's sponge cake, warm sultanas/golden raisins, caramel and banana. Syrupy and intense on the palate, with controlled and well-dispersed heat; the lingering taste is that of macadamia brownie, violet, coconut and sweet tomato.

JIM BEAM SIGNATURE 12-YEAR-OLD (43% ABV)

Vibrant. Pistachio ice cream and big vanilla, bursting with fresh cherries and blueberries, drifting into perfumed nutty musk. Surprisingly light and clean on the palate, like hot stones, with anise and minty coolness. The finish is old, dry wood and stewed damsons.

JIM BEAM SIGNATURE SIX GRAINS (44.5% ABV)

Sour cream and buttermilk, then there's a distinct musty plastic note that reminds me of an old action figure I owned as a child. Hot on the palate, with spiced molasses cake, brown sauce, chewy apricot and dates.

OTHER PARTS OF THE USA

* *

In 2003, when the American Distilling Institute (ADI) was founded, there were a handful of small independent distilleries in the USA. Today there are probably over 600 of them, with the number increasing weekly. Where the saturation point is and what the total figure will rise to is uncertain; 600 seems like a lot already, but when you consider that in 1890 there were more like 5,000 distilleries across the US, the room for growth does seem to validate the current state of the growing market.

Certainly the craft spirits movement can trace its roots to the craft beer movement, which had a good 15–20 year head-start, and even the craft wine movement, which takes us back even further. The same entrepreneurial spirit has driven craft distilleries over the past decade, through the increasing American demand for organic, artisan, locally sourced, genuine food and drink. The ever-present tension that exists between the American people and 'the man' has spurred many, particularly among the middle classes, to shun the big brands and look closer to their homes for everything and anything. So, perhaps 'craft' is about legitimacy of a product, honesty and integrity; these are, incidentally, the foundations upon which many of the larger organizations are built, which does pose the question: when is craft no longer craft? The answer is elusive. According to the ADI, craft amounts to: 'the products of an independently owned distillery with maximum annual sales of 52,000 cases where the product is physically distilled and bottled on-site.' Loopholes can be found, though, like Tuthilltown's 2012 sale of the Hudson Whiskey brand (but not the distillery), to William Grant & Sons.

The range of products made across these distilleries is vast, from fruit brandies and liqueurs

through to gin, vodka, rum and sugar-cane based spirits. The ADI's database of craft distilleries (which is not exhaustive) lists 320 registered craft whiskey products at the time of writing, mixed between bourbon, rye and malt whiskey products. Of course, any distillery founded in the past two years, of which there are over 100, won't have had time to bottle a whiskey just yet, and many of these operations are essentially clock-watching while sitting on maturing stocks. What some of the fledgling operations have done is to release 'work in progress' expressions, not yet classifiable as whiskey.

Perhaps the most interesting thing about the craft movement is the influence it has exerted over larger distilleries, where we are seeing more boutique and experimental expressions entering the liquor-store shelves. This can only be a good thing, as consumers are presented with the option of exploring new faces or rediscovering old friends. Where this will all lead to in the end is uncertain, but I do expect to see bigger companies wading in further to the craft movement, buying up promising small distilleries and exploring further opportunities to leverage demand for craft products in their own ranges. For the craft movement itself, there will be winners and losers, distilleries that are left behind and distillers who are elevated to stardom. This can and will only be achieved through delicious-tasting products, which means the future looks good for us!

Picking four to feature in this book was a daunting task, given the options out there, so I settled on one from the east, one from the west, one from the south and one from the north.

Below The St. George Distillery in California is a striking contrast between clinical steel architecture and warm copper distillation apparatus.

USA

• High West

• St. George

• Tuthilltown

• Balcones

I first came across Balcones (*Bal-ko-nez*) at London's Whisky Live Show in 2011. Amid the anxious clusters of tweed jackets, there stood Chip Tate, a man who looks exactly like you would imagine a man with such a name would look: T-shirt and beard. As the founder and president of Balcones, Chip's appearance is as refreshingly disruptive to the pretentiousness that often plagues the whisky fraternity as his whiskey is to the sanctioned archetypes. Experimental, new-wave... call it what you will, Balcones is becoming one of the most talked-about whiskey brands around.

This all started in the small city of Waco, Texas. Now, Texas has no real connection with whiskey – the choice tipple there is tequila. Chip Tate moved there in 2008 with grand idea of starting a brewery, but when his plans were put on hold, he turned his attention to whiskey. He acquired a little old welding shop, and he and his family went to work renovating it by themselves. Once it was watertight, Chip went all MacGyver on the place, and with a welder and a hammer, hand-built everything, including the stills and condensers. It's important to note at this point that Chip had to teach himself how to weld in order to achieve this. This puts a

Above The Texan heat affords Balcones single malt a lot of wood character, and its fair share of dark, brooding colour, too.

whole new slant on the concept of 'craft', as most start-up distilleries simply pass a catalogue around and take delivery a few months later. But what Chip didn't know back then is that he wasn't just building his own distillery – he was creating, from scratch, a whiskey culture in Texas.

The Balcones range now includes two varieties of blue corn whiskey, the first Texan single malt, some special-release bourbons and a smoked corn whiskey (whereby the liquid is smoked over Texas scrub oak chips). The current 610-square metre (2,000-square foot) space has become insufficient to hold Balcones' growing mantelpiece of awards, never mind all the casks, so in 2015, Balcones will unveil its new distillery, roughly 30 times the size of the current set-up. Stills will be purchased from Forsyth's in Scotland this time, and while this may upset the romantics out there, Chip's attitude is that he only hand-made the stills and condensers because he didn't have enough money at the time – now that the world has stood up and taken notice of Texan whiskey, I'm not sure money is a problem anymore.

It might be worth getting your Balcones purchases in now, as one day, whiskey collectors may look back wistfully at the Balcones whiskies that were made in Chip's welded copper stills.

TEXAS SINGLE MALT (53% ABV)

On the nose we find coconut oil, dusty flaked almonds and a light spreading of chocolate spread. Sweet orange oil and treacle/molasses are awarded to those who are persistent. Hot tree bark, burnt cedar and a whole ton of residual sugar in the taste. The sweetness carries through a long, toasted finish of grape skin, luscious caramel and maple syrup.

BABY BLUE (46% ABV)

Steamed asparagus, hemp oil and green banana skins are the first to show in the smell. Sweet cut grass and baked sponge cake come next, with thyme, cornbread and vanilla. There's a texture of coagulation on the palate, like it is self-aware and unwilling to be swallowed. The finish is breezy, sweet and really rather moreish.

Dubbed as America's first 'craft distillery', the story of St. George dates back to 1982, so if you're in any doubt about the shelf-life and legitimacy of the craft movement over there, know that it is at least as old as the author of this book. Of course, 'craft' has existed in the US since long before you or I were born. In fact, the foundations of American distilling are built upon small operations operated by farmers attempting to get by. Many of the new craft distilleries today are boldly replicating the traditions and techniques of old – proudly declaring that there is more to American whiskey than bourbon.

An aircraft hangar might not seem like the most obvious location for a distillery, but it seems to work quite well for St. George, if only in its aesthetics. The spectacle of seeing casks racked alongside copper stills is quite remarkable. There are few distilleries that have encapsulated the process in a single room such as this, but the benefits are undeniable, and I expect to see it happening more as new craft producers establish themselves.

Given that this is an American craft distillery, the most straightforward first port of call would naturally be bourbon whiskey – so it is of no surprise that St. George bottles one. What is surprising is the name: 'Breaking & Entering', – a fitting name, though, as this is not their own stuff and is in fact pilfered from distilleries in Kentucky.

It's the malt whiskey that St. George produces that gets me really excited, however. Now in its 13th year, St. George has developed a serious reputation for quality malt whisky, and in my opinion this is about as good as it gets in North America at present. That statement alone doesn't quite do the liquid justice, though; this is American malt whiskey, and something is noticeably different about the product. Quite an achievement. The whisky is currently a blend of 3–14-year-old whiskies, has no age statement and is simply labelled according to its release number. Some of the malt used to make the St. George whiskey is smoked over alder and beech woods, giving a

chocolate, nutty character to the dram – one of the factors that clearly sets it apart from Scottish malt. Lance Winters, the master distiller, has a background in brewing, too, so proprietary yeast is used sensitively to mash and convert the barley into a sweet and delicate wash.

ST. GEORGE LOT 13 CASK STRENGTH

The initial slap of tropical fruit quickly fades, and a punchy, dark/bittersweet chocolate note that is highly reminiscent of Belgian beer takes over. Mushroom soup and there's fruit here, too, though – apricot and raisins – which are reflected in the mouth, along with a certain dental mouthwash (perhaps cinnamon) sting. The finish is wonderfully crisp and elegant, gently slipping into a lingering sensation of sweet and nutty woodland mushroom.

Right If you want to understand the American malt whiskey style, look no further than St. George.

Tuthilltown Distillery shouldn't actually exist. Ralph Erenzo's plan was to turn his newly purchased estate in the Hudson Valley, about 144 km (90 miles) north of New York City, into a ranch for rock climbers. Difficult neighbours scuppered the plans, though and, under financial duress, Ralph began selling off parts of the property to pay the mounting bills. Another option was urgently needed. Turns out that the old Tuthilltown site had a few hidden treasures, including a grist mill dating back to 1788. The possibility of distilling whiskey caught hold of Erenzo, and he started experimenting.

With the help of Brian Lee, Ralph got a distilling licence, and in 2003, he opened New York State's first new whiskey distillery since 1919. Ralph and Brian spent months learning the intricacies of whiskey-making; they even managed to source an heirloom varietal of corn from a local farm that had been cultivated since early colonial times. In 2009, the distillery harvested rye grown in the farm, which you'll be tasting in the current rye bottlings.

The warehouse is littered with sub-woofer speakers blasting out hip-hop music, with the aim of agitating the liquid in the cask and accelerating maturation. As ludicrous as this might seem, the logic is sound – keep the liquid moving even slightly and it will permeate the wood more effectively.

The distillery and farm continue to remain in the hands of Ralph Erenzo, but William Grant bought the Hudson Whiskey brand in 2012.

FOUR GRAIN (46% ABV)

Get beyond the typical new-oak, vanilla/wood notes and there's a herbal note here, like a herb scone with lashings of butter, or thyme-scented cornbread. The taste loses some of the subtle top-notes however, revealing liquorice, treacle and spiced fudge.

MANHATTAN RYE (46% ABV)

This rye sits in the spicy camp, more than the fruity: black pepper, cayenne and hot coals. On the palate there's a peppery olive-oil taste, which is reflected in the glossy, furniture polish mouthfeel, too. The finish is dominated by char and a spiced nutty linger.

SINGLE MALT (46% ABV)

Like a harvest festival, this whisky is all cereals, oak, and warm autumn fruits. There's poached pear, pine nut, pine cone and some delicate florals that would be better at home in Scotland than New York. The palate is all wood upfront, leading into leather and vanilla, then finally revealing just a touch of soft tropical fruit and finishing on the dry side of things.

HUDSON MAPLE CASK (46% ABV)

Wood, and more wood. The maple syrup is clear and present, but the double maturation has imparted a huge oak influence, with cigar bog, oak flooring and dusty old planks of wood. On the palate there's little change; its tannic and bitter with oak influence and fortunately some sweetness that partly balances it.

Below Tuthilltown products are renowned for their simple packaging, but the whiskey itself is anything but simple.

HIGH WEST

There are one or two distilleries in this book that I am happy to concede defeat to, and this is one of them. I have not been to the High West Distillery in Utah, mostly for the reason that it is in Utah, which is a long way from anywhere, and I assumed there wasn't a lot else to do in Utah. Or so I thought...

Utah is actually one of the most geologically diverse states in the USA, sporting arid red deserts, sprawling pine forests and of course, the Rocky Mountains. It's on the western edge of the Rockies, on the Wasatch Range to be precise, that the High West Distillery and saloon are located – the world's first and only 'ski-in' whiskey distillery, and the first distillery to open in Utah since 1870. You'd have to say that given its location and its altitude (2,100 metres/6,890 feet above sea-level), it is undeniably both 'high' and 'West'.

Trace back the history of whiskey in Utah and you'll find that it has a lot to thank the Mormon movement for. Brigham Young, also known as the 'American Moses' was a leader of the Mormon pioneers, the founder of Salt Lake City and a rampant polygamist. He also enjoyed a whiskey or two and, despite his faith, was known to go to great lengths to get it – a fact confirmed in the following line from his *Journal of Discourses* (1862): 'When there was no whisky to be had here, and we needed it for rational purposes, I built a house to make it in.' A sensible move, I think you'd agree.

In 1868, Young founded ZCMI (Zions Cooperative Mercantile Institution), which was dubbed 'America's first department store' and known to stock a range of whiskies. It was there that pharmacist C. E. Johnson began selling his own brand of 'Valley Tan Mormon Whiskey'. *Valley Tan* was a Mormon term, traditionally applied to any product that was made locally. According to Mark Twain's *Roughing It* (1871), though, Valley Tan is a 'kind of whisky, or first cousin to it; is of Mormon invention and manufactured only in Utah. Tradition says it is made of (imported) fire and brimstone.' Whatever that means.

Valley Tan is also High West's first expression, which, unlike the rest of the aged whiskey products, is made entirely at its Utah distillery. The mash bill comprises 85% oats, and it's matured for just under two years in refill rye casks; it's all sold out, mind you, but the distillery is now distilling seven days a week for the next round of releases.

Also in its portfolio is a serious selection of products, the components of which are bought in from other distilleries and, at present, make up the vast majority of High West sales. They include straight bourbon whiskey, straight rye whiskey, blended ryes, and blends of bourbon and rye, literally culminating in the enigma that is 'Bourye'. More recently still, we have seen the release of 'Campfire', which builds on foreign relations by combining bourbon, rye and a peated Scotch malt whisky. I personally feel it should have been called 'Ryebourley' – but hey, I'm no marketeer.

RENDEZVOUS (46% ABV)

Guns and roses: gun oil, leather and hot plastic, swimming in a vat of rose water. There are soft tropical fruits, too, including lychee and melon. On the palate the whiskey is sweet and juicy, erring on the fruit side of things and drilling home some good spice to boot. Long finish of oak lollipop.

CAMPFIRE (46% ABV)

The name says it all. White chocolate, hot honey and banana, melted plastic and a subtle whisper of smoke on the finish. Concentrated spice up front in the mouth, leading into sweet and juicy cantaloupe melon and then trails of smoke. Like someone struck a match on your tongue.

VALLEY TAN (46% ABV)

Green and creamy. Pistachio, porridge/oatmeal and some soft vanilla lead into spearmint and soft greasiness. Luscious texture on the palate, like buttery mashed potato, with a good amount of heat to remind you it's there.

CANADA

In Canada, the approach to making whisky has, for the most part, continued to involve making the components of the product separately, then blending them to form a house style. Blending options are the name of the game: some producers will mature their spirit in a range of different casks, while others will start with a range of base spirits, further broadening the possibilities of maturation.

This ability to diversify was a feather in the cap of Canadian producers during the 1960s and 1970s, when they reacted quickly to the consumer demand for lighter, vodka-style spirits. Mainstream Canadian distillation continues to see success in traversing the tightrope between white and dark liquor.

Canadian whisky has a reputation for its accessibility and mixability. It is particularly popular in the USA, which accounts for almost 80% of all Canadian whisky exports. Of the remaining 20%, most is sold in Canada, leaving only a little for Sweden and France, as well as fast-growing markets like Mexico. For me, I must confess that the strong stigma of blandness and bad wood have been my traditional associations with the Canadian spirit, but things are quickly changing and it's not all mass-market and insipid.

The craft movement has gained good traction in Canada, and at the time of writing there are around 25 distilleries, some of them producing their own interpretations of the Canada style; many are now supplementing their whisky offerings with gin, vodka and liqueurs. The multi-category tactic has been bred more out of legal necessity than entrepreneurship, as Canadian whisky must be at least three years old, so it makes sense to produce a range of cheaper (and quicker) alcoholic drinks to offset the cost required to produce whisky. Clear Waters and Shelter Point distilleries are good examples, selling a proportion of their unaged malt whisky as (quite expensive) malt vodka.

Terminology of labels has been a source of confusion over the years as, for many folk, Canadian whisky in the past (and today) was known simply as 'rye'. The reason for this was that many distilleries back then were making two types of whisky: one with rye and one without. The whisky made with rye became the more popular choice, noted for its richer flavour. With the exception of a handful of Canadian distilleries that make 100% rye whiskies, most Canadian rye whisky usually contains only a small proportion (typically under 10%) of rye in the bottle, leading to complaints from American distillers that Canadian 'rye' whisky is not (by US standards) 'true' rye. Some Canadian producers defend this, by arguing that their rye, which is grown in much colder climes than that of the US, is spicier so has a greater presence in the spirit. Canadians can also make the point that their use of ex-bourbon and refill casks means that the wood exerts less impact than an American straight rye (which makes use of new casks), allowing the rye to shine through more in the Canadian product.

Canadian law does permit the addition of flavouring and colouring in whisky products. This has been a controversial topic of conversation

Left Unashamedly modelled in the Scottish mould, Glenora in Nova Scotia was Canada's first malt distillery.

among Canadian distillers and whisky purists for some time now, the latter of which believe that whisky should be bottled in its natural form and not tarnished by a sweet and fruity paintbrush. As is always the case, though, legal definitions do not restrict what producers can do to a product, only what they can call it. Some Canadian distillers staunchly oppose the broadness of Canadian whisky classification by effectively adhering to the Scotch rulebook. Still Waters Distillery, for example, advertises its malt as being non-chill-filtered and having no colour or flavours added.

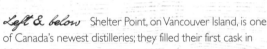

CANADA

Shelter Point

Hiram Walker

Left & below Shelter Point, on Vancouver Island, is one of Canada's newest distilleries; they filled their first cask in 2011.

HIRAM WALKER

Canada's most famous, longest-surviving and largest whisky distillery was actually first established by an American. Hiram Walker was born in 1816, just outside Boston, and moved to Detroit to set up a grocer's shop when he was about 30. The shop sold whisky, too, as was the way back then, and just like his Scottish counterparts, Hiram got to work blending and 'rectifying' (filtering and flavouring) his own whisky products for his customers. Inspired to set up his own distillery, but wary of ludicrous laws and the mounting Temperance movement in the US, Hiram decided to build his distillery in 1858 just across the border on the outskirts of Windsor, Canada. Hiram spent almost his entire working life commuting across the border between his home in the US and his distillery in Canada on a ferry service that he established for that very purpose.

The original distillery was equipped with a 10-metre (33-foot) high wooden column still and a copper doubler, which could get through 16,000 gallons of wash a day. Whisky was sold unaged with just a drop of caramel for colour. The site also operated for 30 years as a flour mill, which was removed in 1878 when demand for Walker's whisky had become too large to warrant the dual-purpose set-up. Around the same time, Hiram Walker built a town to offer accommodation for the numerous people on his payroll. This town had its own church, post office, school and hospital and was fittingly named Walkerville. The town has since been swallowed up by the city of Windsor, but its population continued to grow up until the 1930s when it had swelled to around 10,000, no doubt because it became a key border town for the smuggling of Canadian whisky into the US.

In 1882, five years prior to the introduction of compulsory maturation laws, Walker launched a new product into the American market. It was the first Canadian whisky to be sold in a bottle and was called 'Club'. The whisky was a blend of high rye- and high corn-containing spirits that had been matured for a short period in oak. Sales grew

Below A bird's-eye view of the buildings and grounds of the H. Walker & Sons Distillery with the Detroit River in the background, taken around 1913.

through the 1890s, despite the better efforts of the American distillers to discredit it.

Hiram Walker died in 1899, and the empire was passed on to his three sons, and later Hiram's grandson, Harrington Walker, who sold the business to Harry Hatch for $14 million in 1926. This was a substantial amount of money for those times (in the region of $184 million now), but a good deal from Harry Hatch's perspective, despite the fact that the American market was still suffering during the Prohibition era. Hatch was well versed in the art of whisky-running, having commanded a fleet of 42 boats used to transport whisky to the USA when he was employed at the Corby Distillery near the northern shore of Lake Ontario.

Hatch turned the Walkerville Distillery into an empire, and the family continued to operate the plant until 1987. Since then, the distillery has changed hands a few times, ending up in the grasp of one of the multinationals. But in this case it's not quite as simple as that. Currently the distillery is owned by Pernod Ricard, but operated by Corby Distillers. Corby makes the Wiser's and Gibson's range of whiskies there, but also makes Canadian Club, which is, confusingly, owned by Beam, Suntory, Inc. rather than Corby or Pernod Ricard.

Today the distillery is capable of outputting 55 million litres (58 million quarts) of pure alcohol a year between its columns and pots, but currently only operates five days a week. Interestingly, the Hiram Walker Distillery is the only distillery in Canada (and the only distillery featured in this book) that uses no malted barley, whatsoever. The diastase needed during the fermentation process is fronted up by malted rye instead.

The flavour of Canadian Club owes a lot to Hiram Walker for his 'barrel blending' program, which was introduced at some point in the late 19th century. The unique process is an ingenious yet very simple method of diversifying the distillery's range of stock by creating casks of varied flavours. New-make whiskies of different characters are blended before maturation, resulting in whiskies that follow dramatically different tangents over the years Once fully matured, sets of casks are vatted together to make the different Canadian Club expressions.

If you're partial to a swig of CC and find you have some spare time on your hands, Canadian Club

Above There are still nine cases of Canadian Club hidden in hard-to-reach parts of the world. Go and find them!

launched a worldwide treasure hunt in 1967. Twenty-five cases of whisky were hidden in remote locations around the world. Nine cases remain undiscovered to this day.

CANADIAN CLUB (40% ABV)

Boiled sweets and musty hay on the nose, like a childhood treehouse. There's wood too, but it's cedar rather than oak. Sweet, light and crisp on the palate, some spice and a slight molasses/rum note. Best used for mixing.

1977 VINTAGE BOTTLE (43.4% ABV)

Pencil shavings and stationery tin dominate the nose on this old bottle. The wood aroma feels half-hearted, yet somehow highly resilient.

Vancouver Island is now host to a truly Scottish-style distillery. Shelter Point began distilling on 5th June 2011, but the product, when ready, promises to be an accurate replica of some of the earliest Canadian grain distillates – only this time they will be fully matured.

The distillery was originally a joint venture between Jay Oddleifson, a local businessman, Andrew Currie, founder of the Arran Distillery in Scotland, and Patrick Evans, a local farmer and the owner of the site. The well-respected Scottish distiller Mike Nicholson was brought in to man the stills, having recently moved to Vancouver Island to retire. The partnership didn't work out, though. Mike Nicholson returned to his retirement, Jay Oddleifson pulled out, and Andrew Currie has now moved on to other projects, namely the upcoming Lakes distillery near the Cumbrian Fells in England.

As with other subscribers to the new malt whisky revolution, they're into self-sufficiency and local sourcing here – even the stone and timber used to construct the distillery were cut nearby and the effect is one-part Scottish farmhouse and one-part log cabin. Of course, the tall and narrow Scottish-made stills, 4,000 and 5,000 litres (4,227 and 5,283 quarts) in size – built by legendary copper shaper Forsyth's – also adds to the effect. The pair of stills were shipped by container from Scotland all the way through the Panama Canal and up the west coast of the US. The story goes that when the ship docked in Los Angeles, the stills were either seized as illegal distilling equipment, or presumed to be part of some kind of terrorist plot; they were eventually released after four weeks, looking more than a little jaded for their time spent in detention.

There's barley growing right outside the distillery, but it's merely a decorative addition, since there are no maltings on Vancouver Island and it's unfeasible to send it off the island all the way to Calgary. The only solution would be to open their own maltings and process everything in-house, but for now it's a Pilsner malt bought from Calgary maltings that currently fills the mash tun.

Maturation is in former Jim Beam and Jack Daniel's casks for now (although there is some experimentation with casks that previously held locally made fruit liqueurs). According to tour guide Brian Ingle, the team is placing some faith in its close proximity to the sea imparting some maritime nuances to the finished product: 'Grassy, fruity, sweet from the cotton woods, and please god, maybe a little salt – that's what we're hoping for!' says Brian.

While the whisky waits it out, the guys at Shelter Point are bottling and marketing a 'Stillmaster Vodka' to help with cash-flow. I had the chance to taste a two-year-old cask sample (see tasting notes, below).

22-MONTH CASK SAMPLE

Bourbon sour. There's a good hit of 'obvious' vanilla here upfront, but it drifts away quickly into lemon verbena, waxy lemon skin and some buttery cereal aromas. It's youthful on the palate, which presents itself in a herb cheese biscuit kind of way. But vanilla and caramel also shine through nicely, too, much like a custard tart. Finish has just a touch of bitter dark chocolate and some more resinous wood notes just beginning to interfere.

Left & right With barely any visible pipework, Shelter Point has managed to contain everything within one room and successfully demystify the entire production process.

JAPAN

It was about 11 years ago in one of my first bar jobs that I first became aware of Japanese whisky as a serious contender. I think I had read a magazine article and decided to track down a bottle for the bar. I remember a regular coming in that evening who was a keen malt whisky drinker, so I took the opportunity to test the water and try him with this Japanese dram. He scoffed at the idea of an Asian whisky, finished the glass quickly and said to me, 'I'd drink it if I was lost in a desert.' So the bottle was relegated to the back of the shelf. The following year that same whisky – Yamazaki 12 – picked up a gold medal at the International Spirits Competition, marking the beginning of Japanese dominance at single malt's highest level.

Ironically it was 1983, a dark year for Scotch whisky, that the Japanese whisky boom topped out. Back then, the industry was producing six times its current levels to keep up with the huge domestic market for blended whisky. Hardly any of it was exported. The 20 years that followed saw a steady decline in sales, but things have been on the up again more recently, driven by marked improvements in quality and the new-found fame of Japanese single malts. Today the pillars of Japanese whisky – Suntory and Nikka – are themselves forces to be reckoned with, but these are now accented by Chichibu, Fuji-Gotemba, Eigashima and the highly sought-after products of the now-closed distilleries of Hanyu and Karuizawa. In 2012, whiskies from Suntory and Nikka scooped the top three prizes at the World Whiskies Awards. Every distillery presents a clarity of character that gives definition to the broadening

Below There are few distilleries that can challenge the stunning location of Hakushu in the Japanese Alps.

SHOP
IN THE BARREL

network of whisky-making craft in Japan today.

As with Japanese culture in general, the whisky made here is familiar, but somehow gracefully unnerving at the same time – like an almost imperceptible corruption of an otherwise ordinary situation. Subtleties and implications that would normally be overlooked in the process of Scottish malt whisky-making are quietly scrutinized and amended, through a carefully considered and almost balletic production process. It stands to reason, I guess, as this attention to detail and pride in one's endeavours are also evident in many historic aspects of Japanese culture, like the formal elegance of miniature gardens; the ritual of a tea ceremony or a Geisha's diligent plucking of the *shamisen*. Those are examples of old practices for an old culture, however, and despite whisky-making being nearly 100 years old in Japan, by Japanese standards, it's still quite young.

The art had to be learned, first by the Japanese whisky pioneers Masataka Taketsuru and Shinjiro Torii, and now by progressives like Ichiro Akuto. Japan has not allowed itself the benefit of time and tradition on this occasion, as some things have been sensitively borrowed from abroad, but all the time the influence of Japanese geography, flavour and culture makes itself known. Sympathy, awareness, control and development are the resounding messages I get from every distillery. Yes, there is an element of science in it – Japanese distillers are funding studies on oak sustainability and composition, on Japanese barley genetics and terroir to name a few – but the respect for process and tradition is not at all lost.

Like the *katana* possesses an alluring finesse and dignity that is so utterly Japanese, the whisky also carries a level of calm and refinement that is hard to match. But also like the sword, whisky-distilling here is still fundamentally based on older practices, and in this particular instance, those practices came from Scotland.

JAPAN

Hakushu ·· Chichibu

· Yamazaki

Left A privately-owned cask, signed by the lucky so-and-so, at Hakushu.

Right Traditional wooden washbacks at Hakushu Distillery ferment four mashes of varying peatiness.

Right The stills at Chichibu Distillery. Fresh samples of spirit are taken intermittently through each spirit run at Chichibu, since all spirit cutting is conducted by the nose, rather than by the clock.

YAMAZAKI

Japan's first whisky distillery was built by Shinjiro Torii in 1923. Today it is the largest malt distillery in the country, producing around six million litres (6.35 million quarts) of alcohol a year, which, for the sake of context, makes its capacity similar to that of Glenmorangie in Scotland. The similarities end there, however. Yamazaki comprises a series of enormous red concrete buildings, monolithic in their stature, like huge mid-century Methodist churches, flanked on two sides by bamboo-clad hills and sufficiently well elevated above the small town of Yamazaki, on the outskirts of Kyoto.

It's amazing to think that this distillery once conducted its own floor malting from Japanese barley – a practice that continued up until the 1960s – and housed industrial maltings until 1971. Self-sufficiency was the name of the game in the post-war era. Trade remained difficult though the 1940s and 1950s, which became the catalyst for yet another example of politics steering whisky style. The Japanese oak 'mizunara' cask was first used by Suntory during this period and for some time it was the only type of cask that the distillery filled. Today, mizunara accounts for only 0.5% of the 800,000 casks owned by Suntory. 'Mizunara barrels cost around five times the price of a Sherry butt', Seiichi Koshimizu, Suntory's master blender, tells me. He continues: 'Most of the oak in Japan grows on the hills, it twists and contorts and takes around 200 years to reach maturation. It's more difficult to raise a cask from this type of oak, too, and the labour costs are much higher than in Spain and America."

Only 15,000 casks are held on site at Yamazaki, with another 400,000 held an hour up the road towards Tokyo, which is where all of Suntory's blending work takes place for its Hibiki range. They comprise mostly ex-bourbon barrels that have been converted into hogsheads, Sherry butts (around 15%) and new American oak puncheons. 'The bourbon barrel is too small for us', says Koshimizu, 'and our whisky needs time and the larger casks give us that.' Of course, there are also various wine casks, and more recently some new-fill French oak casks (watch this space).

What all this means of course is diversity. The mixed bag of effects offered by cask type give Suntory a wide range of styles to draw from. These can be bottled as they are, vatted to create one of the core expressions, or used in a Hibiki blend. But maturation is only the final stage of a journey that presents a multitude of options, even in the early stages. Two types of barley are imported from the UK, one peated and one unpeated. These are mashed separately in 16-ton loads and fermented for three days with a mixture of brewer's and distiller's yeasts. The stillhouse contains a large family of mis-proportioned pots, some direct-fired and some not, meaning that pairs of stills produce seven unique new-make spirits, which can either be matured individually, or in combination with others.

The more you continue to think about it, the more complex the situation becomes. But this is all of Suntory's own making. Yamazaki expressions follow no code of conduct; they are vaguely related but very much individual in their style. For that reason I've chosen to include tasting notes of five dramatically different component whiskies that could be used together to make the 12-year-old, 18-year-old or 25-year-old.

Left The copper stills at Yamazaki takes on an almost golden hue, unlike anywhere else I've seen.

Above The sight of the whisky library at Yamazaki is a good enough reason to visit the distillery.

PUNCHEON (63% ABV)

Distilled in 1995, dumped 2007

Bright green tea, lemon verbena and plenty of sweet floral aromas on the nose. This is a green, sappy-smelling whisky that delivers herbaceous qualities on the palate before drying up in the finish.

SHERRY BUTT (63% ABV)

Distilled in 1984, dumped in 2007

Black Forest gateau, PX wine, moist cigar, cigar box. With water there's roasted pineapple. Begins sweet, with plump fruit spice leading into sticky resin, massive concentration of sweet and dry. Some tannin on the finish.

6 YEARS EX-BOURBON CASK + 6 MONTHS BORDEAUX CASK (44% ABV)

Vibrant strawberry purée, oxblood leather. Strawberry persists with water, this time freeze-dried with fruity cereal notes. On the palate, it's relaxed and savoury, with more red fruits coming through – jammy and sweet.

Above The architecture here is at odds with the surrounding bamboo forest and small town of Yamazaki, but hey – they make great whisky!

1986 MIZUNARA CASK (59% ABV)

Mirror-polished cedar wood and pineapple chunks. Behind this the incense become more apparent – murky and intoxicating. There's frankincense, burnt anise and sarsparilla. Massively aromatic on the palate, with pecan, vanilla and cedar. Develops a milky texture when water is added, like chilled saké.

1993 PEATED YAMAZAKI (53% ABV)

Smoky wool and salted skate jerky. Pineapple again when diluted, smoked and green. Some sappy-ness. Unagi (eel), and just a touch of iodine. Sweet throughout.

⟫⟫⟫ CHICHIBU ⟪⟪⟪

Ichiro Akuto is as close as you're likely to get to whisky royalty in Japan. His family have a background in saké brewing, but in 1980, they decided to equip their Hanyu brewery with whisky-making kit. Hanyu was never much of a success, however, and spent the greater part of its 20-year existence struggling to survive an unexpected decline in Japanese whisky sales. It was only once the distillery closed in 2000 that that foreign demand grew as Europe and America finally cottoned on to the standard of whisky being produced in Japan. Fortunately, Ichiro had kept much of the stock from Hanyu and began bottling and selling special releases that became as highly regarded as they were demanded. Inspired to give it a second chance, Ichiro set in motion plans to open a new distillery in Saitama prefecture, around 90 km/55 miles north-west of Tokyo. And so it was, in 2008, to the chorus of nervous speculation from sweaty-palmed whisky geeks the world over, that Chichibu began making whisky.

Walking around the distillery, the first thing of obvious note is the pagoda roof, a feature that graces many Scottish distilleries. One would assume that it would have no use in the modern era of commercial malting, but it's far more than decorative here. Akuto-san and some members of his team learned how to floor-malt in the UK some years back and used the barley to distil their early 'The Floor Malt' release. Since then, they have built their own floor malting in Chichibu and conducted trials with 70kg (154 lbs.) samples in a small 'draw' kiln... or possibly a large dehydrator; I haven't decided which it is yet. More recently, they have received delivery of a one-ton kiln that, while still quite small, can dry enough malt to fill their mash tun twice and should be sufficiently broken in by the time you read this. A large pagoda roof might be a little excessive for its current output, but it gives a good indication of the ambition of this little distillery. For the time being, Chichibu imports three types of malt, mostly unpeated from

Above The unpretentious pagoda roof at Chichibu gives little away of the alchemy going on inside.

Germany and England, but also around 13% heavily peated malt from Scotland. It's in the milling of these grains that the next point of interest should be noted. In a similar vein to the 'polishing' of rice in saké brewing, mashmen monitor their milling with keen interest, preferring a larger ratio of malt 'husk' than most (up to 35%). This acts as a filtration medium, which ultimately affords them a clearer wort. This is likely at the cost of some fermentable material, but at Chichibu, this is looked upon as a necessary step in the character of their whisky.

Next up are the eight 3,000-litre/3,170-quart capacity fermenters – the first and only washbacks in the world made from Japanese mizunara oak. What effect, if any, this has on the finished spirit would be difficult to determine, but the use of Japanese oak is a pertinent reminder of Ichiro's commitment to applying a Japanese 'twist' to Scottish malt whisky tradition.

Short stills and downward-sloping lyne arms would generally lead to a heavy and characterful spirit, but this is balanced out by the clear worts and the fact that the 2,000-litre/2,115-quart spirit is only filled (by my calculations) with about 700 litres/740 quarts of low wines; this is barely enough to cover the steam coil that heats it, and this makes for proportionately more copper contact per litre/quart of liquid.

Between the numerous conflicting forces at play here – like a child that's subjected to a constant 'good cop/bad cop' approach to parenting – you have to wonder at the character of the new make. But as you might expect, it is full and fruity, but also delicate and floral. It's rich and powerful, while retaining freshness and clarity.

The same well-informed curiosity is liberally applied to the maturation program, too. A broad range of wood is used, but particular favourites include the 140-litre/148-quart 'Chibidaru' – a corruption of the words *chibid* (cute) and *taru* (barrel) – made from a cut-down bourbon cask; wine casks that previously held a type of Japanese muscat; a 1,000-litre/1,055-quart mizunara oak vat that hasn't been emptied in six years and is in a perpetual state of topping up and drawing off; and as if all that wasn't enough already – puncheons raised by Ichiro's own team, who were personally trained by an 80-year-old Japanese master cooper. I'm not kidding.

To simply say that what is happening at Chichibu is exciting wouldn't truly capture the awe-inspiring commitment to the whisky-making craft.

NEW MAKE

Intensely fruity new make. Fleshy stone fruit, like nectarine, orange peel and soft apricot, backed up by some tropicals, especially passion fruit. The taste reveals peach skin, lilac, unpeeled banana and digestive biscuit/graham cracker.

ICHIRO'S MALT 'THE FLOOR MALT' (50.5% ABV)

Polished walnut, peach nectar, and a lot of walnuts and cashew. Water reveals fizzy peach. Seriously finessed. Sticky mouthfeel, with plum wine, prune juice and wasabi spice. The finish is soft and squishy.

'PORT PIPE' (54.5% ABV)

Everything pink that you can imagine, beginning with massive plum jam and rose syrup on the nose, both of which seem impossibly focused. Cereal notes and youth then come through.

REFILL HOGSHEAD (63.2% ABV)

Parmesan shavings, tomato and miso – incredible character despite the youth. A second sniff brings more floral and citrus top notes like yuzu and grapefruit… almost hoppy. This leads into a darker area of cappuccino and white chocolate, where hazelnut rules with a praline fist.

CHIBIDARU (53.5% ABV)

Heady florals of elderflower, vanilla blossom and honeysuckle, backed up by tangy grapefruit zest and banana. The taste is soft and constant, coming through in waves; it's fragile yet resolute.

ICHIRO'S MALT 'CARD' HANYU – FOUR OF SPADES (58.6% ABV)

Shiny old leather, sandalwood and candle wax, followed by butter-glazed carrots. Rich and treacly on the palate, gaining traction and leading to Sherry-soaked fruit trifle. The finish is expansive leaving spiced tobacco leaf, bay and chilli/chile.

Below Lifting the lid on one of Chichibu Distillery's mizunara oak washbacks.

Suntory's other malt distillery is about two hours north of Tokyo and a mere 56 km (35 miles) from Mt. Fuji, settled in a region known as the Japanese Alps. At 700m (2,300 ft) above sea level and hidden deep within a woodland area like some kind of jungle village for Peter Pan and the Lost Boys, Hakushu possesses some of the finest air that I have ever had the pleasure of breathing, and a setting that is in stark contrast to its older urban sibling at Yamazaki. The water used here is thawed snow from Mount Kaikoma and there is, not to put too fine a point on it, a superbly tranquil feeling about the place. Hakushu is to me one of those rare examples of a distillery that has somehow drawn upon the themes of its surroundings and successfully bottled them in whisky form. The whisky made here is, more often than not, green, light, lucid and fresh. The question is, though: how do they do it?

'It's the water and the air,' Hiroshi Sano tells me. If anyone should know, he should. He started working at Hakushu in 1973, the same year it opened. Since then he has worked in every stage of production and remains a font of knowledge with regards to the history of the distillery and its technical side. He goes on to tell me about the eighteen 72,000-litre (76,000-quart) washbacks, which are 'made of Douglas fir, just like Scotland, and our fermentation is about three days long. This means we get a lactic acid build-up, which makes our spirit taste grassy, fruity and fresh.' The wash certainly smells fresh, and it tastes a little like a Belgian Lambic beer, with that slightly sour and fruity note. Of course, that was just one of the washes I tasted. There are four different types of barley used at Hakushu, from unpeated through to heavily peated with a couple of intermediate options for good measure.

The stillhouse is a similarly odd-ball scenario as Yamazaki. Of the 12 stills that currently reside there, no two are the same and all of them possess some degree of peculiarity. The reason for this copper-fetishists freak show is again Suntory's demand for diversity of spirit character, with the aim of creating a better composition from a broader palate of flavours. Some stills can be directed toward either worm tub or shell-and-tube condenser, which, coupled with the four levels of peatiness, makes for an incalculable number of potential styles. Four more stills are in the pipeline (so to speak), however, edging ever closer to the dizzy heights of the early 1980s, when Hakushu had a total of 24 stills across two houses. Back then, it was the biggest malt whisky distillery in the world.

Managing stocks here must be a lot of fun, but things do become more automated during maturation, starting with the filling of the casks, which is completed by one-of-a-kind machines that work just like a bottling line. The casks are then organized by a robot in gigantic steel-racked warehouses situated partially underground. Just like any modern automated warehouse, the machine records the details of each cask and can move stock around the place as required. The visual effect could be compared to one of those carparks/parking lots of the future, where your vehicle is snatched away from you and slotted into some barely visible receptacle that's hundreds of meters above.

Left Hakushu's stillhouse contains a selection of copper stills, all for the purpose of product diversification.

Sano-san tells me that, of the 400,000 casks held on the site (some of which are Yamazaki stock), Hakushu uses a larger proportion of ex-bourbon casks because 'It's cooler here than at Yamazaki, the air is lighter, and the temperature moves less. The smaller bourbon cask helps to balance this out and Hakushu prefers the lighter touch that it provides, too.' There are of course Sherry butts and hogsheads, but during a tasting of 100% ex-Sherry cask-aged Hakushu, I did find that the lighter nuances of the whisky were lost a little. A 100% ex-bourbon hogshead, on the other hand, was like a squirrel's banquet – a fantastic mixture of lemon zest, shortbread and acorn paste.

DISTILLER'S RESERVE (43% ABV)

Like scout camp, this malt is all about wet morning campfire, dewy grass and nylon sleeping bags. There's a slightly chilling menthol aroma, too, with some soft green apple and spice bringing up the rear. The palate is warmer, with burnt spices, a lick of smoke and a warm tingle throughout. The finish is salt-and-pepper seasoning and piquancy.

12-YEAR-OLD (43% ABV)

Like a forrest floor, this whisky is green moss and brown leaves. Soft and fragrant as the aroma continues into clean green apple, sage and a more subtle wood-fire note than its non-age-statement sister. Green peppercorns and smoked green banana feature in the taste, which leads to marjoram, shiso leaf and horseradish spice.

HOGSHEAD (56% ABV)

A very soft nose on this cask sample, showing at first lemon, apricot and banana. This leads into some sugared almonds, meadowsweet and cut green grass. The taste is also gentle, with lots of sweetness and a well-structured matrix of fruit, floral and wood spice.

18-YEAR-OLD (43% ABV)

Cut green melon, dessert apple, fennel and green tea are accompanied by a waft of soft smoke and slight waxiness. The taste is clean and grassy, with some tropical fruit and a prolonged arrival of woodsmoke. Elegant and crisp.

Above Hakushu is the definition of understated brilliance. Its products sing rather than shout.

25-YEAR-OLD (43% ABV)

Intially warm, spicy and woody on the nose, then comes maple, fudge, oak moss, fennel seed and waxed cotton. On the palate, it's alert and controlled – much like a ninja. It begins with gripping spice, then peach nectar, stewed apple, and Riesling-like oiliness; this then relaxes into supple bamboo and forest floor. The finish is warm and humid.

OTHER PARTS OF THE WORLD

Not so long ago, the concept of 'world whisky' was little more than a joke to those who subscribed to the rule that Scotch whisky was the one to rule them all. Then something changed. Certainly the number of whisky distilleries around the world increased, and with it the number of countries making malt whisky, but most importantly the quality of these whiskies showed marked improvements, too. It wasn't only the quality, though; individual identity emerged – that fascinating and unfathomable DNA marker that so many whiskies exhibit, reminding us of their terroir and the culture that shaped them. You'd think it would have been fanciful to believe that Indian whisky from the Amrut Distillery would possess characteristics of spiced fruit chutney, but that is indeed the case. This growing arsenal of world whiskies is, for the most part, all made the same way, but (like the differences in terroir that gently resonate through the Scotch whisky brands out there) they exhibit significant fluctuations in style based on their own unique gastronomy, geography, ideology and customs.

The expressions of genus and identity that we see in world whisky are not always as obvious as taste profile. In some instances, it can be better-defined as a general approach or mantra to the art of making whisky. In Scandinavia, and particularly Denmark and Sweden, most new producers have joined the ranks of malt whisky producers through a genuine love of the category, rather than as a supplemental product to a well-established range (as is more typically the case in France, Switzerland and Germany). Indeed, some of the Scandinavian distilleries demonstrate what I'd tentatively describe as typically Nordic methodology and reasoning, in which they enjoy a level of harmony and respect for their surroundings that is rarely present elsewhere in the world. As a result, the whisky made in these places is sometimes afforded a certain level of composure and equilibrium that sets it apart from the rest.

There is perhaps no other place that has been drawn to whisky-making over the past few years like Tasmania, in Australia. Now with nine active distilleries, one of which was awarded the best Single Malt Whisky in the World 2014 (Sullivans Cove from the Tasmania Distillery), it's hard to imagine that there were none 22 years ago. It would seem that opening a distillery on a small island off the coast of a Commonwealth country is very much the trend right now.

Where things become especially interesting and are likely to diversify the category even further is in the regional twists applied to the production process. Local water is of course a given, but locally grown barley is the next path that many distilleries are choosing to go down, since importing the stuff is both costly and ecologically unsound. There is an abundance of new oak species being used to manufacture casks too. The Waldviertler Roggenhof Distillery in Austria, for example, is maturing spirit in locally grown Manhartsberger oak, while the Spirit of Hven distillery in Sweden has built a wood analysis test centre where it hopes to test the affects that different oak types have on the aromatic profile of whiskies through the course of maturation.

World whisky is probably the most exciting area of whisky-making today, not because it's better than the Scottish, Japanese, Irish or North American brands, but because it's the underdog. Young, carefree, dynamic and more than willing to take risks, here is the R&D lab for future whisky development. Watch this space, because the older distilleries of this world certainly will be.

PENDERYN

It is said (in Wales, anyway) that legendary Welsh warrior Reaullt Hir distilled *chwisgi* from mead in AD 356 and thus created Wales's first spirit. Whether this is true or not, distilleries in Wales do date back to at least the early 18th century, where we know for sure that the family of one Evan Williams (of bourbon fame) operated a distillery in the town of Dale, Pembrokeshire. Williams himself didn't emigrate to the colonies for another 50 years, so it's entirely possible that he grew up around a Welsh distillery. These distilleries were producing spirit from mead and other forms of fermented honey, though, and the same can possibly be said for the large distillery opened in North Wales at Bala in 1887 (during the Scottish boom time). It was terrible timing on their part, though, as there was a growing movement towards temperance in Wales, stirred up by the Welsh chapel-building craze, and the distillery was subsequently closed by 1906.

In the year 2000, the Welsh Whisky Companies distillery in the village of Penderyn, in the foothills of the Brecon Beacons, began producing the first Welsh whisky for at least 94 years. Being Welsh has its advantages; unlike Scottish malt whisky, there are more relaxed laws governing the production of the spirit, so Penderyn buy in its fruity wash from the Brains Brewery just down the road.

Penderyn called in the help of one Dr. David Faraday, a descendant of Michael Faraday, to design their two-stage pot and column still set-up. The still is unique in that it does the job in one single distillation, although if you look a little closer, you'll see that there's even more going on here. The pot-and-column design shifts spirit back-and-forth, only collecting the vapours that make it up to the seventh spirit plate in the column. This allows for a lot of reflux in the still and the result is a very high-strength spirit of 86–92% ABV, with a fruity and floral note to it. In my mind, it's the relative cleanliness of the spirit that opens the whisky up to the huge influence of wood. It seems that Penderyn are wise to this as well; its releases have explored various types of wood finishing and styles.

 **Above** Penderyn have chosen vodka-esque packaging, but that shouldn't put you off. This is good whisky.

The Madeira, Sherry and portwood cask releases are all different from each other, yet they do share one common theme – they really do not benefit from the addition of water. Maybe it's a general wood influence that seems to run through the range, or perhaps its just some Welsh alchemy that demands that you drink them as the distiller intended.

WALES

Penderyn

MADEIRA FINISH (46% ABV)

Ex-Buffalo Trace cask, then 6 months in an ex-Madeira cask
Pearl barley and black pepper up front, which quickly give way to an estery blast of sweet violet and bright nectarine, with just a hint of wood. On

the palate there's a green melon note and pink peppercorns. The finish dries off and flattens out rather too quickly, unfortunately.

SHERRYWOOD (46% ABV)

70% ex-Buffalo Trace bourbon casks, 30 % ex-oloroso Sherry casks

There's definitely a touch of Black Forest gateau on this, along with ripe red fruits, vanilla and a none-too-subtle chocolate note. The palate is full and fruity, too, with just a suggestion of milky chocolate, leading to white hot pepper and a crisp finish that has a decent length, but ultimately dries out.

PORTWOOD (41% ABV)

Ex-Buffalo Trace bourbon cask, then 6 months in ex-port cask

As if it wasn't obvious enough, looking at the deep red hue of this whisky, cherry tart, complete with marzipan and pastry, rises from the surface of this dram. The wood is playing a bigger part than in other expressions, with an almost rancio Cognac note coming through and a note of chocolate hiding in the wings. This is complex. The palate continues the brandy theme – I would have been fooled by this one without doubt. Juicy stone fruit and plenty of the dried varieties, too.

SINGLE CASK (60.2% ABV)

Ex-bourbon

This is a sweetshop/candy store of a whisky: cinder toffee, cream soda and a touch of plum sherbet on the nose – only a glimpse, mind, as every bit of the 60-or-so % ABV sneaks up quickly on you. Responds well to water, revealing pimento, a big smack of nutmeg and even a hint of saffron. Big in the mouth, with the whole spice draw dominating until it's replaced by wood spice, vanilla and, well, quite a bit of alcohol.

PEATED (46% ABV)

The peat is certainly apparent on the nose – there's sticky rib glaze, with a touch of carpet warehouse mustiness. Little in the way of fruit has survived, but what we do gain is a minerality that is most interesting. The finish is damp, morning campfire complete with blackened fish skin and tobacco residue.

PAUL JOHN

Take a visit to a street bar in Mumbai. Squint your eyes a little, so that everything turns a little blurry, then have a look around at what the patrons of the bar are drinking. They're drinking Scotch whisky. It's obviously Scotch whisky, because the colour suggests that the spirit has been aged and the bottle says 'whisky' on it – the labels even display typically Scottish names like Bagpiper and McDowell's. Now you open your eyes a little more and allow the scene to sharpen up. Something's amiss. The 'whisky' smells a little too light and tastes more like rum. And those names are... well, a little *too* Scottish to be genuine, surely? Welcome to whisky in India today, where nothing is as it seems and where 'malt' means 'molasses' and 'whisky' means 'rum'.

Let's ignore all that for a moment, though, and take a trip back to the 1820s, when Edward Dyer set up the Kasalui Distillery in the northern state of Himachal Pradesh, just on the western edge of the Himalayas. Dyer allegedly imported equipment from Scotland and England and chose the location based on the similarity with Scotland in terms of climate. The distillery is still operational today. Flash-forward a couple of hundred years and spirits account for 95% of all alcoholic beverages consumed in India today, and a large portion of that is Indian whisky. In fact, statistics show that between 2006 and 2011, India consumed 46% of all the whisky in the world. But, and it's a big but, this can mean anything from coloured and flavoured molasses-based spirits, to blended Scotch whisky with molasses-based spirits added to it. It should be noted that whisky is not the only victim here; gin and brandy are victims of this mockery, too, and these drinks are known as IMFL (Indian-made foreign liquor). The popularity of these products is really a story of availability and more recently, economics. Until

INDIA

Paul John

2001, importing foreign liquor was illegal, so domestic stuff was all that was available. After the restriction was lifted, the cost of buying imported liquor was prohibitive since the duty amounted to around 500% of the value of the product. This has since lowered significantly, but still remains around 150% of the value of the product. Even the cheapest blended Scotch whiskies are far more expensive than their Indian-made counterparts. Nevertheless, the emergence of the wealthy Indian upper classes has doubled the quantity of imported whisky over the past few years, and in turn become the catalyst for a better-quality (genuine) Indian whisky.

I first tried Paul John at The London Whisky Exchange Show in 2012, where it took everyone by surprise by being rather good. The John Distilleries Company was founded in 1992 and since then has built a portfolio of IMFL spirits brands under the Original Choice brand name. In only 20 years, Original Choice has topped 10 million cases per year, bottling rum, 'whisky' and 'brandy'. Now, though, it has turned its attention to the noble cause of single malt, using Indian malt at its distillery in Goa. Rather ironically, its single malt is not currently available in India as Paul John believe that domestic demand will only exist once the product has established itself overseas.

The production of Paul John malts is for the most part loyal to the practices of Scotland, but careful attention is given to the maturation process. Temperature and humidity in Goa both fluctuate across the year like the dial is being tampered with. This means rapid maturation times and significant evaporative losses. Paul John use a climate-controlled underground warehouse to mitigate some of this, but five years (as is the case with Brilliance and Edited) seems to be an adequate period of time for a balanced product. Scottish peat is being used for their peated expression and a small portion of peated malt makes up the Edited expression, too.

BRILLIANCE (46% ABV)

Initial bright tropical fruits lead into proper malted cereal notes and chocolate and caramel shortbread. The mouthfeel is full, creamy and very well balanced indeed, leading into classic wood spice,

Right Paul John is in mnay ways the diamond in the rough that is the Indian whisky market.

sticky prune, malty sweetness and a good finish. Nothing new to see here, but perfectly executed.

EDITED (46% ABV)

A wisp of nutty smoke underlies the aroma of this whisky, accompanied by a touch of almond butter and red apple. Smoke begins to build as the more delicate aromatics drown in it. The taste is deliciously sweet and dry, with a lip-smacking earthy smoke accompanied by wood tannin and barbecued peach.

CASK STRENGTH UNPEATED (55.2% ABV)

Distilled in 2009, bottled in 2013

Coconut husk and barley water are suppressed by the spirit energy contained in this one. Pineapple and orgeat syrup dominate the palate, which eventually gives way to a granola crunch. The addition of water uncovers candied pineapple.

CASK STRENGTH PEATED (55.5% ABV)

Distilled in 2009, bottled in 2013

The smoke here is initially sweet and round, like barbecued paneer. It changes, however, into something derived from an old cellar or basement – musty and wise. Cheese is back in the taste at first, leading into dried dark fruits and spiced chutney. Water reveals a new-carpet note and plenty of sweet florals on the palate. Delicious.

BOX

Dubbed by many as the 'most exciting whisky distillery in the world today', Box near Ådalen in Sweden is only just bottling its first official product. Founded in 2005, by brothers Mats and Per de Vahl, the operation is currently the most northerly whisky distillery (or *destilleri*, as it's spelled there) in the world and contained within a solitary box-like building that previously housed a sawmill and a power plant. Box is really just the tip of the iceberg that is the Swedish distilling movement, as there are now 16 dedicated malt distilleries in Sweden. Couple that with the fact that 15% of the whisky consumed in Sweden is single malt (the highest percentage relative to a country's total whisky consumption of any country in the world), and you have perhaps one of the most important whisky-drinking markets out there today.

They're not messing about with their home-made stuff, either. It all started with the Mackmyra Distillery, which began production in 1999 and has recently opened a second site, affording it a production capacity similar to that of Benromach in Scotland. Now we are seeing the likes of Bergslargens Destilleri in the wooden town of Nora, which has a capacity of 1.2 million litres (1.27 million quarts) of alcohol a year and matures its spirit in a 400,000-square metre (4.3-million square foot) underground bunker – although the future of that particular operation is in question. Then there's the remote Gotland Distillery off the coast of Stockholm in the Baltic Sea; those guys are even floor-malting their own barley using a custom-built robot that does the job of the maltman.

Robots aside, no other distillery is getting whisky geeks as sweaty under the arms as Box is. The reason for this is that Box is itself operated by whisky fanatics. 'Made for whisky geeks, by whisky geeks' ought to be their tagline. Unlike the distilleries mentioned above, there's no single element that sets it apart, but it's more that every stage of production has been painfully researched and placed under intense scrutiny.

Three different two-row spring barley varieties are being used for their unpeated whisky – types of malt traditionally used for brewing beer. 'Pilsner malt gives us lower yield but better body and flavours in the spirit', the distillery manager, Roger Melander, tells me. A Bobby mill is used to grind the malt down and fermentation is conducted using a French brewer's yeast, specially selected for the fruitiness it provides.

The shell-in-tube condensers use the nearby Ångermanälven River water that is either often frozen solid or close to it, and at some times of the year the condensers' temperatures hover just above 0°C (32°F). That makes for highly efficient condensation, and reduced copper contact. Even the new make is only just above 0°C (32°F). To counteract this effect, the distillation is purposely drawn out slowly to remove sulphurous compounds through extended copper contact.

Left Is it a church? Is it a power station? No, it's the future of whisky distilling in Sweden.

SWEDEN

Box

Stockholm

Right Precision and, dare I say, curiosity, is what elevates Box whiskies to a new level of finesse.

Below & below right Roger Melander, the master distiller scrutinizes every step of the maturation process at Box Destilleri.

The cask program that Roger Melander is managing is a unique combination of the traditional and highly progressive. Roger says, 'The Swedish cooper, Johan Thorslund, makes the best casks we have ever bought. He resizes most of our smaller bourbon casks and makes new casks in different sizes from Swedish, American, Hungarian and French oak.' Thorslund is also, especially for Box, creating 40-litre/42-quart 'anchor' casks, to conform to an old Swedish standard dating back to at least 1665. A range of toasting levels coupled with surface char is being explored, too, and just when you thought things had got extreme enough – the new oak casks are seasoned for six months, not with bourbon or wine, but with new-make spirit from Box itself. This is then dumped and the cask filled with fresh new-make spirit.

As a reflection of all these inquisitive trials, the team at Box released a limited run of five 20cl (7 fl. oz) bottles entitled 'Box Advanced Masterclass: Toasting'. It's likely to be the first of many, dare I say, 'educational' releases, the aim of which will be to demonstrate how different decisions adjust the flavour of the final product. Releasing a series like this also gives some insight into the meticulous thought that the distillery is taking with the development of its core range of bottlings. Speaking of which, the first official bottling in the 'Early Days Collection' has just been announced, under the appropriate title of 'The Pioneer' – You don't say.

UNPEATED (53.4% ABV)

40-litre ex-bourbon cask sample, roughly 3 years old
Golden delicious apple purée, lavender honey, brown butter, dried toothpaste and eventually some new-make lingering malty digestive biscuit/graham cracker characteristics. It's light and young on the palate, too, but with a soft precision, exhibiting poached pear, butter beans and minty white chocolate. The finish is surprisingly long, fresh and exceptionally clean.

THE LONDON
⋙ DISTILLERY ⋘
COMPANY

Snoop around the backstreets of Battersea in south-west London and you'll find something interesting happening on the old Ransome's Dock – previously one of the busiest in the city. This little area used to be alive with industry, and, as it transpires, there is still some action taking place in the area – The London Distillery Company.

As the youngest distillery to be featured in this book, The London Distillery Company is the first whisky distillery to open in London for over 100 years. In the eyes of the distillery's founder, Darren Rook, it doesn't seem quite so young, however. I have known Darren for a few years now and I am more than aware of the hoop-jumping that has been required on his part to get the place licensed and to generate the capital needed to get things up and running.

In long-established distilleries, you get the feeing that they were built bit-by-bit, like important equipment was just accumulated along the way. The London Distillery Company, on the other hand, is a showcase of sparkling new whisky-making apparel – from the little mash tun and array of washbacks to the beautiful copper pot still. The place has a London 'hipster' look about it, too. Where there would normally be operations manuals, there are cocktail books, and where a high-visibility jacket would normally hang, there's a tweed blazer. The iMac in the corner of the room completes the scene.

I was lucky enough to drop by on a random afternoon in early December 2013 and by pure chance the boys were conducting their first spirit run on the still. It's the first time I've ever tasted a virgin spirit run and it was quite a special moment for everyone present. We got to chatting about the process that the team had followed to get the outcome they were looking for, and yeast seemed to be the main topic of conversation. 'No one really thinks about yeast,' Darren told me. 'We're planning on trialling five contrasting yeast strains before we nail one down.' The proof was in the pudding of course, and the first yeast they had gone with was aptly named 'orange esters' - and orangey it was, even through to the new make, but it was immediately dismissed by Darren and his team.

I was inspired by the positive morale that the team displayed, even so early in the distillery's lifespan. How do you motivate yourself to create a great product, knowing that much of it won't be tasted for at least three years? For me, it was a poignant reminder of the lengthy contract that any distillery commits today. Nobody opens a whisky distillery to make money – it's a lifestyle choice, not a profession. But I suspect that the long-term rewards make it a very worthwhile endeavour.

ENGLAND

The London Distillery Company

⋙ LARK ⋘

For most of us, Tasmania might not seem like the obvious place to make malt whisky, having been traditionally better-known for its apples and, well, devils. But the mild climate, fresh air and diverse geography, not to mention plenty of peat, mean that 'Tassie' is not at all dissimilar to Scotland.

Despite only making whisky for 22 years, this diffident and unassuming island is now producing some of the best whiskies in the world. In 2014, the expression 'Sullivan's Cove French Oak', won the World Whisky Awards' coveted 'Best Single Malt' prize, the first time a whisky from outside Scotland or Japan has ever won the award. Strewth!

The population of Tasmania sits at 500,000 people, but given its huge area, it works out as approximately seven people per square kilometre. That's only a slightly higher population density than Islay, and given that Tasmania now has nine distilleries compared to Islay's eight, as well as the fact that both are relatively remote islands of the coast of their home nation, there do seem to be a few comparisons that can be drawn.

The varied styles of whisky made on Tasmania do not conform to the Islay mould, however. Most of the distilleries buy in their malt from the Cascade Brewery in Hobart, which also happens to be the oldest brewery in Australia. For me, it's perhaps the barley that really sets Tasmania apart; there is a distinct malty flavour in the finished product that is usually lost in Scottish malts. Peat is commonly used, but more as a seasoning than a significant part of the meal, with some of the distilleries opting to smoke-finish malt over peat reek, seeing as it isn't introduced during the drying phase.

William McHenry and Sons, which is currently the most southerly whisky distillery in the world, uses a unique 500-litre (528-quart) water-jacketed, electrically heated still, allowing for very precise control over the whole process. Then there's the Nant distillery, located in the Tasmanian Highlands, which uses a 180-year-old watermill to grind its malt, and is attempting to build a Highland category within Tasmania using, in their own words, 'million-year-old glacial water'. They will soon be growing and malting 100% of their barley, too.

Bill Lark is the man credited for starting all this, a one-man whisky industry and the godfather of Tasmanian whisky. He originally licensed his own house in Kingston, back in 1992, after petitioning to his local MP to change the Distillation Act of 1901, which required that any distillery used stills of a minimum 27,000 litres (28,530 quarts). Bill was successful, but since then has moved to more serious digs. Bill Lark tells me

that 'The only malt we've been able to obtain is from one of the local brewers, and we're using a traditional brewing barley.' The remoteness of Tasmania gives distillers and brewers little choice in the matter, but it would seem that backing the Tassies into a corner is the way to get good results. Ten years ago, Lark bought his own peat bog at Brown Marsh, which they estimate has around 500 years' worth of supply based on current requirements. In 2007, they purchased Tasmania's only cooperage and are in the process of installing a floor-malting program that will process all of their farm-grown barley. Once all the pieces fit together, Lark will be among the most self-sufficient whisky distilleries in the world.

LARK SINGLE CASK (43% ABV)

Sweet trolley/cart. Big flapjack and malty/oaty aroma to begin with, with added helpings of golden/light corn syrup. Moves on into burnt fruit cake, fig, prune and warm spices. On the palate, there's a shade more smoke than the nose suggested – hot, spicy and greasy, lingering away into Tasmanian apple pie, cloves and nutmeg.

Below Lark have paved the way for new Tasmanian distilleries, and surprised almost everyone in the process.

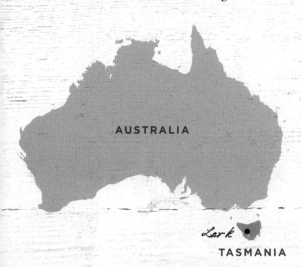

AUSTRALIA

Lark

TASMANIA

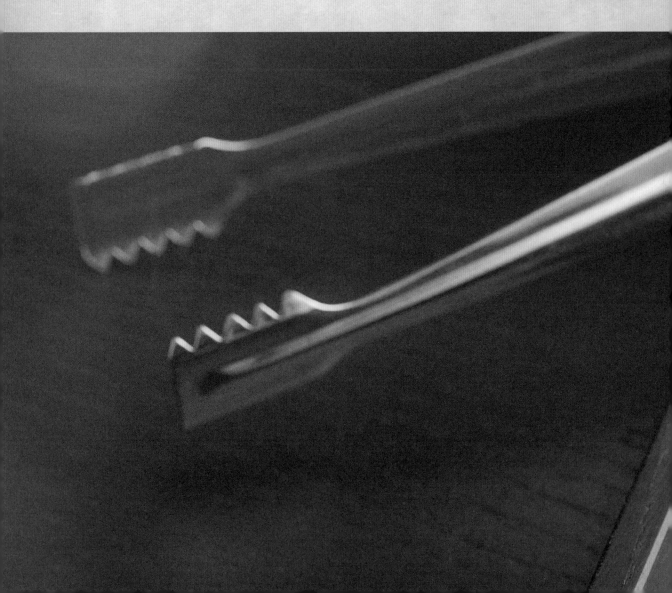

Part Four
Blends & Cocktails

How to Enjoy Whisky

Now listen: I enjoy a dram or a shot as much as the next person. The fact that I have spent so many pages exploring the history, science, production and nuances of whisky is testament to this fact. During the making of this book I sampled over 1,000 whiskies, and some of them benefitted greatly from a splash of water to awaken the serpent and reveal the more elusive elements of the spirit. For many people, water or ice are the only modifiers to be granted an audience with a glass of whisky; anything else is considered devil worship. For the real purists among us, the mere suggestion of water can be too much to stomach, confirming the old adage that there are only two things that a Highlander likes naked, and one of them is his whisky.

I have witnessed first hand the mood of a Scottish bar turning sour at the suggestion of mixing a malt whisky, but the Irish don't seem to care how you consume their whiskey, as long as you consume it. Lots of it. The Japanese take a more zen-like approach to things – for them, it's not what you mix whisky with, but rather how you mix it. In the US, rules about bourbon consumption are scarce, but it tends to fall into one of two categories: mixed and sweet, or straight from the bottle.

The truth is that the best way to enjoy whisky is the way that you most prefer it. Ignore the rule book and don't listen to the purists. Enjoyment cannot be learned or acquired; it's entirely subjective, so do it your own way – or don't do it at all.

Indeed, even the people who make the stuff cannot agree on the best way to analyse whisky, or to enjoy it. I have taken part in tastings with whisky distillers and blenders at which all samples were diluted by 50%, and others at which samples were served strictly at bottle or cask strength only, and covered for a minimum of 30 minutes before nosing commences.

My one and only tip for assessing whisky is to ensure that plenty of air flows through your mouth and out of your nose while tasting. This has the effect of carrying a good concentration of the volatile aromatic molecules over your smelling apparatus. It probably won't involve the wine-tasters 'slurp', but might mean a bit of 'swishing' and a lot of creepy heavy-breathing.

In the following section I've included a selection of mixed drinks and preparations that do a good job of celebrating the unique character of whiskies from all over the world. Some are for classic cocktails, and also include a little history and commentary. Others are original recipes or my own take on classic recipes. It's a pretty eclectic selection, but there should be something for everyone.

My Blends

The blending of whisky is something quite close to my own heart – after all, I've made a career out of combining things in an effort to create something greater than the sum of its parts. Blending your own whisky can be a very rewarding experience, but it can also be a waste of good booze if you get it wrong. One of the biggest traps I fall into when blending is knowing where to draw the line and admit that the mixture in front of you is doomed to fail, that no amount of sprucing up with other whiskies can save it. When that happens, remember you can always use a failed blend in cocktails or highballs – a good way of covering up a blending blunder!

Over the next few pages I have included five tried-and-tested blend formulas you can rely on. The proportions I've used give a good indication of the balance between grain and malt whisky in a typical blend, and also highlight some of the malts that add key aromatic and taste parameters to my own formulas. You can use them as they are, or take them as inspiration for your own creations. Most commercially sold blends are made up of anything from 20–60% grain whisky; my blends are at the lower end of this scale, which gives the malts an opportunity to sing a little bit louder.

You might also notice that most of my blends contain only five or six whiskies, as opposed to the 20-plus that sometimes make up popular blends. As with cocktails, I generally prefer to keep things simple, for several reasons. Firstly, it's unlikely that anyone will be rushing out to buy 20 different bottles of whisky just because I say they combine nicely. Secondly, the likes of you and me don't need to hedge our bets with a wide range of blended whiskies in the hope that one or two will become popular, like the commercial distilleries do. And thirdly, I honestly don't think that good blends need countless whiskies to taste good. Most malt whisky tastes great as it is, so why bother condemning a good dram to obscurity by spreading it too thin?

All the blends, except Grand Old Lustre, contain some grain whisky, which forms the backbone of the liquid. Grain whisky is becoming more readily available, but it is not something you're likely to find on a supermarket shelf. Cameron Brig is a grain whisky product that shouldn't prove too hard to track down, but if you are really struggling you can try using an Irish whiskey such as Bushmills Original (which contains a large proportion of grain spirit) as your grain base.

The first blend, Highland, is a typical balanced blend of whiskies that aims to highlight all that is great about Scotch whisky. The other four blends are more specific and explore specific families of flavour; they are unnatural and blatant abuses of the blender's art in an attempt to make something really special. These blends make interesting cocktail ingredients, too, since they provide a highly focused flavour to the drink, allowing for fine tuning by balancing the other ingredients.

HIGHLAND BLEND

250 ML/8¾ FL. OZ. CAMERON BRIG

100 ML/3½ FL. OZ. MORTLACH 18-YEAR-OLD
Meatiness, Fruit, Sherry

100 ML/3½ FL. OZ. MACDUFF 16-YEAR-OLD
Green, Mossy

100 ML/3½ FL. OZ. ARDMORE TRADITIONAL
Smoked Fruit

200 ML/7 FL. OZ. TEANINICH 10-YEAR-OLD
Herbal, Grassy

200 ML/7 FL. OZ. LONGMORN 16-YEAR-OLD
Nettle, Oats, Honey

150 ML/5¼ FL. OZ. OBAN 14-YEAR-OLD
Earth, Smoke, Rope

This Highland Blend is what I consider to be a day-to-day drinking blend. It really captures the essence of the whisky-making tradition, and in some ways emulates the classic blends of old. All the whiskies in this blend are from the Scottish Highlands; some are fruity, some nutty and a couple of them slightly smoky.

When drinking this blend I am transported to a misty Scottish morning. The air is settled, but moisture fills it and the heather is wet with dew. There's a faint smell of peat bog and the warm fragrance of rotting vegetation underfoot. The effort of walking causes a rush of heat through the bloodstream, which is tempered by the gurgling sound of clear cold water twisting through the glen. From my pocket I produce a hip flask, and this is what's in it.

ENGLISH COUNTRY GARDEN

300 ML/10½ FL. OZ. CAMERON BRIG

100 ML/3½ FL. OZ. LOCH LOMOND
Esters, Juniper

100 ML/3½ FL. OZ. CLYNELISH 16-YEAR-OLD
Honey, Wood

150 ML/5¼ FL. OZ. CARDHU
Grass, Apple, Pear

150 ML/5¼ FL. OZ. OLD PULTENEY NAVIGATOR
Blackberry, Honey, Rose, Salt

100 ML/3½ FL. OZ. HIGH WEST RENDEZVOUS
Rose, Lychee

50 ML/2 FL. OZ. GLENFARCLAS 30-YEAR-OLD
Allspice, Patchouli, Wood

50 ML/2 FL. OZ. ARDBEG
Smoke, Citrus

Floral, grassy and herbal characteristics are normally best when balanced out by solid wood notes and vanillin. This blend aims to do the complete opposite, however. I wanted the aroma and taste to be as fragrant, sweet and inviting as possible, even if it meant losing balance in the process. This whisky is nothing short of a garden perfume made from ingredients foraged by a six-year-old girl: flowers, grass, herbs, moss, a touch of fruit and busy bees.

This is a wonderful blend to drink with soda, since the bubbles lift some of the floral notes and the dilution serves to heighten the fragrant qualities of the whisky, knocking back any heaviness that manages to slip through.

FRUIT & NUT

300 ML/10½ FL. OZ. CAMERON BRIG

200 ML/7 FL. OZ. LONGMORN 16-YEAR-OLD
Porridge, Apple, Honey

200 ML/7 FL. OZ. DAILUAINE 16-YEAR-OLD
Esters, Fruit cake

100 ML/3½ FL. OZ. JURA 16-YEAR-OLD
Granola, Hazelnut

100 ML/3½ FL. OZ. ABERFELDY 21-YEAR-OLD
Fig, Lemon, Wood

100 ML/3½ FL. OZ. BALBLAIR 1997
Lemon, Mango, Apricot

This was a fun and relatively simple blend to come up with; after all, fruit bowls are fairly consistent from household to household, and the concept is less subjective than others. Imagine a fruit bowl furnished with a selection of your favourite fresh and dried fruit, then select the whiskies that best embody those fruits. The trick is not to get carried away with too many, which can result in a muddy, fruit-salad effect that tastes fruity, but not of any one fruit in particular.

The most common fruits to crop up in malt whisky are plum, apricot, fig, raspberry and apple, but they can take many shapes and forms. Plums, for example, can be fresh, stewed, preserved, folded between pastry, or dried into prunes. In this blend I aimed for a mixture of fresh and dried fruit.

Scotch Blend IV

Sweetshop

500 ml/17½ fl. oz. Girvan No. 4 Apps Grain Spirit
Pink prawns/shrimp, Banana candy

50 ml/2 fl. oz. Aultmore 15-Year-Old (Master of Malt Bottling)
Juicy fruit gum, Banana bread, Krispy Kreme doughnut

200 ml/7 fl. oz. Deanston 19-Year-Old (Master of Malt Bottling)
Dr. Pepper, Cinnamon, Buttercream frosting

100 ml/3½ fl. oz. Highland Park 10-Year-Old
Sponge cake, Cherry gum, Menthol

50 ml/2 fl. oz. Glencadam 21-Year-Old
Orange soda, Wood

50 ml/2 fl. oz. Springbank CV
Sugared pastry

100 ml/3½ fl. oz. Macduff 15-Year-Old
Cream soda, Lime oil, Moss

One of the most exciting things about whisky is its ability to conjure up childhood memories, especially that of the sweet shop/candy store. There's a whole ton of aromatics in malt whisky that are actually used to flavour candy, such as esters like isoamyl acetate (banana, pear drops) and isobutyl formate (raspberry sherbet), and other compounds like ethyl maltol (candy floss/cotton candy) and benzaldehyde (marzipan). The idea of this blend is to create a whisky that tastes like an all-out sweet shop assault, with that blast of warm candy aroma that hits you when you walk in, accompanied by the almost tangible feeling of sugar in the air and on your skin. All of the whiskies I have used are floral, fruity or sweet, and combined they have a long, syrupy linger.

Grand Old Lustre

500 ML/17½ FL. OZ. Clynelish 16-Year-Old
Wax, Honey, Glue, Wood

100 ML/3½ FL. OZ. Talisker 18-Year-Old
Mahogany, Tobacco, Chocolate

150 ML/5¼ FL. OZ. Aberfeldy 12-Year-Old
Saddle leather, Honey

250 ML/8¾ FL. OZ. Glencadam 21-Year-Old
Caramel, Varnish, Orange

50 ML/2 FL. OZ. Glenfarclas 21-Year-Old
Polish, Nectarine, Wood

50 ML/2 FL. OZ. Highland Park 40-Year-Old
Oak toast, Tea, Spice

The fifth and final blend is aptly named Grand Old Lustre. It is a combination of whiskies displaying plenty of polished wood, glue and gloss, finesse and age. My good friend Craig Harper describes this kind of whisky as 'like licking a sideboard'. I find this sort of thing delicious: various varieties of wood, from cedar to maple, walnut and, of course, oak, meld together to give a sense of wealth and grandness. Additionally, sweetness and tannin interplay with ethyl acetate, wood spice, nutty Sherry notes, leather and fruit esters to reinforce the notion of a richly furnished stately home.

This is a whisky to be savoured on its own, not because it contains expensive malts (which it does), but because the delicate aromatics that it holds are as fragile as the old furniture it aims to mirror. You'll also notice that there is no grain whisky in this blend; it's a blended malt.

This would be an expensive whisky if it was on sale commercially – the inclusion of Talisker, Highland Park and Glenfarclas make sure of that. Interestingly, though, it would legally only be able to label itself as a 12-year-old, because that is the age of Aberfeldy, the youngest malt in the bottle. But for me it's not the same without the creamy youthfulness that the Aberfeldy bestows, and it just goes to show that age statements should never be a mark of quality.

BEER & BUMP

Back when I opened my first bar, Purl, we were lucky enough to ride the crest of an unprecedented creative wave. Ideas for new drinks concepts came to us thick and fast, and while some of them were madcap, hair-brained designs, others had legs and became awesome cocktails that made it onto the list.

One such drink was inspired, in part, by the Boilermaker (see page 242). The concept was based around the ritual (perhaps a loose sense of the word) of American street drinking: that is, the stereotypical bum, clutching a bottle of hooch in a brown paper bag. 'Brown-bagging' is a loophole in the law governing open alcohol containers in public spaces in the US. We thought it would be fun to serve a drink in a bottle wrapped in brown paper, so that the guests would feel as if they were partaking in a barely legal activity while enjoying the drink. If we could have given them a park bench, we would have. The drink itself contained bourbon, apple juice, cardamom and apricot brandy. The bottle was beer-bottle sized and it

combined the two parts of the traditional Boilermaker into one not-so-neat package. We sprayed beer onto the brown paper for aromatic effect and served the drink at the table on a square of newspaper in place of a regular napkin.

Around a year later, we were ready for the second incarnation of the drink, and it was renamed Beer & Bump. This time the drink came in two parts: a shot of Jack Daniel's and a beer-flavoured drink in a bottle. We wanted to serve a 'beer' that was flavoured with ingredients complementary to the Jack. Looking at the flavour profile, we picked out characteristics such as banana, maple, oak and spice. Now the challenge was on to flavour a suitable beer, one that would complement Jack Daniel's from the get-go, and present the two alongside each other. Here is my updated recipe for Beer & Bump, which I think works a treat. The flavours infused in the beer do a wonderful job of softening the alcohol in the Jack Daniel's, so that the two drinks bounce off one another and beg you to keep on sipping!

35 ML/1¼ FL. OZ. JACK DANIEL'S OLD NO. 7 • 200 ML/7 FL. OZ. BUTTER BEER

•

For the Butter Beer:

50 G/3 TABLESPOONS BUTTER • 10 G/SCANT 1 TABLESPOON SUGAR

5 G/1 TABLESPOON DRIED BANANA CHIPS • 2 G/½ TEASPOON SALT

2 WHOLE CLOVES • 1 CARDAMOM POD • 2 SAGE LEAVES

500 ML/17 FL. OZ. DARK BELGIAN ALE (LEFFE BRUNE IS GOOD)

•

First, we need to flavour the butter. Melt it in a pan and add all the dry ingredients. Heat gently for 5 minutes, being careful not to burn the butter. Leave to stand for a few minutes, then pour off the clarified part of the butter into a separate bowl, leaving behind the milk solids and all the spices. Add the clarified butter to the beer and give it a vigorous stir. Seal it in a wide-necked vessel and put it in the fridge for 12 hours. The butter should solidify, allowing you to scoop it off the top. Pass the beer through a fine sieve to remove any extra lumps of butter, then keep in the fridge for up to a week.

Glass: Shot glass and bottle wrapped in brown paper

Garnish: Beer aroma and newspaper square

BOILERMAKER

1 BOTTLE MILLER LIGHT • 25 ML/1 FL. OZ. JIM BEAM WHITE LABEL

Serve the beer ice-cold from the fridge, and the bourbon in a short, thick shot glass.
Consume both liquids as you see fit. Make another.

Glass: Shot glass

Many of my American friends would surely argue that the Boilermaker is not a cocktail. And given that the drink normally comprises a shot of bourbon and a bottle of beer, they might be right. However, sometimes the most simple drinking rituals resonate more powerfully through bar culture than complex cocktails.

Popular wisdom tells us that a true Boilermaker should be a shot of bourbon dropped into a glass of beer. The drinker is then required to down the mixture in one. I personally prefer either shooting the bourbon and then sipping the beer, or sipping alternately between the two glasses. The night tends to last a little longer that way, too!

If you're still doubtful as to the cocktail credentials of this fantastic beverage, know this: the drink featured in the 1932 book *The Art of Mixing* by James Wiley and Helene Griffith, albeit under the name Block and Fall (walk a block, fall, walk a block, fall, and so on).

According to the *Oxford English Dictionary*, the term 'boilermaker' was first defined as a steam locomotive engineer almost 100 years previously, in 1834. It seems to make sense that a 'why have one drink when you can have two?' beverage such

as the Boilermaker shares its name with a sweat-stained, coal-smeared grease monkey. There is one tall tale that suggests the name Boilermaker (Beer & Bump) predates the boilermaker (Gear & Sump). It's a story I'm inclined to disbelieve, since it originates in my home county in the UK and people in those parts are often guilty of a little romanticization.

It's Christmas Eve, 1801, and we're in Camborne, Cornwall. The town's blacksmith, Richard Trivithick, has just finished engineering an early steam engine and plans to test it by driving it up Camborne Hill. The engine, known as the Puffing Devil, comes to a halt outside the local pub, and much celebration ensues, right on through until morning, the choice tipple for the evening being beer and whisky chasers with roast goose. Sadly, the story ends in disaster: the engine was parked up and the boiler allowed to burn dry, resulting in fire and the total destruction of the engine. A powerful reminder of the pitfalls of drinking one too many Boilermakers! Regardless, the story became one of Cornwall's best-loved drinking songs, *Camborne Hill*.

BLOOD & SAND

35 ML/1¼ FL. OZ. DEWAR'S WHITE LABEL

35 ML/1¼ FL. OZ. CHERRY HEERING LIQUEUR

35 ML/1¼ FL. OZ. MARTINI ROSSO VERMOUTH

35 ML/1¼ FL. OZ. FRESH ORANGE JUICE

•

Shake all the ingredients with ice and strain into a chilled martini glass.

Glass: Martini   **Garnish:** Cherry

This drink was on the menu at the first cocktail bar I worked at. It was my least favourite of all the cocktails we served and I distinctly remember it reminding me of vomit. I came to love it later, however, and more than most I think this drink is a great reflection of its name. Now that I've sold it to you so well, let's discuss its origins and ingredients!

The drink was named after the 1922 Rudolf Valentino film of the same name. It's a silent movie about a bullfighter, which explains the blood and sand connection. Exactly who invented the drink is not known, but the first time the recipe was published, like so many other drinks, was in the 1930 *Savoy Cocktail Book*.

The drink calls for equal parts Scotch, cherry brandy, sweet vermouth and orange juice, which might go some way towards explaining my initial distaste – these are not ingredients you imagine would pair nicely. Indeed, it would seem that the bartender responsible committed the cardinal sin of mixing drinks by colour rather than flavour, since the vermouth and cherry brandy are both red (blood) and the Scotch and orange juice are both orange (sand). Serendipity should never be underestimated, however – after all, Teflon, plastic and even the colour mauve were all invented by accident! The same luck was granted to the inventor of the Blood & Sand. He was only looking for a nice-coloured drink, and what he ended up with was a fortuitous and flavoursome combination of ingredients. Whisky is the backbone of this drink, but expect acidity, sweetness and big competition between all the powerful aromatics.

PICKLEBACK

50 ML/2 FL. OZ. JAMESON IRISH WHISKEY
50 ML/2 FL. OZ. DILL PICKLE JUICE

•

Pour the two liquids into separate shot glasses. Shoot the whiskey, then the pickle juice. That's about it!

Glass: Shot glass

I was first introduced to the phenomenon of the Pickleback by James 'Jocky' Petrie of The Fat Duck restaurant. He was sitting at the bar in Purl one evening and after a couple of drinks started raving about a mad drink that combined Irish whiskey and pickle brine. It sounding both disgusting and fascinating, so I immediately sent the barman back out to the shop to buy a jar of dill pickles. Jocky instructed us to pour Irish whiskey into one shot glass and the juice from the dill pickle jar into another. You shoot back the whiskey, then chase it with the sweet-and-sour pickle brine. It was amazing.

So how does it work? It would appear that the intense sweet, sour and saltiness of the pickle juice does a very good job of detracting from the alcohol burn of the whiskey. But not only that, it actually couples nicely with the liquor, leaving a kind of sweet, toffee-apple aftertaste that is far from unpleasant. The ritual is not dissimilar from that of the Tequila Slammer and Sangrita, which achieve much the same thing, albeit with very different flavour combinations.

Now I must confess at this stage to being an Irish Pickleback advocate, which is not necessarily true to the historical roots of the drink. It was T. J. Lynch of NYC bar Breslin who, in 2009, made a Pickleback with Jameson whiskey famous, but it would appear that the practice had been going on with bourbon for at least a year or two before that. According to New York bartender Toby Ceccini (famed for his part in the creation of the *Cosmopolitan*), the drink was first served to him in 2007 with Old Crow Bourbon at the Bushwick Country Club in the Williamsburg neighbourhood of Brooklyn. It seems that the ritual may have been inspired by a culture of chasing liquor with pickle juice adopted by Texan long-haul truck drivers. The salt supposedly helps keep you hydrated, thus preventing a morning-after trucker headache. Since Texas borders Mexico, it seems plausible that the idea originally came from the Sangrita.

Either way, the quality of the pickle juice is far more important than the quality of the whiskey, since the ritual is designed to clear the palate of low-grade liquor, so choose your pickles wisely!

MALT BLANC

20 ml/³/₄ fl. oz. Brewed Milk Oolong Tea

35 ml/1¼ fl. oz. Dalwhinnie 16-Year-Old

120 ml/4¼ fl. oz. Unsweetened Soy Milk

15 g/1 Tablespoon Wildflower honey (according to taste)

●

Brew the tea at 90°C (195°F) at a ratio of one part tea to 20 parts water and allow to infuse for 5 minutes. Strain the leaves out and leave to cool. Combine all the ingredients in a cocktail shaker and shake with ice. Remove the ice, then 'dry shake' the liquid to introduce plenty of air. Pour the drink into a tall glass and garnish with a cinnamon stick dusted with icing/confectioners' sugar.

Glass: Sundae   **Garnish:** cinnamon stick dusted with icing/confectioners' sugar

This is a drink I invented for L'Aubergaude hotel in Morzine, France. The aim was to create a whisky cocktail that was highly approachable, but that also drew influence from the French Alps. The obvious route was to make a white-coloured drink, which typically means milk, cream or yoghurt, but I wanted to avoid the heaviness of those ingredients so instead opted to use soy milk. Soy milk, and rice milk for that matter, do have a certain affinity with malt whisky, a kind of nutty sweetness that tastes very wholesome and 'of the earth'.

That nutty characteristic led me to the next ingredient: tea. Chilled green tea is a very popular whisky mixer in China, where the almost citrus-like grassiness of the tea lengthens the spirit, but remains sympathetic to its character. Green tea didn't deliver quite the flavour I wanted, though, so I turned to oolong, and more specifically, milk oolong. This particular type of is prized for its

milky texture; it's oily, naturally sweet and not at all bitter when prepared correctly.

The drink required some sweetening, which would improve the texture, and also balance out the dryness of the other ingredients and suppress some of the volatile alcohol characteristics. I quickly found that too much alcohol heat in a milky drink was especially unpleasant – milk shouldn't burn; it simply isn't natural. I settled on wildflower honey, which contributed fruitiness along with its delicate sweet flavour, once again making a good partner to malt whisky.

Speaking of the whisky, I chose Dalwhinnie 16-year-old. There were two good reasons for this, the first being Dalwhinnie's dessert-like qualities of caramel, chocolate and silky vanilla custard. The second, less important but very apt, reason is that Dalwhinnie is Scotland's highest distillery – the perfect choice for a drink named after the highest mountain in Western Europe.

Peat & Melon

30 ml/1¼ fl. oz. Mortlach 16-Year-Old • 20 ml/¾ fl. oz. Talisker 10-Year-Old

20 ml/¾ fl. oz. Merlet Melon Liqueur • A Tiny Pinch of Salt

•

Stir the whiskies together with ice, the melon liqueur and salt for 1 minute. Strain into a chilled glass and garnish with the rocket/arugula leaf and a small blob of olive oil.

Glass: Tulip glass   **Garnish:** Rocket/arugula leaf and peppery olive oil

Although many of my creations have been inspired by food, I'm always quick to stress that the influence the kitchen has on the bar is not as straightforward as some people might have you think. Taking the essence of a dish – the interplay between ingredients, the sweet and sour balance, the correct use of seasoning – is a tricky art to master, but rewarding when done well.

One of my few truly successful attempts at transforming a food concept into a drink is Peat & Melon. The food in question is the delicious Parma ham and melon salad I scoff every time I go to Italy. The genius of the salad is the salty, meaty taste of the ham coupled with the intoxicating, sweet and slightly acidic melon. Salt and sweet are under-recognized bedfellows – where would we be without salted caramel? – and cocktail bartenders are missing a trick by under-using salt in their creations. When I created the Peat & Melon back in 2010 I aimed to correct this.

It only became possible once Merlet melon liqueur was released. Merlet is the only brand I recognize as coming close to the naturally vibrant melon flavour you find in a ripe honeydew melon. Sure, you could muddle or juice a melon, but that's

a total hassle and the chances are your drink will end up cloudy or lumpy – not desirable traits. In short, no other melon liqueur will do, especially not the toxic green one that shall remain nameless. With the melon box ticked, it was time to choose a whisky or whiskies that best represent salty cured ham. This was all about keeping the flavour delicate, but decidedly animal-like.

Whiskies with a meatiness about them tend to be formed from sulphurous new-make spirit. This means minimal copper contact and probably a 'worm tub' condenser. When whisky blenders are looking for meaty, there's one distillery they will always turn to: Dufftown's oldest distillery, Mortlach. The brawn of Mortlach is a powerful backbone to many blends and it was the obvious choice for this drink, but I also needed something a little more funky and salty to provide the spice, fruit and smoke that is also present in Parma ham. For this I turned to Talisker. Talisker is made on the Isle of Skye, and is a great example of whisky that has taken a good look at its surroundings, then concentrated them into the bottle. It's peppery, fruity, smoky, and most of all, noticeably salty: perfect for my cocktail.

WALKER'S GINGER BREW

When I visited the Cardhu Distillery in Scotland's Speyside region I was also shown around the Johnnie Walker museum. Cardhu is considered the spiritual home of Walker after it was bought by them back in 1893. While I was being shown around the relics, the discussion moved on to other products that the Walker family had made during the 19th century. John Walker himself started out as a tea blender and grocer, and many of these items continued to be sold, even after the whisky business had taken off. One such product was ginger beer, and when I returned from the trip I got in touch with the Johnnie Walker archives to find out more.

Deep in rural Scotland there is a building housing the largest collection of historical alcohol-related documents in the world that date back hundreds of years. The archive is strictly closed to the public, but I have on occasion been granted access. It's here that the only known document with John Walker's signature exists.

The archives also record the brewing of Walker's ginger beer. An 1825 stock inventory shows that Walker had two casks for the brewing of fermented ginger beer and a number of bottles intended for its packaging. Thirty years later in 1857, the store still held stocks of ground ginger, whole ginger and preserved ginger, presumably either for general sale or for the production of ginger beer.

Pairing whisky with ginger is nothing new, since the two have a strong affinity with one another, and 'Scotch and dry' is one of the most widely consumed whisky drinks in the world. For my version of Walker's Ginger Brew I have brewed a ginger beer in the traditional manner, with the exception of spiking it with some Johnnie Walker Black Label.

To do this you need to make a 'ginger beer plant' (GBP), which is basically a living culture of yeast and ginger. The living ingredients are used in a similar way to a sourdough starter for baking, comprising a mixture of ground ginger, sugar, yeast and water which, when left to react, encourages acid build-up through the interaction of the ingredients. The good news is that, just like sourdough, you can keep this culture fed and use it over and over again, marvelling as the flavour develops.

For the GBP

200 ML/7 FL. OZ. WARM WATER • 7G/¼ OZ. CHAMPAGNE YEAST

50 G/2 OZ. SUGAR • 25 G/1 OZ. GROUND GINGER

•

Put the water, yeast, 10 g/⅓ oz. of the sugar and 5 g/⅙ oz. of the ginger into a sterilized container and stir well. Set aside in a warm place, covered. Every day for 4 days, add a further 10 g/⅓ oz. sugar and 5 g/⅙ oz. ginger. After 5 days you will have a finished GBP, which should be visibly alive and bubbling away nicely. This can then be refrigerated, or fed every few days to maintain a healthy culture.

For the Walker's Ginger Brew

1.5 Litres/1½ Quarts Water • 10 g/⅓ oz. Sliced Medium-Hot Red Chilli

20 g/¾ oz. Finely Grated Fresh Ginger • 20 g/¾ oz. Grated Lemon Zest

3 g/½ Teaspoon Cream of Tartar • 240 g/1¼ Cups Caster/Superfine sugar

60 g/2¼ oz. GBP • 240 ml/8½ fl. oz. Johnnie Walker Black Label

•

First, sterilize a pair of 1-litre/1-quart plastic bottles. Bring a third of the water to the boil and add the chilli, fresh ginger, lemon zest and cream of tartar. Immediately remove from the heat and allow to cool for 10 minutes, stirring continuously. Pass it through a sieve, then dissolve the sugar in it. Add the rest of the water, along with the whisky. Finally, whisk in the GBP and transfer the liquid to the bottles.

Leave in a warm place for exactly 2 days, then transfer to the refrigerator for 1 day. Drink within 2 weeks. As with anything involving yeast, there's always an element of unpredictability (explosions are not unheard of), so the best practice is to store bottles far away from anything valuable.

IRISH COFFEE

60 ML/¼ CUP DOUBLE/HEAVY CREAM

150 ML/5¼ FL. OZ. ETHIOPIAN COFFEE
(such as Yirgacheffe, or something similarly floral and peachy)

35 ML/1¼ FL. OZ. GREEN SPOT IRISH WHISKEY • 5 G/1 TEASPOON SUGAR

•

Put the cream in a cream whipper (or beat it by hand in a stainless-steel bowl) and warm it in a bowl of hot water for 30 minutes. Brew the coffee, then add the sugar and whisky and allow to cool in the cup for 5–10 minutes. Dispense the warm cream on top and serve immediately.

Glass: Beer mug

I have long preached that Irish coffee is one of the world's biggest abominations. Indeed, even the finest Irish whiskey and most delicious coffee can often do a very good job of obliterating each others' redeeming features, resulting in slightly alcoholic coffee with a peculiar, 'woody' taste to it.

Now that I've finished burying the entire concept of an Irish coffee, it's time to reveal the only recipe that I would ever use to combine the two in liquid harmony. To explain, first let's look at the origins of Irish coffee to understand the reason for its existence.

It's the famous wet winter of 1942 and consequent grounded planes at Shannon Airport in Ireland that force delayed passengers to hole up in the airport bar. Bartender Joe Sheridan observes his weary patrons and takes the unprecedented step, which eludes so many bartenders, of inventing a classic cocktail. Whether it was known to him or not, the combination of sugar, fat, alcohol and caffeine provides everything the body needs in situations that demand extreme levels of pick-me-up-ness.

The key to making a great Irish coffee is matching the coffee and whiskey sympathetically. To do this we must first find the character traits they have in common. This might be the caramel character shared by Redbreast 12-year-old and a single-origin coffee from Guatemala, for example. I also believe that lighter whiskies and coffees tend to work better, which is as good a reason as any to continue using Irish whiskey.

The second important consideration is temperature. Make the drink too hot and it becomes spirity and unpleasant, requiring more sugar to counteract the dryness of the alcohol. It must be balanced with the cream on top, which acts as a kind of insulation blanket for the lips as you sip through to the main event. I prefer to serve the cream and coffee at the same temperature. I would always recommend making the coffee in a cafetière/French press, which gives the greatest clarity in the cup and allows the flavour of the coffee to shine through. Use white sugar, not brown, which will distort the flavour of the both the coffee and the whiskey.

WHISKY GUMS

200 ml/7 fl. oz. Whisky (see below) • 30 g/1¼ oz. Powdered Gelatine
180 g/½ Cup Liquid Glucose • 150 g/¾ Cup Sugar
5 g/1 Teaspoon Malic Acid • Icing/Confectioners' Sugar, for Dusting

•

Put half the whisky in a saucepan and heat it to at least 60°C (140°F) with the gelatine, whisking until fully dissolved. Remove it from the heat and set aside. Add the remaining ingredients, except the icing/confectioners' sugar, to another pan and heat until they form a caramel, removing it from the heat only once it reaches exactly 126°C (259°F). Allow to cool to below 100°C (212°F), then quickly mix in the gelatine mixture and pour into greased chocolate moulds. Place in the fridge for a few hours, then turn out and dust with icing/confectioners' sugar.

Credit where it's due: this idea came from a visit to the Fat Duck restaurant in Bray, England. My good friend Jocky Petrie was head of the development kitchen at the restaurant and I was lucky enough to spend a day working with him in 2010. One of the innovative courses they had devised there aimed to recreate the classic wine-gum candy, only this time it had real booze in it and it was whisky!

The Fat Duck made four different 'whisky gums', each from a different single malt, and I found it an excellent way to appreciate the differences in flavour without having to sip my way through four whole glasses. Also, the fact that the alcohol was evaporated off and tempered by some sweetness meant that some flavours were made more apparent than they would normally be. The flip side was that the drop in alcohol also dumbed down some of the more complex spice, tannin and dry fruitiness you might expect to get from a good glass of whisky. I think there's also something to be said for the mouthfeel and thick texture in this recipe; when coupled with the usual whisky characteristics, it highlights a sort of primal, nectar-like quality that I think is present in all malt spirits, but usually only as a distant backdrop.

The Fat Duck's recipe for these gums makes a melt-in-the-mouth jelly that softens as soon as it hits the palate, then lingers around, getting more and more gloopy as it melts. Although this is delicious, I wanted my gums to be more reminiscent of the jaw-achingly chewy gums I remember buying in twisted plastic packets when I was young. I've also included a couple of extra ingredients that give that mouth-puckering sweet-and-sour effect.

The whisky that you choose is your own choice, but I recommend making a selection of gums that cover a broad spectrum of flavour. Stand-out gums for me have been Lagavulin 16-year-old, Highland Park 18-year-old, Glenfarclas 15-year-old, Jameson Irish Whiskey, Four Roses Yellow Label and Jack Daniel's Gentleman Jack.

HET PINT & COG

200 ML/7 FL. OZ. HIGHLAND PARK 12-YEAR-OLD • 50 ML/2 FL. OZ. SWEET OLOROSO SHERRY

400 ML/14 FL. OZ. SINCLAIR BREWERIES RED MACGREGOR ALE • 100 G/3½ OZ. CASTER/SUPERFINE SUGAR

3 ALLSPICE BERRIES • 3 CLOVES • 1 LARGE CINNAMON STICK

•

Put all the ingredients in a saucepan, cover with a lid and heat gently. Monitor the temperature using a thermometer, and once the mixture reaches 75°C (167°F), scoop out and discard the spices and serve. You can use other beers, but Sinclair Breweries Red MacGregor from Orkney is the real deal and the only true Orcadian way to make a Cog. Serves 6

When I visited the island of Orkney and the Highland Park Distillery, my good friend Daryl Haldane let me in on a little Orkney tradition of drinking whisky from a cog. I must confess that I'd never heard of this ritual before. Further research revealed that no one outside of Orkney had ever come across it, let alone written about it. For that reason, I believe this to be the first and only whisky book to include a cog recipe.

The cog itself looks like an ornate bucket, and is very similar in style to a classic Viking bucket. No surprises there, given the level of Scandinavian influence on the island. The bucket is distinguishable by two, sometimes three, vertical handles that follow the angle of the bowl. Usually cogs are large, capable of holding around two or three litres of liquid, but smaller ones (like the one pictured) are also available. It's possible that the cog is named after the cog boat from the 10th century, since the bucket is somewhat reminiscent of the protruding bow and stern.

It's customary to serve a cog at weddings on Orkney, where it acts like a kind of shared punchbowl. Traditionally, there are three cogs that circulate around the room, the geud (best) man's, the priest's and the bride's. When the cog is passed on, the guest grips the handles and quaffs a mouthful of punch, then passes it on to the next guest. The three-handled versions are rare and were apparently created so that the bride's father could grip the spare handle and prevent over-eager guests from sampling more than they were due!

The drink that goes into the cog is reminiscent of some old Scandinavian beverages, but the fact that it contains whisky tells us that there's no small amount of Scottish influence here, too. The drink is very similar to the classic het pint, which is traditionally drunk during the Scottish Hogmanay (New Year). Where they differ is that cog doesn't normally have egg in it, unlike the het pint, which is more of a beer and whisky eggnog. Cog recipes vary across Orkney, and some families have a proprietary formula that they guard with their lives. This recipe is based on a combination of some of the recipes that I overheard in Orkney, with a few extra flourishes.

MIZUWARI

50 ML/2 FL. OZ. NIKKA FROM THE BARREL

150 ML/5¼ FL. OZ. SCOTTISH MINERAL WATER (OR WATER OF YOUR CHOICE)

•

Put a few chunks of hand-cracked ice in a highball glass; if you can get hold of the crystal-clear stuff, then all the better. Add the whisky and water and stir for 1 minute. Japanese tradition dictates that you should stir only 3½ times, but I feel it benefits from a little extra chilling. Try not to disrupt the ice too much; it should be a quiet process. Remove the spoon and serve with a warm oshibori (towel).

Glass: Highball tumbler

The Japanese ritual of *mizuwari* is a great example of the simplicity of whisky winning through. On the face of it, this drink is nothing more than whisky, water and ice, but if there's one thing that the Japanese do well, it's ice. If there's another thing they do well, it's whisky. And they're not bad at water, either.

I was intrigued the first time I was served a Mizuwari by legendary bartender Kichi-San in Tokyo's underground Star Bar. Suntory Yamazaki, hand-cracked ice and crystal-clear water were added to a glass, and the concoction was silently and skillfully stirred for just the right length of time. A quick sniff alerted me to some faint aromatics of whisky, but it was in the taste where I was really surprised. The liquid itself was very cold indeed, and whipped around my mouth with tropical fruits like pineapple and lychee, then slipped away like a fruity little serpent. The other surprising thing was the sweetness – oh, the sweetness! – despite having had no sugar added at all. I put much of that down to the gloopiness of the liquid post-chilling. Since then I've often heavily diluted whisky to see what effect it has on the flavour. Take it (almost) out of the

equation, and you have the opportunity to experience whisky in a whole new light.

Bourbon & Branch is a similar drink traditionally drunk in America. I was first introduced to it by the Ian Fleming novel *Diamonds Are Forever*, in which Bond orders one because it is 'fashionable in racing circuits'. The author goes on to explain that 'real bourbon drinkers insist on having their whiskey in the traditional style, with water from high up in the branch of the local river where it will be purest'. It seems that whisky-drinkers in the 1960s were a discerning crowd.

I've seen many a distiller and blender brooding over the effect that different types of water have on whiskies. Once water becomes 75% of your drink, things like the pH, mineral content and TDS (total dissolved solids) begin to have a big impact on flavour perception. Mineral salts are very much like table salt, and so can accentuate certain characteristics as well as providing a harder, more chalky texture. Soft water, with a lower TDS, tends to feel sweeter as it slinks around your mouth, and water with a high (alkaline) or low (acid) pH can give a boost to spicy flavours and smoke.

Hot Toddy

500 ML/17½ FL. OZ. THE BALVENIE DOUBLEWOOD • 100 G/3½ OZ. HONEY • 100 G/½ CUP SUGAR

150 ML/5¼ FL. OZ. FRESHLY SQUEEZED LEMON JUICE • 3 LARGE CINNAMON STICKS

5 WHOLE CLOVES • 1 STAR ANISE POD • 5 SPRIGS OF LAVENDER • LEMON SLICES, TO GARNISH

Put all the ingredients in a sealable bottle and give it a good shake. Allow to sit for a good week before using. To prepare the drink, pour 60 ml/¼ cup Toddy Infusion into a mug and top up with 150 ml/⅔ cup hot water. Garnish with a slice of lemon.

Take a quick flick through the history pages of this book and you're likely to find more than a couple of references to the medicinal uses of whisky. There's a reason that they call it 'Grandpa's old cough medicine': only 80 years ago it would have been possible, in the US, to get a prescription from a doctor for medicated whiskey. These days we are quite rightly aware of the negative impact that alcohol can have on our health, but for short-term gains whisky should not be underestimated.

In fact, as I write this very line I regret to inform you, dear reader, that I have been overcome with a bout of the common cold. Needless to say, I have taken measures to relieve my condition by way of carefully (self-) prescribed whisky. I am pleased to report that it has lifted my mood and settled my ailments.

The hot toddy is not the only antidotal whisky-based drink out there – whisky on its own does a pretty good job – but it is perhaps the best of them. Thought to be named after the Indian drink 'toddy', made from fermented palm sap, the Hot Toddy is a veritable dream-team of medicinal heavyweights. Hell, I don't think I've ever drunk one when I didn't have an illness of some sort!

There's an old Scottish cold remedy that instructs the patient to retire to bed with a large whisky toddy, to hang a bowler hat at the foot of the bed, and drink until there appear to be two hats. Obviously the chief ingredient here is whisky, and the alcohol contained within is a one-two punch of antiseptic and anaesthetic. Next is the lemon, full of vitamin C (which is also an antiseptic) and sour, to refresh the mouth. Then there's sugar or honey, which balances the lemon, but more importantly, provides instant-access energy. Spices augment the ensemble though anaesthetic effect (cloves) and heated invigoration (cinnamon). Lastly, there's hot water, which extracts and interacts with all the other ingredients, then vaporizes them to form hot steam that cleanses the olfactory system and soothes the throat.

My recipe sticks to the basic toddy formula, but I've included a few additional ingredients and tweaked some others. The recipe calls for making your own Toddy Infusion, and this is by far the best way to do things, because you only need to add hot water in your hour of need, rather than messing about with all those spices.

IRISH CREAM LIQUEUR

First, let me tell you that I am not the greatest advocate of off-the-shelf cream liqueurs. It's not so much to do with the flavour – I actually quite like the taste of Baileys and its close relatives – it's more to do with the audacity of the whole thing, that someone, at some point, deemed it OK to combine Irish whiskey and fresh cream in a shelf-stable bottle. God knows what sordid procedures the manufacturers of these products have developed to make the stuff last so long. Deals have been made with the devil, though, and even an open bottle is guaranteed by the manufacturer to taste good for at least two years. If the nukes hit tomorrow, the surviving cockroaches could live off Baileys.

The stability of the product is helped along by the alcohol content, which stops the cream from souring, but there is also a complex series of homogenization (refining particle size) and emulsification (preventing separation of fats) processes that depend on added emulsifiers and vegetable oil, among other things. So it struck me that it would be nice to make an Irish cream liqueur that forgoes the shelf life, but tastes delicious while it lasts.

The first Irish cream liqueur was Baileys, which was launched in 1974. Its origins can be found in such drinks as the 'flip' (eggs, sugar, spirit, spice) and of course in Irish coffee (see page 254). In a sense, it is a cold Irish coffee that has been stirred together to form a kind of a coherent, milky mass. The difference with the liqueur is that it must be composed of at least 40% Irish whiskey – by my reckoning – to achieve the necessary alcoholic strength. If the strength of the liqueur is below 16%, it is at a greater risk of spoiling quickly.

My recipe includes a selection of spices and flavourings, too, which both enhance and balance some of the flavours present in the cream and the whiskey. The quantities of these ingredients are my own recommendations, and you can adjust them if you want to knock back or lift up a specific flavour.

800 ML/3½ Cups Whole Milk • **0.5 G Vanilla Seeds** • **25 G/1 OZ. Cacao Nibs** • **200 G/1 Cup Sugar**
5 G/1 Teaspoon Salt • **15 G/½ OZ. Freshly Coarse-Ground Coffee** • **400 ML/1¾ Cups Bushmills Black Bush**
150 ML/⅔ Cup Double/Heavy Cream • **2 G Sodium Alginate (Optional)**

•

Sterilize a suitable bottle to hold your liqueur, either by boiling it in hot water or using a sterilizing solution.

Put the milk, vanilla and cacao nibs in a pan and bring to a simmer. Hold it there for 30 minutes, then strain through muslin/cheesecloth. Return the liquid to the pan along with the sugar and salt, and allow to reduce slowly for an hour, or until you are left with half the liquid – about 450 ml/2 cups in total. Turn off the heat and allow to cool for a minute, then add the coffee. Stir well and after 5 minutes, strain the liquid through a fine sieve/strainer or tea strainer. Allow to cool down, then stir in the whiskey.

Put the mixture in a jug blender (or use a jug and an immersion blender) and blitz for 20 seconds while steadily pouring in the cream. Stop the blender and pour the finished liqueur into the sterilized bottle. Keep refrigerated for up to a month. If you want to make the liqueur thicker, try adding a gram or two of sodium alginate during the blending stage. It's a natural thickener of dairy products that gives the impression of a more fatty consistency without actually increasing the fat.

It keeps for at least a week in the fridge – any longer and you're not doing it right! You can serve it over ice, mix it into your cappuccino, or pour it over your dessert.

Makes approximately 1 litre/4¼ cups

Glossary

Amylase Malting enzyme that converts starch into its soluble form; also found in saliva.

Bære Oldest variety of British barley.

Backset see sour mashing.

Beta-glucan Starch family prevalent in rye grain; partly responsible for its gluey consistency when mashed.

Bourbon cask 180–200-litre (90–211-quart) charred American oak cask.

Bushel Old unit of measurement equivalent to eight gallons and used commonly for cereals.

Butt Large 500-litre (528-quart) cask traditionally used for storing Sherry.

Caramel Non-sweet colour additive used to add the effect of longer maturation and for colour consistency. Not permitted in bourbon and straight whiskey.

Charring Non-penetrative and aggressive flame burning of the internal surface of a cask to liberate flavourful compounds and aid with spirit interaction; barrels may be charred to various degrees.

Chill filtering Controversial finishing process used for some whiskies wherein the liquid is cooled to below 0°C (32°F) and filtered to remove flavourless residual haze that can be unsightly. Critics believe the process also removes body and flavour.

Cooper/cooperage Maker/raiser of barrels for the wine and spirits industry.

Diastase Malting enzymes that are naturally present within cereals.

Doubler Pot-still used in the distillation of American whiskey through which the alcohol from the continuous-still passes to create the final spirit.

Draff Spent cereals left over after mashing. High in fibre and protein, these are processed into animal feed.

Drum malting Think tumble/spin dryer that turns and cools barley grains during malting.

Ester A chemical compound formed by the interaction of an acid and an alcohol; typically smells fruity and floral.

Feints The last alcohol to come through on the final (typically second) distillation. Low in alcohol and high in fusel oils, these are mixed with foreshots and redistilled in the next spirit run.

First-fill A barrel that is being filled for the first time with malt whisky/Irish whiskey, but has typically already been filled with bourbon or Sherry – so actually it is a second fill!

Foreshots The first spirit to emerge during the final (typically second) distillation. High in alcohol and some dangerous volatiles, these are redistilled with the feints in the next spirit run.

Floor malting Traditional process of malting barley, where the grains are spread evenly across a large floor space and regularly turned over, typically over a week-long period (but it varies).

Germination Hormonal trigger that kicks-off growth mechanisms in barley during malting.

Gramineae Family of grasses to which all major cereals belong.

Green malt Malted barley before it has been dried.

Hogshead 250-litre (264-quart) cask made from American oak, usually by adding extra staves in to a bourbon cask.

Kiln drying Process of halting the germination and malting process though heating with or without peat.

Lauter Filtering screen in the base of a mash tun.

Lyne arm The elbow at the top of a pot-still that carries alcohol vapour from the body of the still to the condenser. Lyne-arm angle and gauge affects the character of the spirit.

Malting Process of enzyme-based cell-wall destruction, typically in barley.

Mothballed A distillery that has ceased production, but not been decommissioned.

Peat Plant matter that has decomposed over thousands of years in an acidic environment with poor drainage. When cut, dried and burned, it is a crude fuel source, traditionally used to dry malted barley, which imparts a smokiness into the finished whisky.

Phenol/Phenolic Organic compounds derived from peat reek that imparts tarry, smoky, charred and burnt characteristics to a whisky.

PPM Phenolic parts per million. The industry-standard measurement for smokiness in peat-dried barley. A 10ppm malt sample contains 10 phenolic parts for every 999,990 non-phenolic parts. PPM is almost always a measurement of malt phenolics, not the phenolic part of a finished whisky, which is usually much less.

Reek The phenolic smoke produced by burning peat.

Reflux The (repeated) condensing of vapours within a still before it has reached the condenser proper. Reflux is controlled by temperature and time and is one way of producing a lighter spirit.

Rummager Turning chain in a still that helps to prevent build-up of residue on the inside of the base.

Saladin box Large-scale malting that takes place in cooled troughs and turned by a large corkscrew.

Seasoning Practice of filling a new-oak cask with spirit or wine (bourbon, Sherry, Madeira etc.) prior to actual maturation of the product to extract 'new wood' influence over the spirit.

Shiel Shovel-like tool used to turn barley grains when floor malting.

Solera From the Spanish word meaning 'ground', or 'earth'. This is a system of cask maturation whereby casks are filled in tiers from top to bottom with the lower tiers being filled from the upper. Spirit is only removed from the bottom tier, hence the name solera. Each tier is never completely emptied, meaning that some small amount of whisky will remain in the system throughout the lifespan of the system, aiding in consistency and in a way doing the job of a whisky blender.

Sour mash American whiskey process of adding the sour leftovers from the previous distillation into the fermenter along with the next mash. This lowers the pH and promotes good fermentation.

Sparge Wetting cereals in a mash tun to extract fermentable sugars.

Stave Shaped piece of wood used to construct a cask.

Tannin Coloured substance extracted from wood that gives a sensation like a drying bitterness on the tongue. Derivative of gallic acid.

Thumper A doubler containing water, which helps to remove some heavier alcohols and 'cleans' the spirit a little bit.

Toasting Penetrative heating of the internal surfaces of a barrel to liberate flavourful compounds and aid spirit interaction; barrels may be toasted to a variety of different degrees.

Volatile Molecules with evaporative tendencies that distil easily and, assuming they are not odourless, can also be smelled easily.

Wash Alcoholic beer produced from the fermentation of wort; in the US it is referred to simply as 'beer'.

Worm tub Traditional manner of converting alcohol vapour into liquid. A 'worm' is a coiled pipe that sits in a 'tub' of cool water; as the vapour passes through the coil it condenses into new-make spirit. Worm tubs typically give a heavier, more sulphurous spirit.

Wort Sugar rich liquid drawn from the cooking of cereal grains in a mash tun.

GLOSSARY OF DISTILLERIES

SCOTLAND

ISLAY

Ardbeg The darling of Islay and the only whisky on the International Space Station (undergoing a scientific experiment, no less). Ardbeg is characterized by lots of peat and light body. Uiegaidail is a particularly good release form this distillery.

Bowmore A pioneer in every sense, Bowmore is one of the oldest Scotch distilleries, and was one of the first to achieve cult status in the 1990s. The distillery still has an active floor maltings and the location is nothing short of breathtaking. I highly recommend old Bowmore from the 1970s.

Laphroaig The crown prince of peat. Almost half of all the whisky bottled and sold as malt from Islay has a Laphroaig label on it, with the 10-year-old and Quarter Cask both being very popular expressions. Like Bowmore, Laphroaig still operates a floor malting.

SPEYSIDE

Aberlour France's most popular malt, Aberlour has achieved more than any other mid-century Speyside distillery. Why? Well, it would have to be its herbal, fruity and green character – ideal for blenders and excellent as a stand-alone malt, especially when mixed with Sherry wood.

Alt-a-Bhainne Major contributor to the Chivas blend, but available as a malt bottling under the 'Deerstalker' brand.

Ardmore Big contributor to the Teacher's blend, owned by Beam Inc. Ardmore was the last Scottish distillery to abandon direct coal-firing in 2002, so look out for older independent bottles. Unusually for Speyside this dram tends to be slightly peated.

Auchroisk Pronounced *au-thrusk*. Big distillery and under-represented Speyside dram that contributes to Diageo blends. Unique clingy mouthfeel and cheesecake qualities.

Aultmore Looks like a school, tastes like a sweet/candy shop. Big contributor to Dewar's blends, but has been available in a 12-year-old bottling since 2004.

Balmenach Former family-owned distillery of the great Sir Robert Bruce Lockhart, now run by Inver House and also used to produce Caorunn gin. Almost everything made here finds its way in to the Hankey Bannister blend. Sulphury new make.

Balvenie The smaller sibling to Glenfiddich and producer of the ever-popular Doublewood bottlings. Still run by David Stewart, the longest-serving distiller in Scotland (52 years!). Balvenie is the great absorber of wood.

Benrinnes Another Diageo-owned hidden gem, being as close as you're likely to get to Mortlach for sheer meaty nutrition, which is probably at least partly down to a proprietary distillation process. Some excellent Independent bottles available from Master of Malt.

Braeaval Located in the Braes (high valley) of Glenlivet, this distillery was formerly known as the Brae O' Glenlivet. It's the same elevation as Dalwhinnie at 355 m/1,165 ft. and adheres to the contemporary Speyside style.

Cragganmore Founded in 1870 by John Smith, of The Macallan, The Glenlivet and Glenfarclas fame. Unusually, the stills here have flat tops and use traditional worm-tub condensers. A very decent dram.

Craigellachie This big Dewar's contributor shares the town of Craigellachie with the better-known The Macallan Distillery, as well as the famous Craigellachie Hotel, which sports one of the best whisky bars in the world.

Dailuaine The first distillery to be fitted with a pagoda roof, back in 1889, Dailuaine is typically honeyed, grassy and fruity. Over 98% of Dailuaine's 3.4 million litres (3.6 million quarts) a year of alcohol goes in to Diageo's blends. Pretty good stuff.

Dufftown Besides being the chief fellow in Diageo's Singleton label whisky, Dufftown is also the most environmentally sound distillery in all of Scotland. All but 3% of their product goes into blends.

Glenallachie Rarely bottled as a malt, this distillery, which was opened in 1967, is owned by Pernod Ricard and contributes virtually all of its product to the Chivas blends. Gloriously unexceptional.

Glenburgie Grassy, agricultural and silage are all words that I would use to describe Glenburgie. As unappealing as that might sound, this distillery does manage to secure some individuality in a section of Speyside that is guilty of slipping into blind mundanity.

Glendullan Dull by name… dull by nature. In the past, Glendullan has been bottled under Diageo's 'Singleton' label, but for the most part this is a blend filler, fruity and green.

Glen Elgin The glint in the blender's eye, Glen Elgin now enjoys pride of place within Diageo's Classic Malt range.

Glen Grant Light, thanks to nice, tall stills and purifiers. Glen Grant used to describe its whisky as 'pale with a colourful past'; colour is added liberally these days, however. But it's still one of the cleanest new-make whiskies in Scotland today.

The Glenlivet A distillery that has earned its place in history (see pages 122–23), but hasn't earned a place in the coveted whisky tour section in this book. The Glenlivet is truly the benchmark Scotch malt, the second-biggest malt whisky distillery in Scotland, and the most popular Scotch in the USA bar none. Floral and orchard fruits define the distillery.

Glenlossie Diageo's Glenlossies Distillery stores over 200,000 casks – big by Scottish standards. The tropical-tasting whisky itself is rare, however, and only currently available as a Flora & Fauna bottling.

Glen Moray Located in the heart of Elgin (and surrounded by a housing estate) the whisky from Glen Moray tends to be about as exciting as its location suggests.

Glenrothes Like Balblair (see pages 140–41), Glenrothes is another flag-flyer of vintages over age statements. The distillery is owned by Edrington (The Macallan, Highland Park) but all official bottlings come from Berry Bros.

Glen Spey A feeder for the J&B blend, very little Glen Spey sees daylight through a bottle that isn't green. Expect to find nutty, greasy, almost bourbon-like characteristics.

Glentauchers Founded by blender extraordinaire, James Buchanan, in 1889. Exceptional only for its unnatural and unsuccessful experiments with continuous distillation of malt whisky in the early 20th century.

Inchgower Diageo-owned distillery and a harlot of the blending world, being used for both its owners stock as well as selling out to rival firms. Fairly tasty, though, and unique in that it was for a short time in the 1930s collectively owned by the town of Buckie.

Kininvie Lesser-known runt of the William Grant litter (Glenfiddich, Balvenie) Kininvie is an unabashed blend jockey, but not a bad dram in its own right… if you can track a bottle down. Dufftown, Banffshire.

Knockando Run of the mill at its very best. It was the first distillery in Speyside to have electricity, however… that's about it.

Knockdhu Also known as anCnoc (Gaelic for 'the hill'). This distillery changed its name in 2001 after Inverhouse bought it. Still a good dram.

Linkwood An under-represented dram if ever there was one. Linkwood is a massively subtle, complex and fragrant dram, with a great weighty mouthfeel. I expect to see more in the future.

The Macallan The Sherry-cask whiskies generate a good deal of hype among those with deep pockets. Which makes it all the more surprising that it's the third-largest distillery in Scotland. The 6-litre 'M' decanter holds the record for the most expensive bottle of whisk(e)y ever sold, having been auctioned in Hong Kong in 2014 for £393,109 ($669,020). Unusually, The Macallan is labelled as a highland malt, despite being right in the middle of Speyside.

Mannochmore Yet another phantom Diageo distillery, which proves more useful as a cask stash than it does as a producer of anything especially noteworthy. That's not to say it's bad, however; expect to find delicate spice and good flavour clarity.

Miltonduff Not to be confused with the Milton (Strathisla) Distillery (which is also owned by Chivas) or Macduff Distillery (owned by Dewar's). Miltonduff has a peppered history, having once conducted a triple distillation and at another time owning a pair of Lomond stills, which were used to produce a malt called Misstowie. One to watch.

Speyburn An underachiever, this one. Creating a fruity and well-bodied style, partly thanks to the worm tub, this distillery was the first (in 1897) to have a drum malting on site – in a time where everyone else was still raking floors (some still are).

Speyside Ironically, this distillery in Glen Tromie, which only began production in 1990, is barely within the walls of the Speyside region, being stuck right out on the south-western border. Unfortunately, it's not a stand-out dram, either.

Strathisla Oldest operating distillery in the Highlands, dating back to 1786. Most goes to Chivas blends. The 12-year-old release is all about pickled walnuts and Chardonnay.

Strathmill Another Diageo blend-donkey. You can find a 12-year-old Flora and Fauna release, which is clean, dry and nutty.

Tamdhu Large-scale, but unremarkable distillery, recently brought back from the dead by Ian Macleod Distillers in 2012. Tamdhu was the last distillery to conduct malting in Saladin boxes.

Tamnavulin Light and malty, just like its 1960s brethren, Tomintoul and Tormore (below), Tamnavulin is innocuous almost to the point of cowardice.

Tomintoul With the self-prescribed sub-heading of 'the gentle dram' you might expect this to sit alongside light Speyside representatives, but Tomintoul also produces a heavily peated variation, which is smoked using locally sourced peat.

Tormore Designed by Sir Albert Richardson, Tormore is perhaps my favourite-looking distillery in Scotland. It dates back to 1960, which makes it the first truly new-built distillery in Scotland in the 20th century. It looks like an art deco fortress and is hard to miss if you're driving through Speyside on the A96. Lightly peated and mostly agreeable expressions.

HIGHLANDS

Aberfeldy Core malt of the Dewar's blends, which has seen little limelight itself up until recently. That's about to change, however, so keep an eye out for this pleasantly nutty, apple-y, honeyed malt.

Ardmore Teacher's pet (blend monkey). Heavily peated, yet delicately aromatic, Ardmore is one of Scotland's largest distilleries and still has its own cooperage, which is used for cask repairs. Stills were coal-fired until 2001, so I wouldn't be surprised to see a subtle change in recent younger expressions.

Blair Athol The home of the Bell's blend. An easy distillery visit from either Edinburgh or Glasgow. While you're there be sure to pick up a bottle of the distillery-only cask-strength first-fill Sherry bottling.

Dalwhinnie The meeting place. Possibly Scotland's most gazed-upon distillery, positioned only a few hundred meters off the western side of the A9. Joint highest in Scotland (with Braeval). Sat between the Cairngorm and the Monadhliath ranges, it is isolated, cold and very tasty. Chocolate, honey, orange.

Deanston Another surprising distillery. Deanston generates all its electricity requirements (and then some) from turbines in the River Teith. The whisky is good, too: docile, warm and a little waxy.

Fettercairn A distillery that's seen its fair share of ownership over the years. There's been some interesting kit here, too: soap grinders on the side of the stills (to reduce frothing), stainless-steel condensers (replaced with copper in 1995) and a kind of cold-water cooling system that runs down the side of the stills. A weird one.

Glendronach A whisky that loves ex-Sherry casks and that has the muscle to keep them at bay. Old expressions are fantastic. Recent investment in 2009 means we can probably expect to see some new additions to the range soon.

Glen Garioch Scotland's first gas-fired distillery (in 1982) produces a powerful, rich dram that does well over long periods of maturation. At 25,000 litres (26,500 quarts) it also has one of the biggest wash stills in Scotland.

Glengoyne You'd never know that you're only 30 minutes from the centre of Glasgow in this picturesque distillery, complete with waterfall. There's more than just a pretty setting to Glengoyne, mind you; the 17-year-old is a great dram. Pay close attention.

Glenlassaugh Despite being nearly 140 years old, this distillery has only been active for 64 of those years. It still remains to be seen what the new Dutch owner will do with it.

Glenmorangie Another poster boy/girl that didn't quite make it into the whisky tour chapter of this book. The clue is in the name when it comes to flavour: the exceptionally tall stills afford this dram notes of orange sorbet, mango, toffee and anything else orange you care to think of.

Glen Ord Somewhat of a monster, thanks to the large Glen Ord drum maltings that provide malt for at least six of Diageo's distilleries. Glen Ord recently found brief fame under the 'Singleton' label, which was readily available in the USA for a time. Green, damp and slightly smoky.

Glenturret Built on the same site as the Hosh Distillery, which was founded in 1775 and closed in 1921, Glenturret tenuously claims to be the oldest distillery in Scotland. Popular with visitors, Glenturret is the home of The Famous Grouse 'experience'.

Loch Lomond Weird and wonderful, Loch Lomond uses eight varieties of malt and sports three different types of still (column, pot, Lomond-esque) across four sets, meaning it can output a huge variety of products. The Inchmurrin malt is one such product produced at this distillery: clean, cool and green.

Macduff Load-carrier for the William Lawson's and Dewar's blends, but nay-a malt in its own right (officially bottled as Glen Deveron). Richer and rounder than many of the other 1960s distilleries.

Oban Distillation historian Alfred Barnard called Oban the 'Charing Cross' of the Highlands, and rightly so – Oban is one of the few distilleries in Scotland that is located right in the middle of a bustling town. It's currently the only Diageo malt that is 100% bottled as malt whisky.

Royal Lochnagar A contender for Scotland's most beautiful distillery. Lochnagar produces a fresh and clean new-make, despite its slight stature (it's one of the smallest in Scotland). Of the 450,000 litres (457,500 quarts) of alcohol made here, some go to the Vat 69 blend.

Teaninich An oily, cutting, thick, slick dram that probably deserves more attention than it gets. Think lawnmower underbelly and you're pretty much there.

Tomatin This distillery started with two stills, and by 1986 it had 23! The same year it was bought by Takara Shuzo (the first Asian company to own a Scotch distillery – not the last) to fulfil blending needs in Asia. Sweet and fragrant.

Tullibardine Converted from a former brewery, this distillery came under new management in 2003 and, since then, has been producing some decent whiskies under former Cardhu distiller John Black.

CAMPBELTOWN

Glen Scotia Living in the shadow of its more famous Campbeltown brother, Scotia is a good example of survivalism. The whisky is definitely worth a try; keep an eye out for the 7-year-old peated expression.

ISLANDS

Abhainn Dearg Pronounced *aveen jarek*. This 'Red River' distillery is on the Isle of Lewis and is the most westerly distillery in Scotland and the furthest from the mainland. Stills that look like they're out of a Tim Burton movie. Early releases are… interesting.

Arran The only distillery on the Isle of Arran and a relative newcomer to island distilling. Cream, spice and fruit are common descriptors of Arran malts.

Scapa A very different dram to the 'other' Orkney malt. When Scapa was founded, it was one of the most advanced distilleries of its day, and the first to use steam-coil-heated stills. Today Scapa is one of only a handful of distilleries that uses a Lomond still.

Tobermory The only distillery on the Isle of Mull produces two malts: Tobermory (unpeated) and Ledaig (lightly peated), the latter of which is the better, in my opinion and is named after the distillery's original name.

LOWLANDS

Ailsa Bay Don't expect to see any bottling of Ailsa Bay any time soon. In a similar vein to Diageo's Roseisle Distillery, this distillery aims to produce a variety of styles to fulfil its owner William Grant's blending needs.

Bladnoch Ill-fated and oft-overlooked Lowland producer with a capacity of just 250,000 litres (264,000 quarts) per year. Bladnoch has had at least 10 owners over its 200-year-existence, and is up for sale again as we go to print.

Daftmill Tiny newcomer that produces 20,000 litres (21,000 quarts) promises to be a classic of the future. The owners are in no rush to release anything, it seems, despite their 10-year-old stocks in the warehouses now. Keep your eyes peeled.

NORTH AMERICA

There are a lot of new distilleries in North America and quite a few have a whisky product on their books. Many more are working on a rye, corn, malt, wheat or bourbon, and releasing vodkas, gins or liqueurs in the meantime. This glossary is a fairly comprehensive list of the distilleries that have a whisky available to buy in 2014, but it is by no means exhaustive. I am sure to have missed a few and for that I apologize.

ARIZONA

Arizona Distilling Company Currently making malt whisky from a mash brewed by the local Four Peaks Brewery, this distillery is also readying a durum wheat whiskey, as well as bottling its Copper City Bourbon, which is distilled in Las Vegas.

Hamilton Distillers Producer of Del Bac Whiskey. Barley is malted in-house and dried with mesquite smoke. There are also unaged and unsmoked variants.

Thumb Butte Distillery First legal distillery in Prescott's own 'whiskey row' since Prohibition. Working on 1888 Rodeo Rye, Bloody Basin Bourbon and Central Highlands Single Malt.

ARKANSAS

Rock Town Distillery First legal distillery in Arkansas since Prohibition. This distillery makes wheated bourbon, a hickory-smoked wheat whiskey, a rye and a corn whiskey, and is working on a four-grain bourbon. Corn and wheat are both sourced from local farmers.

CALIFORNIA

American Craft Whiskey Distillers A distillery using Germain-Robin's Cognac stills to make Low Gap Whiskeys, including a 2-year-old wheat whiskey.

Anchor Distillers Of brewery fame, these guys turned their attention to distilling in 1993. Their Old Potrero Single Malt Rye (named after the hill upon which the distillery sits) has been joined by a straight rye and a single malt aged for 11 years.

Ballast Point Spirits This brewery and microdistillery makes Devil's Share Whiskey, a malt whiskey and Devil's Share Bourbon, both of which are aged in heavily charred American oak casks.

Charbay From the wine-growing region of Napa County, this distillery, celebrating its 30th year has put out two releases of its barley-based, hop-flavoured whiskey, as well as Charbay Double and Twisted Light Whiskey.

Lost Spirits Distillery This distillery makes peated single malt whiskies under the labels Seascape, Leviathan (aged in botrytized Sémillon wine casks) and Ouroboros, which is made from Californian barley, smoked with Californian peat, and matured in charred ex-Sherry Hungarian oak casks… unusual.

COLORADO

Leopold Bros. A whole host of products are made at this distillery, but they include a corn-based American whiskey, a rye and a number of flavoured whiskies made from new-make spirit.

Peachstreet Distillers Producer of various fruit- and plant-based products, including Colorado straight bourbon, which is made from locally grown corn.

Stranahan's First distilled in a horse stable, Stranahan's has now filled over 5,000 casks with malt whiskey, which are being released in batch numbers. The bottle has an elongated cap, making it look rather like an alien.

Wood's High Mountain Distillery This distillery makes Tenderfoot malt whiskey, which is in its sixth batch and contains a small amount of malted rye and wheat in its mash bill.

ILLINOIS

Blaum Bros. Distilling Co. This distillery is in the early stages making its own bourbon, rye, wheat and malt whiskey. In the meantime they have released some sourced whiskies, including Lead Mine Moonshine, distilled by Flagler Spirits, and Knotter (i.e. 'not our') Bourbon and Rye, distilled by MGP. One to watch on account of one of the brothers having a substantial beard.

Few Spirits This well-thought-of distillery in the Chicago suburbs is named for the initials of Francis Elizabeth Willard, the lady who championed the Temperance movement with the Women's Christian Temperance Union. They make very nice bourbon, malt and rye whiskies.

Koval Distillery Producer of a range of different cereal-based whiskies, including bourbon, rye, millet, oat and four-grain. All are matured in small new casks, so tend to be heavy on the vanilla side of things. Lovely packaging, though.

INDIANA

Midwest Grain Products Ingredients (MGP) Located near the Kentucky border, this powerhouse produces spirit for over 30 different bourbon, rye and corn whiskey brands. If you're not sure where your whisky was made… it's probably made here.

IOWA

Cedar Ridge Distillery This winery makes Iowa Bourbon, Reserve Bourbon, Griff's Cowboy Whiskey, Short's Whiskey, a wheat whiskey, a malt whiskey and a white whiskey. Plans are afoot for a rye malt whiskey, too.

KENTUCKY

Alltech Lexington Brewing & Distilling Co. This brewery makes a malt whiskey, Pearse Lyons Reserve, and Town Branch Bourbon and Rye.

Barton Distillery aka Tom Moore (established in 1899) Kentucky's least-known distillery yet one of the most historic. Only one of its (many) brands is marketed outside of Kentucky: 1792 Ridgemont Reserve. If you're in Kentucky, get a hold of a bottle of VOB (Very Old Barton) – it's great!

Corsair Distillery This distillery has big plans for bourbon. So far, they are marketing Triple Smoke, a malt whiskey; Wry Moon Unaged Rye Whiskey; Rasputin, a hopped whiskey; and an early version of James E. Pepper Bourbon.

Heaven Hill The largest independent and family-owned distillery in North America. Most famous for production of the Evan Williams and Elijah Craig brands of bourbon, among almost 50 other bourbon, rye, and blended whiskey products.

Kentucky Bourbon Distillers Also known as Willet Distillers established in 1935. This family-owned distillery employs around 15 people and makes over 20 different bourbon and rye labels, most of which are revivals of long-gone pre-Prohibition brands.

Maker's Mark Famous for being really rather tasty, but perhaps even more famous for its wax-dripped bottle. In 2013, the brand announced plans to reduce the alcohol strength of the product from 45% to 42%; it was met with outrage from Maker's fans, causing Beam Inc. (the owner) to reconsider. Cynics consider the whole debacle to be an elaborate marketing exercise.

Old Pogue Distillery The original Old Pogue Distillery closed in the 1940s and the brand survived for years as an independent bottler. In 2012, the Pogue family opened a new distillery in Maysville, where they make Limestone Landing Rye and Five Fathers Rye.

Wild Turkey Most of the bourbons and rye whiskeys made at this Lawrenceburg distillery carry the Wild Turkey name, though they have recently begun to market Russell's Reserve as a separate brand. They also make Duke Bourbon.

MARYLAND

Lyon Distilling Co. Maryland was once the fifth-biggest whiskey-producing state. This distillery makes Maryland Free State Rye, which is currently only available in unpaged form, but give it a little time…

MASSACHUSETTS

Bully Boy Distillery This distillery is named after an old workhorse that used to tend the farm of Will and Dave Willis. They make a white whiskey and an aged wheat whiskey.

Nashoba Distillery This winery-turned-distillery uses a combination of new oak and ex-wine casks to age its single malt whiskey for five years.

Ryan & Wood Distillery Producer of a few different distilled products, including a rye whiskey that was launched in 2011 and is made in a 600-litre (634-quart) alembic still with an attached rectifying column.

Triple Eight Distillery Cog in the machine that is the Nantucket Vineyard and Cisco Brewers, this distillery produces a 10-year-old single malt called 'Notch' (i.e. not Scotch.) They also bottle a bourbon called Nor'Easter, named for the legendary storms that have battered New England for centuries.

MICHIGAN

Grand Traverse Distillery With plenty of locally grown rye and perhaps the best cherries in North America, it's hardly surprising that these guys, who set up in 2007, make a great rye whiskey and a flavoured cherry whiskey too. They also bottle a 3-year-old bourbon.

Journeyman Distillery This organic distillery is constructed largely from salvaged materials, giving it a strikingly beautiful look. Some of its early products are salvaged, too, like Ravenswood Rye, the first batch of which was made at Koval in Chicago, with successive batches being made at Journeyman. They are also releasing a four-grain whiskey called Silver Cross, Featherbone Bourbon, Flat Landers Bourbon, Buggy Whip Wheat Whiskey, Three Oaks Single Malt Whiskey (made from two row barley) and a wheat whiskey. Oh, and they have a bar there, too.

New Holland Brewing Co. This brewery-turned-distillery produces some bizarre whiskies, including Malthouse Brewers Whiskey, made from malted barley, smoked barley and rye; Barrel Hatter Royale, which is a hopped whiskey; and Beer Barrel Bourbon, which is fairly self-explanatory, I think.

MISSOURI

Square One Distillery Another brewery-cum-distillery. Square One release spirits under the 'Spirit of St. Louis' brand, including J.J. Neukomm Whiskey, which is made from malt that has been smoked with cherry wood and aged in Missouri oak casks.

NEVADA

Las Vegas Distillery Established in 2011 by a first-generation American Hungarian family from Transylvania, this small distillery makes 2-year-old Nevada 150 bourbon from local yellow corn. There are a few other products, too, including something called 'Rumskey'…

NEW MEXICO

Don Quixote Distillery Dr. Ron Dolin, the proprietor of this distillery, had a long career in engineering and is something of a tinkerer – he made a solar-powered still when he was just 19. Since establishing the distillery, Don has built (from scratch) no fewer than seven stills, which are apparently optimized to deal with the Jemez Mountains and the distillery's altitude of 2,225 metres (7,300 feet). The distillery makes blue-corn bourbon.

Santa Fe Spirits Established by Englishman Colin Keegan in 2010, this distillery has just released a single malt whiskey called (wait for it…) Colkegan. The whiskey is made from barley that has been smoked with mesquite and matured in a climate-controlled warehouse.

NEW YORK

Hillrock Estate Distillery Definitely one to watch. This distillery in the Hudson Valley is not only floor-malting its own barley, but growing it on its own estate, too. Future releases aim to explore the estate's terroir. While it matures, they have released the only 'solera'-aged bourbon that I have ever come across.

Long Island Spirits Established in 2007, this distillery makes Pine Barrens Single Malt Whiskey and Rough Rider Bourbon, which would appear to be bought in and extra-matured in brandy casks.

Van Brunt Stillhouse This hipster distillery opened in April 2012 and has already released a rather tasty 9-month-old malt whiskey. And a bourbon. Their first rye-based endeavour launched as we went to press and there's a four-grain American Whiskey on the cards, too.

OHIO

Staley Mill Farm & Distillery Located on the site of a historic family-owned farmstead, this distillery was constructed in 2011 by an Amish crew and aims to capture the essence of Ohio's distilling tradition. Currently they source heirloom rye and corn varieties, but wheels have been set in motion to grow their future requirements on the farm itself.

John McCulloch Distillery This distillery makes Green River Whiskey, a reincarnation of the popular pre-Prohibition John McCulloch brand, also known as 'the whiskey without a headache'.

OREGON

Clear Creek Distillery Maker of McCarthy's Oregon Single Malt, which was released way back in the 1990s. It is a 3-year-old whiskey distilled from a wash of peated barley that is sourced from Scotland and fermented by the Widmer Brothers Brewery in Oregon. Oregon oak is used for maturation.

Edgefield Distillery A distillery on a golf course. Edgefield makes Hogshead Single Malt and a number of small-release whiskies under the Devil's Bit label. Currently they are all only available to buy at McMenamins entertainment spots.

House Spirits This one is on my 'one to watch list'. Current releases include the Westward malt whiskey, which is made from American barley, ale yeast and aged in new American oak casks.

Ransom Spirits For me, this distillery is better-known for its fantastic 'Old Tom' gin, but it also makes bourbon under the Henry DuYore's label, and Ransom Emerald 1865 Whiskey, an Irish-style whiskey made with rye, barley and oats to an original recipe from 1865.

Rogue Spirits Perhaps more famous for its beers, this field-to-glass brewer and distiller makes Rogue Dead Guy Whiskey, a four-grain whiskey and Chatoe Rogue Single Malt Whiskey.

Stein Distillery This farm-to-bottle distillery, grows its own rye and corn, which goes into Stein Straight Bourbon and rye.

PENNSYLVANIA

Mountain Laurel Spirits 'Live & Let Rye' craft producer of excellent rye whiskies, including a delicious vermouth cask-finished expression.

Pittsburgh Distilling Co. In 1794, Phillip Wigle defended his right to distil and tussled with a tax collector. He was hanged. Over 200 years later, in 2011, the Pittsburgh Distilling Co. (which is completely unrelated to Phillip Wigle) began releasing whiskey under the Wigle brand name. It now makes rye and wheat whiskies.

RHODE ISLAND

Sons of Liberty Spirits Co. If death metal was a distillery… These guys use beer as the focus and make Uprising Whiskey, a whiskey distilled from stout and aged in a combination of American oak and French oak; and Battle Cry single malt, distilled from a Belgian-style beer that has been fermented with Trappist yeast. They also release seasonal whiskies, one of which is hopped.

TENNESSEE

Corsair Distillery This distillery makes Triple Smoke, a malt whiskey; Wry Moon Unaged Rye Whiskey; Rasputin, a hopped whiskey; and they have plans for many other whiskies including an oatmeal stout and a chocolate mocha porter. They also distil the Collier & McKeel whiskey brand. This is their second distillery; the first is in Bowling Green, KY.

TEXAS

Garrison Brothers Distillery Progressive producer of Texan bourbon, they currently have a range of products with names that play nicely to the Texan stereotype, such as The Young Gun (young bourbon) and The Cowboy (barrel-strength bourbon).

VERMONT

Silo Distillery This distillery produces a bourbon made from both corn and rye grown around the Connecticut River Valley of Vermont.

VIRGINIA

A. Smith Bowman Originally founded in 1934 and now owned by the Sazerac Company A. Smith Bowman redistils whiskey originally distilled at the Buffalo Trace Distillery (also owned by Sazerac) in Kentucky. It markets bourbon under the labels Virginia Gentleman, Bowman Brothers and John J. Bowman.

Catoctin Creek Distillery This Virginia distillery makes Roundstone Rye, which is available in 40%, 46% and barrel-proof (58%) strengths. Solar power accounts for 85% of the power used at Catoctin Creek.

Copper Fox Distillery Rick Wasmund took a six-week internship at Bowmore on Islay back in 2000; five years later he fired up the stills at the Copper Fox Distillery at the foot of the Blue Ridge Mountains in Sperryville, Virginia. The distillery malts its own barley and dries it with cherry and apple-wood smoke for Wasmund's single malt whiskey. Copper Fox Rye Whiskey is made from a mash of ⅓ malted barley and ⅔ Virginian Rye.

George Washington Distillery Rather unbelievably, this distillery was founded in 1797 by President George Washington. He employed a Scotsman named James Anderson to build it, and two years later it was the largest distillery in North America. The distillery burned down in 1814, but was excavated in 2000 and a near-replica rebuilt in 2007. Most recently, 1,000 bottles of the original recipe unpaged rye whiskey were released on 16th May 2014, available to buy only at the distillery.

Reservoir Distillery Founded by Jay Carpenter and David Cuttino, this Richmond distillery makes bourbon, rye and wheat whiskey. Richmond, Virginia.

WASHINGTON

Bainbridge Distillers A USDA-certified organic island distillery that makes Bainbridge Battle Point Organic Whiskey, a whiskey made mostly from Washington white wheat and matured in 10-gallon American Oak barrels made by a family-run cooperage in Hot Springs, Arkansas.

Heritage Distilling Founded by Jennifer Stiefel, this distillery holds more trademarks than your average multinational corporation, including 'Your Whiskey, Your Way'™, 'My Batch'™, 'Cask Club'™ and 'Field to Flask'™. What does all this mean? Not a great deal, except for the fact that you can enrol in a DIY whiskey programme at the distillery. They currently make Elk Rider's blended whiskey and Commander's Rye, which is based on George Washington's Mount Vernon recipe.

Oola Distillery This craft distillery makes Waitsburg Bourbon, which is a blend of bourbon sourced from elsewhere and bourbon made at the distillery.

Woodinville Whiskey Co. 'Bigger Dreams, Smaller Batches'. Working with Dave Pickerell of Maker's Mark fame, this distillery makes Mashbill No. 9 Bourbon and 100% Rye.

WISCONSIN

45th Parallel Spirits At 45th Parallel, the corn, wheat and rye are all bought in from Strate Farm, which is a mere 13 km (8 miles) down the road and situated on the 45th Parallel itself (halfway between the North Pole and the Equator). The spent grain is trucked to another local farm as cattle feed. The distillery makes Border Bourbon and New Richmond Rye.

Yahara Bay Spirits Jack of all trades. These guys make Yahara Bay Whiskey and 'V Bourbon' Whiskey and more recently, a single malt. They also bottle Charred Oak Bourbon and rye for RJR Spirits and make Death's Door Whiskey for Death's Door Spirits.

THE REST OF
THE WORLD

ARGENTINA

La Alanza Argentina's first dedicated malt whisky distillery is located in Patagonia and began distilling in 2012. The owner, Pablo Tognetti, sources his barley locally and casks include ex-bourbon, PX and Malbec (of course) varieties. Production capacity is around 10,000 litres (10,570 quarts) per year.

AUSTRALIA

Bakery Hill These guys produce a small range of single malt whiskies, including a peated, unpeated and a double-matured whisky (finished in a Sherry cask). American oak casks are re-coopered in to 100-litre (106-quart) barrels, which coupled with the temperature of southern Australia, makes for a somewhat accelerated maturation process.

Black Gate New South Wales' first distillery was founded in 2012 and has supplemented its maturing malt stocks with a range of quick-to-market liqueur and vodka offerings. Whisky is matured in 100% Sherry casks and should be released in 2015.

Castle Glen Whiskey seems to be spelled with an 'e' here in Queensland, despite the Scottish distillery name. Wine and beer are also brewed, as well as absinthe, rum and a whole bunch of liqueurs. The first release was a 2-year-old in 2012.

Great Southern Distilling Company Very old port and Sherry casks, coupled with an unusually long fermentation (7–10 days) make GSDC an interesting one to watch. Whisky is currently bottled under the Limeburners label, but they also bottle a bourbon-style whisky called Tiger Snake.

Hellyer's Road By far the biggest malt whisky distillery in Australia, with a single wash still that weighs in at 40,000 litres (42,500 quarts) – bigger than any in Scotland. Distillation is very slow, so copper contact is significant (despite the bottom half of the stills being made from steel), which is apparent in the light new-make spirit.

Nant On the site of an old water mill, the Nant Distillery in Tasmania only conducted its first spirit runs in 2007. Get used to the name though, as Keith Batt, the founder, plans on opening over 20 Nant whisky bars around the world over the coming years.

New World Whisky Distillery Like St. George, in California, NWWD calls an old aircraft hanger its home. This distillery was founded in 2008 by David Vitale, a former Lark Distillery employee (Bill Lark helped him set his own operation up). The beautifully packaged 'Starward' is the distillery's first release, aged for roughly 4 years in ex-Sherry casks of various sizes.

Old Hobart Formerly known as the Overeem Distillery, Bill Lark, from the nearby Lark Distillery, lends a hand here by processing all the mashing and fermenting to the exacting requirements of Old Hobart's owner, Casey Overeem. The Port Cask release from 2011 (60% ABV) was a beauty.

Tasmania Distillery The Sullivan's Cove whisky produced here won the prestigious World Whisky Awards 'Best Single Malt' award in 2014. That particular whisky was distilled before the current owner, Patrick Maguire, took over. I suspect he fully intends on landing more awards in the future, though.

Timboon Railway Shed The Pilsner malt used here is sourced from the Red Duck microbrewery; the spirit matures in very small 20-litre (21-quart) casks that have been resized from larger barrels that previously held Tokaji wine and port, among other things.

William McHenry & Sons McHenry first considered leaving his sensible job in biotechnology back in 2006, and in 2011, he moved his family to Tasmania to do it. His 500-litre (528-quart) still is heated electrically and he currently holds the title of the most southerly whisky distillery in the world. McHenry also makes vodka and sloe gin.

AUSTRIA

Whiskydestillerie J. Haider Austria's first whisky distillery was founded by Johann Haider in 1995 and released its first whisky in 1998. Austrian oak is used to mature the single malt, and a malt made from roasted barley, as well as a rye whisky are also produced here.

Reisetbauer Although this distillery was founded in 1994, they only began supplementing their fruit brandy offering at the end of the following year.

BELGIUM

The Owl The stills at this distillery were sourced from the demolished Caperdonich Distillery in Scotland, and it's these that are used to make The Belgian Owl, which was Belgium's first single malt when it launched in 2007.

Het Anker Brewer-cum-distiller, Charles Leclef, officially founded this distillery on his family's estate in 2010, although he had previously made the Gouden Carolus Single Malt back in 2008, which was distilled at a nearby genever distillery. Leclef uses an unhopped beer from his brewery as the wash.

BRAZIL

Union Distillery Long-time, large-scale producer of malt whisky, most of which goes to blends, but they do also bottle a Brazilian single malt under the Union Club brand.

CANADA

Glenora Canada's first malt whisky distillery is modelled on the Scottish blueprint, even in its name. Glen Breton was their first (10-year-old) bottling back in 2000, but has been supplemented by numerous other expressions, including Glen Breton Ice, a 10-year-old aged in an ice wine barrel.

Still Waters Located on the northern outskirts of Toronto, Still Waters is the brainchild of Barry Bernstein and Barry Stein, who started out as independent bottlers. Their current single malt bottlings are sourced from other Canadian distilleries while their own stuff matures.

CZECH REPUBLIC

Gold Cock Originally founded in 1877, Gold Cock is one of the oldest whisky distilleries in Europe outside of Ireland and Scotland. They make a 3-year-old blended whisky and a 12-year-old single malt.

DENMARK

Braunstein This micro-distillery produces both peated and unpeated whisky, the former being bought in from Port Ellen Matlings on Islay, no less. They have released a number of expressions since 2010, including whiskies finished in oloroso, Sherry and rum casks.

Fary Lochan Destilleri Hot off the bottling line, owner Jens Erik Jørgensen released his first 'lightly smoked' whisky in 2013, which partly comprises Danish malt that has been dried over a nettle fire.

Ørbæk Bryggeri The father-and-son team on the Danish island of Fyn operate both a brewery and a micro-distillery, which produces painfully small quantities of whisky under the Isle of Fionia label.

Stauning Self-sufficiency in tiny quantities, Stauning floor-malt their own Danish barley and dry some of it using Danish peat, too. The four stills (two wash and two spirit) afford them an annual production of only 15,000 litres (15,850 quarts). A rye whisky is also made here, too.

ENGLAND

Adnam's Copperhouse Long-famed for brewing, Adnam's completed works on its distillery in 2010 and, master distiller, John McCarthy, bottled its first whisky in 2013. Erring towards the American style, Adnams use a combination of column and pot as well as new oak for their single malt and three-grain whiskies.

St George's England's first whisky distillery for over 100 years is steaming ahead in terms of both its expressions and its sales, having topped over 100,000 bottles sales of both peated and unpeated whisky (bottled under the English Whisky Company label) in 2013.

FINLAND

Teerenpeli What started as a small whisky project for Anssi Pyysing in 2002, big enough only for the 3-year-old product to be sold in his restaurant, has now grown to a capacity of 30,000 litres (31,700 quarts) per year and includes a small range of lightly peated products.

FRANCE

Bertrand This Alsacian distillery, which started making whisky in 2002, buys its wash in from a local brewery and matures some of its whisky in casks that have previously held Banyuls wine. Approximately 7,000 bottles are currently being produced annually in a town that has two distilleries and only 1,000 inhabitants.

Brasserie Michard Settled within that staple of the French wine and Cognac industry, Limousin (and its associated oak forests), Michard use a proprietary yeast formula and released their first whisky in 2011. The next releases are highly anticipated.

Brûlerie du Revermont Distillers for hire they mat be, but the use of stills designed to make perfume and 114 litre (120 quarts) 'half-casks' at this Comté distillery make the Prohibition brand of whisky that is made here a rather unique proposition.

Brunet Currently Cognac's only whisky distillery, Brunet began bottling Tradition Malt in 2009 and also bottles under the Brenne brand in the USA.

Castan Producer of Villanova Berbie whisky, which will soon come in both peated and un-peated varieties from a third-generation mobile-still.

Claeyssens de Wambrechies One of France's oldest distilleries (dating back to 1817) was previously more famous for its liqueurs, but that changed in 2003 when they launched their first single malt, a 3-year-old. More recently a Wambrechies 12-year-old was released, the oldest French whisky currently available.

Distillerie Gilbert Holl The tiny 150-litre (158-quart) still used by Gilbert Holl was originally purchased in the early-1980s to make fruit brandy. In 2000, Holl began distilling whisky, but bottles are, rather unsurprisingly, very few-and-far-between.

Domaine de Hautes-Glaces Perhaps France's most exciting new whisky distillery, the founders of this purpose built operation, Jérémey Bricka and Frédéric Revol, intend on keeping almost every stage of their malt whisky and rye whisky production in-house, from malting right through to bottling. All cereals are organically grown too. The first (3-year-old) bottlings are anticipated for release in 2015.

Glann ar Mor A perfect recreation of traditional Scottish distillery can be found in Pleubian, in the form of Glann ar Mor. The distillery proudly practises direct firing of its copper stills, and uses cold worm-tubs to condense. Two labels are available, the unpeated Glann ar Mor and the peated Kornog.

Grallet Dupic This distillery was founded in 1860, but whisky production only began ten years ago after the owner, Hubert Grallet, accepted a drunken dare. They now produce peated and unpeated expressions under the G. Rozelieures brand.

Hepp Uberach's 'other' distillery (Bertrand being the rival) produces a trio of single cask whiskies under the AWA (Authentic Whisky Alsace) label, which are finished in noble grape casks (riesling, gerwurtztraminer, pinot gris) and a non-age-statement whisky called simply Tharcis Hepp.

Lehmann The whisky made here (since 2000) is matured exclusively in French white wine casks, exploring the affect that the various wines might have on the maturing product. We have already seen Bordeaux and Sauternes been used to good effect, Coteaux-du-Layon is next to get the Lehmann treatment.

Meyer Originally a fruit *eau de vie* distillery, the 60-year old Meyer distillery turned its hand to whisky in 2007 and now produces a large chunk of the own-label supermarket French malts and blends.

Distillerie de Northmaen Dominique Camus has been releasing 3-year-old whisky (under the Thor Boyo brand) from his craft brewery since 2005. Older releases are beginning to emerge, most recently an 8-year-old called Sleipnir.

Warenghem This distillery was founded in 1900 by Leon Warenghem, but only released France's first single malt whisky in 1988. Warenghem continue to market a range of relatively young malts under the Armorik label, which range from 4 to 11 years in age.

GERMANY

Blaue Maus (Blue Mouse) This new German distillery looks, from the outside, like a new-build home and that's because it is – a new home, for an old distillery, that is. Blaue Maus was first established in 1980 and now has around ten single malts in its range, most of which are matured in German oak.

Hammerschmiede The malt whisky made here (bottled under the Glen Iarran and Glen Els labels) was originally an ancillary product to a great range of bitters and liqueurs, but it is quickly taking precedent as sales grow. The distillery has become famous for its exploration into the journey of production, having released identical expressions with subtle shifts in wood smoke and cask finishing; these form the Journey and Ember range of releases.

Preussische Whiskydestillerie A 3-year-old whisky was released by this distillery in 2012, and followed by three more in 2013. It is unique in its 6x distillation process and use of organic barley. Oh, and its owned and operated by a woman, Cornelia Bohn.

Slyrs Bavaria seems like a fitting place for whisky distillery given the association that the area has with beer. Slyrs celebrates this fact, the malt here is smoked with beech and matured in new US oak. I can highly recommend the PX-finished expression.

Stickum Brennerei This brewery in Düsseldorf, like so many others, turned its attention to whisky-making in 2007. Distillation is conducted in a copper column-still and maturation in various types of new and seasoned oak. A 3-year-old is the only currently available expression.

Sytler Not exactly a distillery, but an interesting anomaly nonetheless. The whisky bottled as Sylter Offshore is actually distilled at the Dolleruper Distillery in Dollerup, then shipped to the northern German island of Sylt for maturation, with the aim of imparting a marine character into the whisky. The spirit is due for release imminently.

INDIA

Amrut Malt whisky has been distilled here since the mid-1980s, and the distillery was originally founded in 1948. Indian barley is used for the unpeated variants, which is malted in Jaipur and New Delhi. The range of expressions is now quite large, with the 8-year-old Greed Angels being the oldest to date; evaporative losses over such a long period in the Indian heat meant that only one-quarter of the contents of the cask survived.

McDowells This distillery was originally established by a Scotsman, Angus McDowell, way back in 1826. It's gone a long way since then, however, and now makes up a large chunk of the United Spirits portfolio, which sells over 130 million cases a year. A mere 1.5% of those cases hold malt whisky, mind you, distilled in Goa and aged for 3–4 years.

IRELAND

Carlow This distillery operation in Bagenalstown is currently nameless, but was formed through a partnership between The Carlow Brewing Company in Ireland and Alltech, an agricultural manufacturer from the US. Alltech also owns the Lexington Distillery in Kentucky, and are now branching out to this new venture which, with stills made in Kentucky, promises to be an Irish/American hybrid. Expect to see the first bottlings of a single malt in late 2015.

Cooley Formerly a diamond trader, gold digger and oil driller, John Teeling founded the Cooley distillery in 1987, at a time when Ireland really needed it. This independent distillery went on to produce a range of different blended and single malt whiskies for a portfolio of clients. More recently the distillery has passed on to Beam Inc. for a rumoured $95 million (£56 million). Word on the street is that independent labels will soon cease production at Cooley, as Beam concentrate on their own brands.

Dingle I wouldn't expect to see any whisky from this distillery until at least 2016, but the new Dingle Distillery in Co. Kerry has been bottling vodka and gin from its distillery installed in the old Fitzgerald sawmill since 2012.

Kilbeggan This much older brother of the Cooley Distillery was brought back from extinction by John Teeling in 2007, exactly 250 years after it was originally built. One of the only wooden mash tuns in the world is still used at Kilbeggan along with stills that pre-date most of the distilleries in this book. Kilbeggan is also now owned by Beam Inc., so its future remains in the balance.

ITALY

Puni Destillerie The Ebensperger family founded Italy's first malt whisky distillery in 2012 and are now producing spirit from barley as well as malted wheat and rye. Stocks are currently maturing (in ex-World War II bunkers) and the first legal whiskies are expected for release in 2015. In the meantime the family have released Puni Alba, which is a 1-year-old expression matured in Marsala casks.

JAPAN

Fuji Gotemba Surprisingly this is Japan's biggest distillery, producing over 12,000,000 litres (12,680,000 quarts) a year including grain whisky. It's American oak only here, however, and only a handful of the range of whiskies made here actually advertise it, including Fujisanroku 18-year-old.

Miyagyiko A fairer touch when compared to its more northerly Nikka brother. In the 1960s Masataka Taketsuru apparently spent three years hunting down the site of this second distillery before he settled on the humid and peaceful area in the Miyai Prefecture. Check out the Coffey grain release, which is all pencil shavings, caraway and menthol. The distillery suffered minor damage in the 2011 earthquake.

Shinshu With production hitting only 25,000 litres (26,500 quarts) a year, Shinshu is Japan's smallest active whisky distillery. After a few recent World Whisky Award wins, this little operation is fast becoming famous for its Mars Maltage blended malt.

White Oak Japan's second smallest distillery (60,000 litres [63,000 quarts] a year) also happens to be its oldest by a clear four years. Their Akashi 15-year-old, which was released in 2013, is matured in konara oak, a relative of the better known mizunara.

Yoichi Coal-fired stills and a traditional approach define the rugged style of Nikka's first distillery, which was founded my Masataka Taketsuru in the 1930s. The distillery is located on the Northern island of Hokkaido, chosen for its similarities to the Scottish Highlands.

LIECHTENSTEIN

Brennerei Telser An unconventional location for a malt distillery it certainly is, but this fourth generation family owned distillery relies heavily on tradition. The tiny pot stills (120 and 150 litres) here are wood-fired after an epic 10-day fermentation (one of the longest I have come across). The spirit is subsequently matured in a 500-year-old cellar, exclusively in ex-pinot noir barrels.

THE NETHERLANDS

Us Heit The first Dutch whisky was bottled at the Us Heit brewery/distillery in 2005, made from locally grown barley malted at the brewery itself using a proprietary technique.

Zuidam Since 2007, this distillery in Holland has been bottling rye and malt whiskies alongside various other grain-and-fruit based products. The current range includes a 5-year-old malt that comes in both peated and unpeated flavours, a 10-year-old matured in new American white oak and a 10-year-old matured in ex-Sherry casks. Zuidam rye has proven itself especially popular amongst bartenders.

NEW ZEALAND

NZ Malt Whisky Co. New investors keep piling in on this operation which no doubt will one day prove to be formidable. In the meantime, older stocks that were inherited from the decommissioned Wilsons Willowbank Distillery in Dunedin. are bottled under various labels, including Milford, South Island, Dunedin, Diggers & Ditch (a blended malt), and Water of Leith (a blend).

NORTHERN IRELAND

Bushmill's Often credited as the oldest distillery in the world, Diageo, Bushmill's current owners, date its history back to 1608. This is a stretch, however, but even at the more realistic approximation of 1784, it's still impressively old. Ten stills and a production capacity of 4.5 million litres (4.75 million quarts) a year affords Bushmill's a wide variety of products, including Black Bush and Bushmill's Original blends, a 10-year-old malt and older malts including a 16-year-old (finished in port pipes) and a 21-year-old (finished in Madeira casks).

NORWAY

Agder Brenneri Norway's first single malt whisky is produced at the Agder Brenneri Distillery and it's in painfully limited supply – current annual release quota is just 1,750 bottles of 3-year-old whisky, which has been matured in a single ex-Sherry butt.

PAKISTAN

Murree Brewery Founded 150 years ago, the Murree brewery supplied beer to the British colonies. Now they make a few single malt expressions, too, among many other things. A cooler climate than India means that maturation can be drawn out a little longer. A 12-year-old and 18-year-old make up the core range.

SOUTH AFRICA

Drayman's This brewery in Pretoria is somewhat of a hidden gem. Their malt whisky production involves a ten-day fermentation process and maturation in French oak casks that have previously held red South African wine. The distillery bottles under the label 'Drayman's Highveld Single Malt'.

James Sedgwick Despite a 25-year history of whisky production, it's sporadic malt whisky releases that seem to have defined this grain/malt distillery over the past decade, but the next instalment of their 10-year-old – matured in ex-bourbon casks – is due in 2015 (after a 3-year wait).

SPAIN

Destilerias Liber Founded in 2001, the smaller of the two Spanish whisky-makers produce a range of spirit categories, inducing a 5-year-old single malt whisky called Embrujo de Granada.

Distilerio Molino del Arco Rather surprisingly, whisky distilling started here in 1962, making Molino del Arco one of the oldest European producers outside of the British Isles. Grain and malt whiskies are made here, with combined production capacity topping 10 million litres (10.6 million quarts) per year. The distillery includes its own maltings too and produces a range of blended and malt whiskies, including a newly released 10-year-old.

SWEDEN

Gamelstilla Handmade and custom designed stills are the order of the day in this new Swedish distillery, which began running spirits in 2012. Expect to see bottles on shelves in 2016.

Gotland Production began at Gotland in May 2012 with a couple of unique talking points. Firstly, all the barley used for their malt whisky is local and organic, malted on-site, and turned by their own custom made 'malt-bot'. Secondly, their ageing warehouse is underground, meaning that temperature and humidity are more constant which, in turn, will steer the maturation in a different direction.

Grythyttan Set on an 800-year-old farm, this distillery also has around 800 shareholders. A cask strength 3-year-old was the first official whisky release at the tail end of 2013.

Mackmyra Sporting an innovative gravity-fed system, contained within its 37-metre (121-feet) high chassis, Mackmyra's new distillery (to replace its older site that was founded in 1999) kicked into production in late 2012. Two styles of whisky are made here, one fruity and the other smoky – derived from burnt juniper wood and bog moss.

Nortellje Brenneri Oloroso and ex-apple brandy casks are on the menu at Stockholm's nearest distillery, which is located on a fifth generation family-owned farm.

Smögen Full-bodied and smoky is the aim for Pär Caldenby's new distillery, which began spirit runs in 2010. Caldenby is a whisky author himself and personally designed and sourced the materials used to construct the distillery. Their first whisky, a cask strength bottling called Primör, was released in March 2014.

Spirit of Hven There's a long list of obsessive goings-on at Henric Molin's distillery in the Island of Hven. The wood policy is extremely regimented, with oak being sourced from the USA, Spain and Japan, before lengthy drying periods and seasoning. Some barley is peated, sometimes burnt with seaweed and seagrass. Then there's the oak laboratory, which completed construction in 2013 and promises to be the go-to facility for research into oaks effect on spirits.

SWITZERLAND

Bauernhofbrennerei Lüthy After four years of whisky production, a floor malting was built at Lüthy in 2009, which now produces the Swiss peated malt requirements for the distillery.

Hollen Purpose-built in 1999, Hollen Whisky Distillery produced the first Swiss single malt. Like most other Swiss distilleries, they use a combination of French red and white wine casks for maturation. There are currently 4-year-old and 5-year-old expressions available.

Langatun Producers of Old Dear (unpeated) and Old Bear (peated) single malt whiskies, which are both matured for 5 years exclusively in Swiss and French oak. They also produce a single barrel rye whisky, called Old Eagle.

Brauerei Locher This brewery was founded in 1886 and recently turned its hands to distilling. Among its repertoire is the practice of using very old beer casks to mature its whisky, but wine and bourbon casks are used, too. Peated and unpeated expressions are available.

Brennerei Stadelmann This distillery was, for 70 years, one of many nomad operations that could be mobilised if the distiller desired. It finally settled down in the new millennium under the guidance of the founders grandson, Hans Stadelmann. A 3-year-old became the first official bottling in 2011.

Whisky Castle Perhaps Swizerland's best known dedicated whisky distillery produces a mere 10,000 litres (10,565 quarts) of alcohol a year, making it smaller than any in Scotland. But they make up for it in variety, having released a range of young expressions since 2004.

TAIWAN

Yuan Shan Distillery Producers of the Kavalan brand of Taiwanese whisky, Yuan Shan is perhaps the most visited distillery in the world, attracting typically over 3,000 visits a day – more than all the distilleries in Scotland put together! Casks here are tied together in groups of four to stop them rolling during earthquakes, and with around a dozen expressions now, there are a lot of casks to protect.

INDEX

Writing a whisky book of this size in only nine months is not an easy task and would certainly not have been possible without the help and support of a small group of individuals – this book is dedicated to you.

Addie Chinn, for the continued development of our symbiotic photo-lingual relationship. Craig Harper, for regular words of support, and for completing a lap of Scotland in four-days. Daryl Haldane, for bringing Orkney to life (and bringing life to Orkney), fact-checking and long conversations about wood. Itoh Takuya and Rogerio Igarashi for handling everything on the Japan leg of the tour and being generally amazing hosts.

Thanks also to the hundreds of brand ambassadors, distillery managers, mashmen, cask-fillers, bottle-cappers and distillery cleaners who have made each and very trip an experience to treasure. You're too numerous a group to list, but know who you are.

Thanks to the team at RPS – especially Nathan Joyce – who I think (like me) got a lot more than they bargained for with this one!

Finally, thanks to my wife and son, for their patience, endurance, and love throughout the long months and late nights of research and writing.

PICTURE CREDITS